PENGUIN BOOKS

THE PENGUIN ANTHOLOGY OF AUSTRALIAN POETRY

John Kinsella has been a Fellow of Churchill College, Cambridge University since 1997, and was made an Extraordinary Fellow of Churchill College in 2008. He is also a Professorial Research Fellow at the University of Western Australia, and Adjunct Professor to Edith Cowan University. He has published over thirty books.

THE PENGUIN ANTHOLOGY OF AUSTRALIAN POETRY

EDITED BY
JOHN KINSELLA

PENGUIN BOOKS

PENGUIN BOOKS

Published by the Penguin Group
Penguin Group (Australia)
250 Camberwell Road, Camberwell, Victoria 3124, Australia
(a division of Pearson Australia Group Pty Ltd)
Penguin Group (USA) Inc.
375 Hudson Street, New York, New York 10014, USA
Penguin Group (Canada)
90 Eglinton Avenue East, Suite 700, Toronto, Canada ON M4P 2Y3
(a division of Pearson Penguin Canada Inc.)
Penguin Books Ltd
80 Strand, London WC2R 0RL England
Penguin Ireland
25 St Stephen's Green, Dublin 2, Ireland
(a division of Penguin Books Ltd)
Penguin Books India Pvt Ltd
11 Community Centre, Panchsheel Park, New Delhi – 110 017, India
Penguin Group (NZ)
67 Apollo Drive, Rosedale, North Shore 0632, New Zealand
(a division of Pearson New Zealand Ltd)
Penguin Books (South Africa) (Pty) Ltd
24 Sturdee Avenue, Rosebank, Johannesburg 2196, South Africa

Penguin Books Ltd, Registered Offices: 80 Strand, London, WC2R 0RL, England

First published by Penguin Group (Australia), 2009

10 9 8 7 6 5 4 3 2

Text design by Nicci Townsend © Penguin Group (Australia)
Cover design by Cameron Midson © Penguin Group (Australia)
Cover image © Shayne Higson
Typeset in 11/14.75 pt Apollo MT Regular by Post Pre-press Group, Brisbane, Queensland
Printed and bound in Australia by McPherson's Printing Group, Maryborough, Victoria

National Library of Australia
Cataloguing-in-Publication data:

The Penguin anthology of Australian poetry / editor, John Kinsella.
9780143008736 (pbk.)
Includes index.
Australian poetry
Other Authors/Contributors: Kinsella, John, 1963–

A821.008

penguin.com.au

To my fellow poets, to Tracy for being there, and to Clive for his belief and support in seeing the job done

contents

eighteenth century

nineteenth century

twentieth century

Introduction

What is an anti-nationalist doing compiling an historical anthology of Australian poetry? In making my selection for this volume, which begins with poets born in the eighteenth century and runs through to one born in the late 1970s, I have tried to avoid popular notions of what Australian poetry is, as well as the prescriptive expectations of the academy and of the poets themselves. This does not mean that old favourites and 'canonical' poems aren't included; they are. There is also conscious overlap with predecessor volumes, especially Harry Heseltine's *Penguin Book of Australian Verse* (1972), and the more recent John Tranter and Philip Mead selection, *The Penguin Book of Modern Australian Poetry* (1991). Various points of contact are essential to me, whether it is including an influential feminist poem such as Judith Rodriguez's 'Nu-plastik Fanfare Red', anthologised by Heseltine, or something more recent such as Ania Walwicz's brilliant 'Little Red Riding Hood', included in the Tranter–Mead selection. Each of these poems speaks of a different moment in women's poetry in Australia, always strong but coming to the forefront from the 1970s on.

It will probably strike readers of this anthology that it is unusual for so many contemporary writers to be represented in an historical anthology. I have done this because I feel that the late twentieth and early twenty-first centuries have proven and are proving to be fertile periods for poetry. I have made a policy decision to use single poems from most contemporary poets. This is not intended to 'represent' their work, but to give a sense of the diversity, strength and uniqueness of the poetry that is available today through books, journals, the internet and performance. A poet having more poems included here doesn't mean he or she is 'better' than any other. I have had to leave out numerous poems I would have liked to include. Omitting any poet from the anthology is not a statement about their relevance or significance; clearly the choices are subjective and personal.

I argue that historically much Australian poetry has been consciously or unconsciously experimental and innovative. Even poems conservative in form are often radical in content. This radicalism does not have to be a major departure from the expected, as over time minor changes can become cumulative. From the earliest Australian poetry – which, of course, we can only trace through received memory, song cycles, rock paintings and traditions of body painting, dance and other manifestations of poetic spirit – through to hypertextual computer innovations, performance and slam poetry, and the increasing move towards international collaboration via the internet, there is a sense of urgency about communicating the uniqueness and significance of the Australian landscape, and the relationship between individuals and community and country/place.

The harsh conditions of convict life throw up a poetics that is adaptable, pragmatic, often ironic and inevitably desperate. 'Frank the Poet' and other convict poets take their skills from the 'old world' and reinvent them to speak out of the new hell. The experience of new environmental conditions, isolation, relationship to 'home', and posturing for power within the colonies, all affect and pressure standard poetries. What we might term the convict poetries of resistance were often consciously written against the poetics of authority. The 'anonymous' poet becomes a figure of alterity in the nation-making canon, at once both claimed as part of the Australian character and identity and often resisting those. Whether anonymous or using a *nom de plume* or their own names, however, poets of the nineteenth century predictably engaged with the social mores of their time. Sadly such social mores inevitably contained strong bigotries.

It is true that in the nineteenth century plenty of Australian verse was purely derivative of British models. But rather than seeing all earlier non-indigenous Australian poetry as poor replications of European, especially 'British', poetry, one could argue that the obvious change towards the local in thematic content also brought with it a change in rhythm and prosody in general. With this change in thematic content, poetry began to include local referents beyond specifically occasional verse such as Michael Massey Robinson's 'Song (To Celebrate the Anniversary of the Establishment of the Colony)'. The inclusion of local referents was not only on the level of scrutinising the 'bizarre' nature of the kangaroo, as in Barron Field's poem, 'The Kangaroo', which has much in common with other colonial poems comparing unusual 'new' animals and plants with the known, either mythologically or in reality. It was also on the level of an Australian 'sensibility' regarding belonging, place (light, flora, fauna) and a consciousness of indigenous presence (the latter evolves most strongly from the poetry of Charles Harpur onward). What are often seen as poorer examples of verse need to be reconsidered in context – looking at the time and conditions and 'receptivity' during which they were written.

The range of experimentation in Australian poetry recognisably changes after Federation in 1901, with the changing nature of communications and connectivity brought by 'nationhood'. There are mutual influences between poetic experiment on the one hand, and visual art, music, and changes in technology on the other. I have included here an über-modernist poem from the 1930s by Furnley Maurice, 'To a Telegraph Pole' – poised between a lyrical ode and a 'found object' poem. Maurice makes use of this symbol of technological progress and mass communication, which has often been called the internet of its time. Regarding technology, we may also note a Sydney Push writer of the 1950s like Harry Hooton (whose poem 'Words' is included here) and his important 'manifesto' piece on 'Anarcho-Technocracy'.

The visual is highly important in the panoramic context of Australian poetry. Large skies, large spaces and drenched colours appear, and all have been treated with varying degrees of sensitivity to whether these spaces are 'empty' or replete. The pastorality of Australian rural verse, and its distortions, has gone hand in hand with a desire to impose order, to make familiar – and this has been a visual process. Dorothy Hewett, always something of a renegade, brought numerous threads of old-world tradition and its new-world variants into play in her (Western Australian) wheatbelt poetry. It is intensely visual, almost painterly, poetry, but is also consciously connected with the Australian balladic traditions, and with a pastiche of gossip, myth-making, Romanticism and hard-nosed left-wing politics.

One might draw a parallel between the introduced monocultures in agriculture that have so damaged the land, such as wheat- and sheep-farming, cane-growing and cotton-farming, and the seeming wish to canonise a certain thread of European poetic practice in anthologies of Australian poetry. So much of Australian poetry *is* concerned with the rural, and specifically a pastoral construct of a European idyll transcribed into Australian conditions. It is often seen that what makes early Australian printed poetry more 'Australian' is the increased number of references to local flora and fauna, local events and so on; whereas, frequently the most radical departures from the norm are when the transcription of this idyll is challenged. You get this in poems of seemingly conservative structure, such as Eliza Hamilton Dunlop's 'The Aboriginal Mother' and 'The Aboriginal Father', which – while obviously including Australian references by lamenting the massacre, mistreatment and abuse of Aboriginal people – shatter the form they are presented in, challenging this western pastoral idyll on all levels.

A comparison may be made with criticisms of Oodgeroo Noonuccal's (Kath Walker's) and Jack Davis's (Nyungar's) poetry – criticisms made by those who see them as supposedly caught within western tradition (and thus compliant with western sensibilities) through their use of traditional English verse structures, rhythms and poetic devices. However, I would argue that by using indigenous concerns as content in such verse structures these poets are consciously undermining the English traditions themselves. These are acts of resistance.

The roots of much modern Australian innovation in poetry can be found in a single document published as a preface to the poems of Adam Lindsay Gordon. Marcus Clarke, primarily known as the author of the novel *For the Term of his Natural Life*, was also a journalist, critic and poet, and one of his poems is included here. Fascinatingly he was a school friend of Gerard

Manley Hopkins back in Britain. His remarks regarding 'weird melancholy', originally made about Australian art – visual art and poetry being inextricably interwoven in the Australian condition – disturbingly pinpoint much of the anxiety of the 'settler condition'. 'What is the dominant note of Australian scenery?' he asks, and then answers himself: 'That which is the dominant note of Edgar Allan Poe's poetry – Weird Melancholy.'

There are conscious breaks within the canonical strand of Australian poetry of European derivation we have been critiquing, and these prove to be intense points of dispersal and redirection. One example, from the mid-nineteenth century (though not published in book form until the early twentieth century, and then rapidly forgotten), is the work of Elizabeth Deborah Brockman, an entirely neglected though major poet from 'bush' Western Australia, who was among other things a translator of Petrarch. Brockman's poem 'On Receiving from England a Bunch of Dried Wild Flowers' fits within a genre of flower poems written in Australia during the period that compares the native blooms of Australia with the delicate beauties of especially British gardens. But the poem carries with it an intensely unsettled sense of belonging and estrangement. It is almost as if a paranoia is being written down, in that the 'old world' is no longer a living reality as the 'new world' is a ghostly reflection of it; it is as if the 'other hands' back in England are feared to be lifeless, even though it's only the speaker's touch they will never again feel:

> But in my hand these frail memorials
> Lie closely pressed; a slight electric link,
> By which thought over-passes time and space,
> To other hands that plucked them: other hands

That never more to any touch of mine
Shall thrill responsive. Blessed be those hands
With prosperous labours, fruitful through long years,
Of all life's truest, tenderest charities.

Brockman's small oeuvre is full of poems of visceral connection to place. I write this introduction sitting in the shadow of the 'purple mountain' she describes elsewhere in her poetry. It is very characteristic of Australian poetry of the period, from any of the colonies, to fuse an immediate sense of place with elements of uncertainty and disconnection. Even the 'native-born' poets (Brockman came to Australia as a child) convey this uncertainty if for no other reason than that they are writing in received/inherited media evolved for other spaces.

Christopher Brennan, writing in the late nineteenth century through to his death in 1932, though completing most of his important work by 1904, is in his assertion of symbolist models both experimenting (and reiterating) and struggling with national identity. The absence of obvious Australian material in his work, though it is there if one looks closely, gives rise to a discussion of classicism and tradition that, reinvented in the Australian writing environment, becomes of necessity textually innovative, even radical. In other words, old traditions can become innovations when decontextualised and reinvented. Mallarmé, new in France, is not simply rehashed in Australia, but reinvigorated and made new again. I have included here one of Brennan's late poems written for his lover, Vie, 'Because She Would Ask Me Why I Loved Her', an exquisite lyric conveying a personal intensity, a Brennan up-close that is often suppressed in his earlier *livre composé*.

World events significantly affect the content of many of the poems in this anthology, especially war – from Leon Gellert's World War One verse through to Kenneth Slessor's 'Beach Burial', written when he was a war correspondent during World War Two, to Bruce Dawe's 'Homecoming' from the Vietnam war, to Yahia Al-Samawy's poem of exile, with its overtones of a war-torn contemporary world. Australian poetry is influenced by the horror, the changing nature of communications and the 'travel' that come about through world events affecting life back home – not only in what is brought home, but in what is sent out (for instance, C. J. Dennis's poetry sent into the trenches of Gallipoli). Though her poem included here may be read as an observational, lyrical 'moment' poem, Jennifer Maiden, a highly innovative contemporary poet, has actually spent her writing life protesting against imperialism and war. Essentially, however, events at home and abroad are but one aspect influencing poetry. The conscious creation of a canon of national literature is the biggest influence on radical experimentation.

When it comes to looking at the modernist period, there are in Australian poetry numerous points of connection and comparison with modernist poetries and poetics outside this country. However, I would argue that Australian modernism had its own directions and triggers, and that any model for comparison needs to be reconsidered in this light. It is often argued that in Australia modernism finds its origins with Kenneth Slessor, and while Slessor is a great exemplar of the 'modernist urge', we might look earlier to the love and anti-war poetry of Zora Cross, or, as I have suggested, to early Brennan. A discussion of what constitutes the origins of modernism is particularly apt when examining Australian poetry. If we look at the Baudelairean dandy of the 1850s as a salient trigger point for European modernism, we might well find a comparison in what the critic Michael Ackland locates as the 'shining band' in Melbourne, with Marcus Clarke and his literary associates.

A specifically Australian literary and cultural 'movement' at a tangent to modernism, the Jindyworobaks (the term means 'annexing') of the 1930s and '40s essentially looked to create a 'prehistory' of connection (appropriation) between settler cultures and tens of thousands of years of indigenous song cycles and other poetries of telling, ceremony and communication. Inevitably this compelled a poetry of the land and 'Australianness', which produced its own shapes of poetry, its own rhythms and content. The crisis of modernism, much discussed with regard to the 'Ern Malley hoax', is crucial to this portrait of experimentation but is really a side journey – an aberration (important, interesting and also hugely influential but still a deviation) while other innovations were, often slowly, taking place.

Considering the role of the expatriate in experimentation, of writers like Ada Cambridge and Peter Porter, allows for comparative models with genuine conduits to what is happening 'over there' and 'over here' to be created. Peter Porter's poetry is often seen as traditionally formalist, especially given his connections with the Movement of 1950s London, but as time has gone on, in relation to his Australian origins this 'formalism' has become not all it seems.

The highly productive and generative period of the 1960s and '70s is one with which many critics of Australian poetry would associate the term 'experimental'. This period's obvious digressions, challenges and deconstructions of 'standard English' poetry have been well anthologised and discussed. Its tendencies are not actually maverick, but are connected to the urge towards innovation prevalent from the earliest poetry written in Australia, and also to that which existed well before the arrival of European-style writing. There is a pre-existing template for innovation prior to European settlement/invasion, and importantly much of the innovation of the mid-to-late twentieth century comes about through the so-called multicultural or migrant voices interacting and rewriting, overlaying English language poetries and poetics.

The desire by both critics and poets themselves to categorise their practice within historical, social and cultural contexts is not unique to Australia. The labelling of 'isms' allows critics and writers to see poets as either belonging to or departing from particular movements, to define them through the activities of their peers. With this in mind, it is not surprising that Les Murray should have connected himself to the nationalist concerns of the Jindyworobaks and their annexing of Australian prehistory, to their agenda of making a new cultural Australianness. Les Murray and Peter Porter famously engendered the debate between 'the Boeotian and the Athenian', the dichotomy between country and city, old world and new world, creativity and rationality.

The term 'Generation of '68', which was first used by Thomas Shapcott in the *Australian Book Review* but is more broadly associated with John Tranter's seminal anthology *The New Australian Poetry* seeks to define itself against such a binary, and contribute to a discourse of deconstruction in Australian poetics, although in many ways one could argue that it remains within the binary, on the Athenian side. The consequence of this is that from the late 1970s on poets are constantly labelled as being in one camp or the other; that is, the rural lyric or the urban non-lyric. Of course, Australian poetry is inevitably a mixture of these, so we see the growing presence of lyrical hybridisers such as Peter Minter, Michael Brennan and M. T. C. Cronin. The critic David McCooey has picked up on this 'new lyricism' that has also been prevalent in American and French poetry over the last twenty years. McCooey's assessment seems to be independent of these tendencies outside Australia.

Contemporary experimentation in poetry is frequently cross-generic and often determines itself as transfigurative or transformative. That is, the end result is to bring not only textual but social change. I would argue this has always been the agenda of innovation and experimentation to differing degrees. What is certainly able to be calibrated is how consciously this agenda is expressed by poets in their poems and commentaries. The meta-textual exploration of the politics of subjectivity necessarily means the separation of the self from text. The concern generated by L=A=N=G=U=A=G=E poetry in America, from the late 1970s on, for the position of the 'Lyrical I', of the unified self, has been the basis of much experimentation in Australia also.

In searching for a linguistically innovative poetry as a response to a set of political and ethical desires or prerequisites, it is necessary to place the canon under pressure. Australian poets have long histories of creating models to work against models: Π.O. in asserting a dialect poetry that transfers performative speech onto the page, or John Tranter as an Australian wrestling with the values of the New York School he esteems and in many ways departs from. Without wishing to contribute to hierarchies, I feel the most vital poet writing in Australia today is the Murri poet Lionel Fogarty. Fogarty, as attested by Mudrooroo, writes a 'guerrilla' poetry that undermines the status quo of English as a dominant language. Fogarty writes in an idiosyncratically creolised English that intentionally follows none of the 'rules' of standard English. Through this methodology he resists the coloniser. For Fogarty, colonisation is not a thing of the past, but an active and ongoing process that must be challenged.

Migrant or refugee poets in Australia, as of old, since all non-indigenous poets here are to some degree of migrant origin, confront the inability of their new country to absorb their differences, as much as they reject certain Australian 'national' values (Ania Walwicz, for example). It is both affirming and negating to refer to a selection of poetry as 'migrant'; the reference identifies in a positive sense but also marginalises in a national context. Ali Alizadeh, an Iranian-born Australian, writes out of his community but also within the broader community. His poem 'Rumi', anthologised here, is specifically about an historical poetic figure, but has obvious subtexts about the Australian landscape and experience.

Ouyang Yu, an Australian poet of Chinese background, has defined his poetics through identifying and resisting histories of bigotry, and affirming alternative canons of Australian literature. He is often seen as rebarbative, but his experimentation has opened new possibilities of discourse that are both outside and belonging at once: he has made his work 'inside-out'. Australian poetry not written in English may become experimental outside its own language-community in terms of the questions it asks of publishing opportunities and venues in a primarily English-speaking country. Eva Sallis's translation of Al-Samawy from the Arabic is an example of this. Of necessity, this volume is primarily an anthology of Australian poetry in English, but I have tried to recognise the impact of different language-cultures on English. Australia is a pluralistic, multicultural and language-diverse country.

The publication or presentation of innovative verse-novels, prose poetry, hypertextual poetry, multimedia and performance poetry, installation poetry, concrete poetry and many other cross-generic forms is standard in Australia now. Experimentation is the expectation rather than the departure, but this surely leads us to question what actually constitutes the experimental, and to begin looking elsewhere for what is truly working against the status quo.

JIMMY MURRAY

Thunder

Mungga walmanyu murrul ngumarrangu
Murrul walmanyu mungga ngumarrangu
Mada nyiburu gubu guraragu

Mina milmindu minba mayjalagu
Mungga walmanyu murrul ngumarrangu
Mada nyiburu gubu guraragu

Mungga walmanyu murrul ngumarrangu
Mada nyiburu gubu guraragu
Mina milmindu minba mayjalagu
Mungga walmanyu murrul ngumarrangu

A mighty noise rises up, roars as it rushes by
Rushes and rises, a mighty noise that roars
Hurl out a leaf that is soaked in sweat

Bolts of lightning strike, and flare
A mighty noise rises up, roars as it rushes by
Hurl out a leaf that is soaked in sweat

A mighty noise rises up, roars as it rushes by
Hurl out a leaf that is soaked in sweat
Bolts of lightning strike, and flare
A mighty noise rises up, roars as it rushes by

(Girramay dialect)

WANGKANGURRA PEOPLE

Songs of the Knob-tailed Gecko

1. Yadná wuRadi pantaná yádnalpántaná
   Yadná wuRadi pantaná.

The Sandhill Lizard, Wakultyuru, was in the fire at the Kudnara camp. He had tried to protect himself with his shield but it was burnt. His skin peeled off. Lying among the ashes he sang this verse.

2. Yadnál' pantaná yadná linthityá,
   Linthítyarará.
   Yadná warará yadná linthityá.

It must have been the day after: he slowly came back to life amid the ashes. He was not yet a Knob-tailed Gecko. He was Wakultyuru, that is, a lizard in the sandhill country. You see him anywhere: he is brown with a big head and a long tail. His burns have made him look different: he was to turn into a Knob-tailed Gecko called Mayipalkuru or Tyarla-tyarla.

3. Linthityalarái yadnáwararái
   Yadná linthityá.

He remained there, he just lay there flat after the fire, not looking anywhere. He lay there and went on lying there. Not that he was sleeping: he was as if dead!

4. Yanpá láthuká, yatú pantaná
   Yadná wuRa
   Yanpá láthuká, yatú pantaná
   Yadná wuRali.

He managed to look up and he saw his own camp; it had been burnt.

5. Mákulyé kulyákulyáidna
Makundnhái tyar'ímpirái.

He gradually recovered enough strength to move. He named himself in a verse. Then he turned the verse around.

5a Tyar'ímparáta ma kudnhá
Mákulyá kulyáidna
Má kudnhái tyar'ímpará
(*half sung*)
Uta thurkaná!

And he arose from the dead.

6. Lingwetyengwé, pályalya lingwetyengwé
Pályala wardity' amánta língwemantá.

This is how he set out and he looked around close by to decide in which direction and which way he should go.

7. Kantiéri yályara ʀambálkulyanái,
Kánti lyalyiyará ʀambálkulyanái,
MáʀRara wílpilpiné.

He went looking for somewhere to camp but the country all around was already in twilight. The sun set. He was looking for a windbreak, for a bit of mulga to break up to make a shelter. Everything had been burnt by the fire. 'Where can I go to settle down among some mulga trees?'

He went on. There was a mulga tree in a swamp, a mulga tree! The swamp had not been burnt, and the tree was standing there, alive. He spent the night by the mulga tree and travelled further southwest into the desert the next day.

8. Pántu Mirláka wára kanpíne
Rityanpiriá kawára kanpíne.

He saw the saltlake Mirlaka then and named it in his song.

9. Purlká nhintya láwurú purlká nhintya
Láwurú lithírkithirké
Purlká nhintya láwurú.

He was still so ill as the fire had burnt his stomach. As he was looking at the lake he turned into a Knob-tailed Gecko because he had been burnt by the fire. He saw that on the other side of the saltlake, not far from the edge, there lay a huge sandhill. He went up on top and looked around the area. He was looking for a place. Where could he go down below the ground and rest for good? He was still sick from having been burnt by the fire, and his tail had dropped off.

9a. Purlká nhintya láwurú lithírkithirké,
Purlká nhintya láwurú lithírkithirké.

10. Tyálara tyálara ruté
Ya tyálara tyálara rut'
Yadnadnámpa kályara runté.

10a. Yadnadnámpa kalyáRa luntáyi
Yadnadnámpa kalyáRa luntáyi
Yátyalára tyarlára luntáyi
Yátyalára tyarlára luntáyi
Yadnadnámpa kalyáRa luntáyi

At last he found a place to camp. He went to lie down below the ground, he dug himself in below the ground, he then pronounced a curse, a magic spell at that place. (The singer does not include the spell, which he describes as having been given to him by his father. It refers to what had happened to the Gecko. It could only be directed against men.)

PADDY LANDO-NADDI

White Engine Against Black Magic

Tabi in Njamal

jarnaŋgalu kardipula
jirdalari jarrawarŋgaga
ŋarlu ŋurndirri
wại̱ama ŋanḏula
ŋai̱arda ŋirrbirikardi
waiĺ̗balalu jiḋirrbalu
pugarkurra ŋaana mii̱akarda
parbarrmarnu
mundagu kardipula pagarrbala
mạparnkarra naalama ŋai̱arda palbarri
kalukalu.

You steer the plane with both arms
Sending it straight through the air.
Inside, what a noise!
We are nobody with our cleverness,
Against the whitefellow.
He can read, and write, and sure enough,
Drive the big things in the sky –
Magic? – He doesn't need it.
Our medicine-men, the whole lot,
Are utterly useless.

WILLIAMS

Whirlwind – Talu

Tabi in Karierra

parlgarragu wạnaŋgurana kanḋii t̲akanna
t́urrańpinna wạnaŋgurana murlimurlimana
parlgarragu wạnaŋgurana kanḋii t̲akanna
t́urrańpinna wạnaŋgurana palbarrguba wạngu t̲akanna
palbarrguba wạngu t̲akanna
ŋai̲inkabu Marbirrimarraŋu

As a whirlwind I grabbed the edge of the plain,
As a whirlwind I sent it whirling around.
As a whirlwind I grabbed the edge of the plain,
As a whirlwind I hurled it,
Caught it at the sky's bend,
Caught it at the sky's bend –

That's how Marbirrimarra dreamt it.

eighteenth century

Previous explorers had 'discovered' Australia from a European viewpoint, but James Cook's 1770 voyage fired the imagination of Empire. He claimed Australia's east coast for King George III. Colonisation and occupation of this 'new' land by the British began with the arrival of the First Fleet at Botany Bay in 1788 and the establishment of the penal colony of New South Wales. What was 'Sydney Cove' to Governor Phillip and the colonists was the land of the Eora people of the Cadigal tribe of the Dharug language group. Despite trade and a certain amount of cultural interaction, even 'sharing', the movement was towards the English language and customs of the invaders. This is not to say the language of the indigenous peoples that the invaders and their prisoners encountered did not influence their written language and speech, but generally it was given little chance. The story is repeated in a variety of ways over the continent through the years of exploration and colonisation.

The poets collected in this section were migrants, primarily born in Britain. Each had his or her own motive for 'migration', be it Barron Field taking up the position of Supreme Court Judge of New South Wales, or Fidelia Munkhouse, who became Fidelia Hill, born towards the end of the eighteenth century in Yorkshire, who arrived in Australia on the *Buffalo* with her husband Captain R.K. Hill. Fidelia Hill was not only the first woman in Australia to publish a book of verse, but also the first to include poems written in the colony of South Australia. After the death of her husband, she eventually remarried and moved to Tasmania.

In the main poets born in the eighteenth century took their sensibilities from being children of the British Empire. Generally, these are poems of colonisers, those who were part of spreading the 'pink' around the globe. They carry points of connection with the southern land, but the values of where they come from still hold the poems firmly in place. They are talking 'home' in so many ways, but this relationship is not necessarily straightforward, and there are differing degrees of participation in colonisation.

Michael Massey Robinson is an interesting case. Oxford-educated, he actually arrived in Sydney in 1798 as a convicted blackmailer, but having clerked on the transport for a judge-advocate was granted a conditional pardon. His duality persisted, for he continued his criminal ways and in 1802 was found guilty of perjury, only to escape sentence again because of his unique skills in a colony hungry for such talent. He was up for forgery in 1805, and was sent to Norfolk Island. Back in Sydney, he was tolerated by Bligh and ended up being head clerk for the Police Department.

Robinson's Odes are often recognised as a beginning of 'Australian literature'. The apparent contradiction of his unreserved praise (as a transportee) for George III and Queen Charlotte certainly captures the anxiety of the colonies to connect to their parents; Robinson's 'situation' also emphasises the irony of this praise. The arrival of these poets in the penal zones defines their relationship to 'home', to what they left behind.

Of course, concurrently tens of thousands of years of poetic and singing tradition continued among the many indigenous tribes throughout Australia. Song cycles, stories of the dreaming, rituals of spiritual significance, the telling of the law all passed through what might be interpreted and respected as the 'poetic'. That is why this volume begins with Aboriginal songs.

MICHAEL MASSEY ROBINSON

Song

(To Celebrate the Anniversary of the Establishment of the Colony)

Philosophers say, and experience declares,
That life is a medley of pleasures and cares; –
That the sunshine which smiles on our prospects to-day,
May be chas'd by the gloom of to-morrow away.

Whilst some, who are strangers to conjugal strife,
Are apt to repine at the loss of a wife, –
There are others (perhaps you may dissolute call 'em)
That are glad to escape from the fetters that gall 'em.

Thus serious and comic, the scene passes on,
The demise of the sire makes way for the son;
When the coffers, by rigid conomy stor'd,
Are squander'd and swallow'd at luxury's board.

For years, on this Isle, a bright Day-star has gleam'd,
And the CHIEF that we hail'd was the Friend we esteem'd;
Now Time, in its triumph, has clos'd his career,
And the smile we have cherish'd – is chang'd to a tear!

Yet, often shall memory cling to THIS DAY,
And often shall gratitude swell the fond lay;
While Australia shall boast, in her annals of story,
THAT HIS SUN, AS IT ROSE – SO IT SET, IN FULL GLORY!

But the shadows that threaten'd our Evening forlorn,
The breath of young Hope shall disperse with the morn;
For grac'd with fresh laurels from Fame's fairest stores,
His Illustrious SUCCESSOR has smil'd on our Shores.

Then, here, whilst in circles of social relation,
Our hearts and our hands join in Commemoration;
From AUSTRALIA'S first dawn – let her trophies proclaim,
That her Standard of WORTH stamps her Passport to FAME.

JOHN GRANT

Verses Written to Lewin, the Entomologist, 1805

Nature! there dwells in these Australian lands
Thy faithful Copyist whose Art expands
Thy novel Beauties o'er our ancient Globe
Who to far distant climes thy Charms derobe.

Modest, laborious, steady in his Plan,
I view, admire and venerate the Man.
And, lest Neglect a tender Genius blight,
Cheer Muse! his Patience; usher him to light!

Lewin: rare, beauteous Plant in Genius Vale!
Painter! Engraver! Nature's wooer! Hail!
Courage! Thy Labours consecrate thy Fame;
Ages to come shall venerate thy Name.

When thy productions European eyes
Gaze on; and Nature, struck with glad surprise:
We think she blossoms but at Lewin's will
Thine imitations mark such wond'rous skill!

Touch'd with delight; involuntary thought
Rebounds to England where, thy labours sought,
Her sons unanimous shall Tribute pay
Thee: wanderer, searching Nature's thorny way.

BARRON FIELD

The Kangaroo

'mixtumque genus, prolesque biformis.'
– VIRGIL Aeneid VI

Kangaroo, Kangaroo!
Thou Spirit of Australia,
That redeems from utter failure,
From perfect desolation,
And warrants the creation
Of this fifth part of the Earth,
Which would seem an after-birth,
Not conceiv'd in the Beginning
(For GOD bless'd His work at first,
And saw that it was good),
But emerg'd at the first sinning,
When the ground was therefore curst; –
And hence this barren wood!

Kangaroo, Kangaroo!
Tho' at first sight we should say,
In thy nature that there may
Contradiction be involv'd,
Yet, like discord well resolv'd,
It is quickly harmoniz'd.
Sphynx or mermaid realiz'd.
Or centaur unfabulous,
Would scarce be more prodigious,
Or Labyrinthine Minotaur,
With which great Theseus did war,
Or Pegasus poetical,
Or hippogriff – chimeras all!

But, what Nature would compile,
Nature knows to reconcile;
And Wisdom, ever at her side,
Of all her children's justified.

She had made the squirrel fragile;
She had made the bounding hart;
But a third so strong and agile
Was beyond ev'n Nature's art.
So she join'd the former two
    In thee, Kangaroo!
To describe thee, it is hard:
Converse of the camélopard,
Which beginneth camel-wise,
But endeth of the panther size,
Thy fore half, it would appear,
Had belong'd to some 'small deer,'
Such as liveth in a tree;
By thy hinder, thou should'st be
A large animal of chace,
Bounding o'er the forest's space; –
Join'd by some divine mistake,
None but Nature's hand can make –
Nature, in her wisdom's play,
On Creation's holiday.

For howsoe'er anomalous,
Thou yet art not incongruous,
Repugnant or preposterous.
Better-proportion'd animal,
More graceful or ethereal,
Was never follow'd by the hound,
With fifty steps to thy one bound.

Thou can'st not be amended: no;
Be as thou art; thou best art so.

When sooty swans are once more rare,
And duck-moles the Museum's care,
Be still the glory of this land,
Happiest Work of finest Hand!

RICHARD WHATELY

There is a Place in Distant Seas

There is a place in distant seas
Full of contrarieties:
There, beasts have mallards' bills and legs,
Have spurs like cocks, like hens lay eggs.
There parrots walk upon the ground,
And grass upon the trees is found;
On other trees, another wonder!
Leaves without upper sides or under.
There pears you'll scarce with hatchet cut;
Stones are outside the cherries put;
Swans are not white, but black as soot.
There neither leaf, nor root, nor fruit
Will any Christian palate suit,
Unless in desperate need you'd fill ye
With root of fern and stalk of lily.
There missiles to far distance sent
Come whizzing back from whence they went;
There quadrupeds go on two feet,
And yet few quadrupeds so fleet;
There birds, although they cannot fly,

In swiftness with your greyhound vie.
With equal wonder you may see
The foxes fly from tree to tree;
And what they value most, so wary,
These foxes in their pockets carry.
There the voracious ewe-sheep crams
Her paunch with flesh of tender lambs,
Instead of beef, and bread, and broth,
Men feast on many a roasted moth.
The north winds scorch, but when the breeze is
Full from the south, why then it freezes;
The sun when you to face him turn ye,
From right to left performs his journey.
Now of what place could such strange tales
Be told with truth save New South Wales? –

ANONYMOUS

To the Editor, *Sydney Gazette*

Australian Aboriginal Song
IMMAH, IMMAH YA,
Gnora worrayn na,
Gnah, bah, yah,
Kummah lah nah,
Towwan kurrah te,
Ure wonnan na,
Undong, undong,
Warrun, warrun na!
Bi yah,
Ko be to
Ting gar rah,

Undong, undong,
Warrun, warrun na!

December, 1825

FIDELIA HILL

Adelaide

'I dreamed a dream last night.'
Romeo & Juliet

I entered the wide spreading streets – methought
    Of a vast city; all was bustle there:
Crowds hurried on with eager looks befraught,
    And hum of many voices filled the air.
Then my eye rested upon buildings rare,
    Circus and crescent to perfection brought,
On splendid stores, where all things rich and rare
    Exposed for sale, by young and old were bought,
While many a rising spire, and spacious dome
    Reminded me of London and of home!

Tho' dear to thought, and to heart doubly dear
    The city of my native land shall be
While memory lasts – there did in this appear
    An added charm perchance 'twas novelty;
Yet all that soul could wish, or eye could see
    For Comfort, ease, convenience, or for cheer –
Treasures for time, and for eternity
    Seemed as by magic art concentrated here.
Proud was the pageant, and a costlier scene
    To mortal sight hath scarce presented been.

And was this Adelaide? then who shall say
(Though but the baseless fabric of a dream)
Young city of the desart, in thy day,
How vast thy grandeur, and thy wealth should seem;
Even from thy early promise we may deem
Great things of thee, for well dost thou repay
The settlers' toil: – on thee may fortune's beam
Rest – and around thy opening prospects play,
Till other lands confess thy rising fame,
And commerce, health, and plenty crown thy name!

ELIZA HAMILTON DUNLOP

The Aboriginal Mother

(from Myall's Creek)

Oh! hush thee – hush my baby,
I may not tend thee yet.
Our forest-home is distant far,
And midnight's star is set.
Now, hush thee – or the pale-faced men
Will hear thy piercing wail,
And what would then thy mother's tears
Or feeble strength avail!

Oh, could'st thy little bosom,
That mother's torture feel,
Or could'st thou know thy father lies
Struck down by English steel;
Thy tender form would wither,
Like the *kniven* in the sand,
And the spirit of my perished tribe
Would vanish from our land.

For thy young life, my precious,
  I fly the field of blood,
Else had I, for my chieftan's sake,
  Defied them where they stood;
But basely bound my woman's arm,
  No weapon might it wield:
I could but cling round him I loved,
  To make my heart a shield.

I saw my firstborn treasure
  Lie headless at my feet,
The goro on this hapless breast,
  In his life-stream is wet!
And thou! I snatched thee from their sword,
  It harmless pass'd by thee!
But clave the binding cords – and gave,
  Haply, the power to flee.

To flee! my babe – but whither?
  Without my friend – my guide?
The blood that was our strength is shed!
  He is not by my side!
Thy sire! oh! never, never
  Shall *Toon Bakra* hear our cry:
My bold and stately mountain-bird!
  I thought not he could die.

Now who will teach thee, dearest,
  To poise the shield, and spear,
To wield the *koopin*, or to throw
  The *boommerring*, void of fear;
To breast the river in its might;
  The mountain tracks to tread?

The echoes of my homeless heart
  Reply – the dead, the dead!

And ever must the murmur
  Like an ocean torrent flow:
The parted voice comes never back,
  To cheer out lonely woe:
Even in the region of our tribe,
  Beside our summer streams,
'Tis but a hollow symphony –
  In the shadow-land of dreams.

Oh hush thee, dear – for weary
  And faint I bear thee on –
His name is on thy gentle lips,
  My child, my child, *he's gone!*
Gone o'er the golden fields that lie
  Beyond the rolling clouds,
To bring thy people's murder cry
  Before the Christian's God.

Yes! o'er the stars that guide us,
  He brings my slaughter'd boy:
To shew their God how treacherously
  The stranger men destroy;
To tell how hands in friendship pledged
  Piled high the fatal pire;
To tell, to tell of the gloomy ridge!
  and the *stockmen's human fire.*

The Aboriginal Father

A transliteration of the Maneroo *dirge*

The shadow, on thy brow my child:
    A mist o'er a clear lagoon,
Steals on with presage – dim and wild;
    Of the *death-god's* direful doom.

Our tribes are falling by their streams,
    Each fount, that fed, is dry!
And the white-man's fire sends forth its gleams
    O'er the *batwan* where they lie.

And thou beloved! the last – the first –
Green branch, of a withering tree
    The stranger's mock will drown the burst
    Of my spirit's lament o'er thee.

WULLATI

Native Poetry

Nung-Ngnun
Nge a runba wonung bulkirra umbilinto bulwarra!
Pital burra kultan wirripang buntoa

Nung-Ngnun
Nge a runba turrama berrambo, burra kilkoa;
Kurri wi, raratoa yella walliko,
Yulo Moane, woinyo, birung poro bulliko,

Nung-Ngnun
Nge a runba kan wullung, Makoro, kokein,

Mip-pa-rai, kekul, wimbi murr ring kirrika;
Nge a runba mura ke-en kulbun kulbun murrung.

Thus '*Translated and Versified by Mrs E. H. Dunlop*,' of Mulla Villa, New South Wales.

Our home is the gibber-gunyah,
  Where hill joins hill on high;
Where the turruma and berrambo,
  Like sleeping serpents lie; –
And the rushing of wings, as the wangas pass,
Sweeps the wallaby's print from the glistening grass.
Ours are the makoro gliding,
  Deep in the shady pool;
  For our spear is sure, and the prey secure . . .
Kanin, or the bright gherool.
  Our lubras sleep by the bato clear,
  That the Amygest's track hath never been near.

  Ours is the koolema flowing
With the precious kirrika stored;
  For fleet the foot, and keen the eye,
That seeks the nukkung's hoard; –
  And the glancess are bright, and the footsteps are free,
  When we dance in the shade of the karakon tree.

Gibber-gunya – Cave in the rock. *Turruna* [sic] and *Berrambo* – War arms. *Wanga* – A species of pigeon. *Makoro* – Fish. *Amygest* – Whitefellow. *Kanim* – Eel. *Gheerool* – Mullet. *Bato* – Water. *Kirrika* – Honey. *Nukkung* – Wild bee. *Kurrakun* – The oak tree.

SARAH COLLINS

Lament

They chain us two by two, and whip and lash along,
They cut off our provisions, if we do the least thing wrong,
They march us in the burning sun, until our feet are sore,
So hard's our lot now we are got upon Van Diemen's shore.
We labour hard from morn to night, until our bones do ache,
Then every one, they must obey, their mouldy beds must make;
We often wish, when we lay down, we ne'er may rise no more,
To meet our savage governors upon Van Diemen's shore.
Every night when I lay down, I wash my straw with tears,
While wind upon that horrid shore to whistle in our ears;
Those dreadful beasts upon that land around our cots do roar;
Most dismal is our doom upon Van Diemen's shore.
Come all young men and maidens, do bad company forsake,
If tongue can tell our overthrow, it would make your heart to
    ache;
You girls, I pray, be ruled by me, your wicked ways give o'er,
For fear, like us, you spend your days upon Van Diemen's shore.

MARY LEMAN GRIMSTONE

On Visiting the Cemetery at Hobart Town

And here, like England's sad exiles, this wild spot
The sad conclusion of their mournful lot, –
Here, a true type of all their griefs I find,
This scene, neglected, naked, and unkind!
Here, as I wander through the weed-grown graves
Of some, perchance, yet loved beyond the waves,
The splashy waters rise at ev'ry tread

As if the tears of the indignant dead
Reproaching, with mute eloquence, the race
That could assign them *such a resting place.*
Where is the decent order that should keep
The last sad home where friends and lovers sleep?
Where is the neatness that should still preside
Where rest the objects of our love and pride?
Ah, my own country, when thy hamlets rise
In all their rural graces to my eyes,
Not such the scenes thy humble churchyards yield
Where love yet guards the tomb that death has seal'd,
Where, hovering o'er the graves of age and youth,
The holy calm still speaks the moral truth,
That all must know full soon, yet learn too late,
The doom of human kind – decree of fate –
Oh, here, where all is young, save grief and crime,
Toil must anticipate the work of time,
Nor were that task less holy which should trace
A decent scene for death's sad dwelling place;
Where grief might look with sad respect, and dry
The tear which starts, unbidden, to the eye:
And where, when years have sooth'd the mourner's pain,
Memory may wake those fond regrets again –
With less of bitterness, while tears will roll,
That purify the heart and soothe the soul –
Where when we quit the house of pray'r we may
With chasten'd spirits through its pathway stray,
And still prolong the feeling we have caught
From the bright altar of religious thought;
Ponder again the precepts that are given
To lead us to the grave, and thence to heaven!

RICHARD HOWITT

To the Daisy

On finding one unexpectedly in Australia, 30 July 1840

Whence was the silvery gleam that came?
A daisy! can it be the same?
– Some fairy from my native land
For me this glad surprise has planned,
Of light and joy a sudden shower,
Or never had I seen this hour,
Our real English daisy-flower.

Daily I meet some shape or hue
That brings old times before me new:
Some token of life's brightest hours,
In streams and trees, in birds and flowers:
The past is by such spells unbound:
But never, until now, have found
What made me feel on English ground.

Of poesy thou favorite child!
First seen when some blest angel smiled!
O'er Britain scattered every where –
But strangely solitary here –
Yet buoyant-looking, brisk and bold,
That with like cheer do I behold
Thy silver rays and disk of gold.

These mosses, ferns, resemble ours:
These sundew, sorrel, speedwell-flowers:
Yet none are in all points the same
As in the isle from whence we came,

Save thee, dear daisy! thee alone, –
Thy crimson tips proclaim thee known;
At once we hail thee, all our own!

Now easy seems it to my mind,
I also may a primrose find
In some shy glen; or it may be
A cowslip nodding on the lea:
All things are possible, it seems,
To him, for whom the fairy schemes,
Whose waking hours are blest as dreams.

O, not miscalled the eye of day –
Sweet gowan of the Scottish brae!
Close shut at eve: with dawning light,
Opening on heathy summits bright:
When first the crimson streaks the gloom,
That very tint dost thou assume,
And sweetly blushest into bloom.

Flower of the dawn, and dawn of song!
O, well may grace to thee belong!
By ancient bards how blazoned wide –
And how by Wordsworth glorified!
And seen by Burns he could not choose
But crown thee with unfading hues –
Thou – loved of every sylvan muse!

In England thou art always seen,
On mead, on moor, on village-green:
In forest glen, on mountain height;
A common thing in common sight;
But here, 'midst flowers superbly dressed,

Shalt thou, and prized o'er all the rest,
Become our cherished garden-guest.

Australian flowers I prize nor scorn;
Let those who in this land were born
Admire them, praise them, pluck and wear
On swarthy brow, in jet-black hair:
I never gathered them, nor knew,
Where I a child to manhood grew; –
What have I then with them to do?

Yet flowers bloom here of loveliest dye,
Where roves and rests the enamoured eye;
Chaste forms, and tints of beauty rare;
For these no fondness can I spare;
Of song they have no generous dower;
No life-long memory, homely power,
Like thee, our darling English-flower.

ANONYMOUS

Scraps from a Bushman's Note Book

Port Phillip! land of many wonders;
Land of lightning; land of thunders;
Land of various reptiles evil;
Land of heat would scorch the devil;
Land of every savage vice;
Land of Christian avarice;
Land of emus, kangaroos;
Land of parrots, cockatoos;
Land of pelicans, black swans;
Land of possums and tuans;

Land of bandicoots, wild cats;
Land of Platipusses, rabbit rats;
Land of march flies and mosquitos;
Land of pumpkins and tomatoes;
Land whose various winged tribes
Are yet unsung by learned scribes;
Land of gloomy desolation;
Land of reckless dissipation;
Land of damper, tea, and mutton,
Enough to satiate a glutton;
On damper, mutton, and bohea,
Poor bushmen fare three times a day.
Land of murderers, burglars, robbers;
Pickpockets, lawyers, and landjobbers.
From every turn my fate directs,
I feel the gloomiest effects –
By day by hosts of flies invaded,
At night by wild dogs serenaded.

JOHN DUNMORE LANG

Colonial Nomenclature

'Twas said of Greece two thousand years ago,
  That every stone i' the land had got a name.
Of New South Wales too, men will soon say so too;
  But every stone there seems to get the same.
'Macquarie' for a name is all *the go*:
  The old Scotch Governor was fond of fame,
Macquarie Street, Place, Port, Fort, Town, Lake, River:
'Lachlan Macquarie, Esquire, Governor', for ever!

I like the native names, as Parramatta,
  And Illawarra, and Woolloomoolloo;
Nandowra, Woogarora, Bulkomatta,
  Tomah, Toongabbie, Mittagong, Meroo;
Buckobble, Cumleroy, and Coolingatta,
  The Warragumby, Bargo, Burradoo;
Cookbundoon, Carrabaiga, Wingecarribbee,
The Wollondilly, Yurumbon, Bungarribbee.

I hate your Goulburn Downs and Goulburn Plains,
  And Goulburn River and the Goulburn Range,
And Mount Goulburn and Goulburn Vale! One's brains
  Are turned with Goulburns! Vile scorbutic mange
For immortality! Had I the reins
  Of Government a fortnight, I would change
These Downing Street appellatives, and give
The country names that should deserve to live.

I'd have Mount Hampden and Mount Marvell, and
  Mount Wallace and Mount Bruce at the old Bay.
I'd have them all the highest in the land,
  That men might see them twenty leagues away.
I'd have the Plains of Marathon beyond
  Some mountain pass yclept Thermopylae.
Such are th' immortal names that should be written
On all thy new discoveries, Great Britain!

Yes! let some badge of liberty appear
  On every mountain and on every plain
Where Britain's power is known, or far or near,
  That freedom there may have an endless reign!
Then though she die, in some revolving year,
  A race may rise to make her live again!

The future slave may lisp the patriot's name
And his breast kindle with a kindred flame!

I love thee, Liberty, thou blue-eyed maid!
  Thy beauty fades not in the hottest clime!
In purple or plebeian garb arrayed
  I love thee still! The great in olden time,
Roman and Greek, worshipped thy very shade
  And sung thy beauty in their song sublime.
'Tis Paradise to live beneath thy smile,
Thou patron Goddess of my native isle.

But he that loves fair Liberty must be
  Virtue's sworn friend. The vicious is a slave
And serves a tyrant, nor can e'er be free.
  Of old her wooers were like Brutus, brave;
Like Marvell, incorrupt; Milton, like thee!
  A recreant race wooes now and digs her grave;
Byron their leader, whose high-lineaged muse
Walks a vile pimp and caters for the stews!

Choice work for British Peers! Baser alliance
  Than Austria's with her band of despot kings!
For he who setteth virtue at defiance
  And holds her dread commands as paltriest things,
Whate'er his rank, learning, or wit, or science,
  Or high pretence of love for freedom, brings
A tyrant worse than Slavery in his train
And binds men with a more ignoble chain.

On Freedom's altar ere I place strange fire
  Be my arm withered from its shoulder-blade!
Yea! were I lord of Great Apollo's lyre,

I'd sooner rend its chords than e'er degrade
Its sweet seraphic music to inspire
One vicious thought! When built on vice, fair maid,
Thy temple's base is quicksand; on the rock
Of virtue reared, it braves the whirlwind's shock.

(1824)

nineteenth century

The nineteenth century was a period of flux in which new colonies were founded and eventually all colonies worked together to become a federation, finally emerging as the Commonwealth of Australia in 1901. This move towards nation brought with it its own problems, though, and the exploration and occupation of indigenous lands continued at a rapid, overwhelming pace. There was resistance and there were massacres. Remains of deceased indigenous people were shipped back to Britain as curios and collectibles, as the centre of Empire took stock of its 'holdings'. It has been convenient to label all indigenous people in Australia as one people, but though there is a sense of shared origin, purpose, celebration and resistance, Australia is a land of many indigenous peoples. The small representation of indigenous-related material here reflects the limitations of such anthologising, and the overwhelming context of the colonial and its control of 'history', reception and voice. There are strong 'colonial' voices of protest as well, however, as is evidenced in Dunlop (see previous section) and others.

Though this is an anthology in English, a significant number of new arrivals traced their origins outside Britain. This was also the century of significant Irish migration. Many of the poems included here are poems of migration, though we also see the first poems of the so-called 'native-born', non-indigenous Australians. It is easy (and convenient for some) to forget that this was also a century of strong Chinese presence in Australia, and that other languages also travelled here.

Those born in the nineteenth century are the generators of what we understand as an Australian literature now. The moderns find their feet here, but so do many who prefer to retain a worldview from previous eras. The post-enlightenment values of science, industry and self are in the mix, but so are the genealogical obsessions of fealty to Church and country, and a classical education. So isolated from the sources of these values, the mimicry of 'old' European models formed hybrids and distortions that necessarily generated their own values and mythologies. By the time we reach the turmoils and affirmations of the 1890s, with strikes and cooperations among workers, and within the machinery of industry (railway lines, telegraphs and so on), in the move towards Federation, the claim to a character that is quintessentially Australian, based on egalitarianism, mateship and other now-clichés of Australian identity, have well and truly been established. Such an identity took characteristics out of their origins, but was in many ways defined against it.

This is the age of the Australian landscape becoming a subject in itself. It is the age of the Australian-born Harpur and Kendall, who so wrestled with the specificities of the Australian environment in their poems – though the old world of which they were never a part constantly reached through to the new world in which they were writing. They were sophisticated poets dealing with complex issues of dispossession and usurpation, with recognition and claim, without fully working out their positions, and they remained caught in the values of expectation – what the readers expected – as well. This is the birth-age of Henry Lawson, born in the bush, out in the New South Wales gold diggings, resentful of the bush evermore, but truly part of it. It is the birth-age of the-city-and-the-bush dichotomy, with all its frictions, and its popular usage in the nation-making agendas.

Some of the greatest Australian poets were born during the nineteenth century. And I believe it's the crash course in modernity mixed with the colonial drag and allure of the bush as a place apart from the rest of the world that makes this mixture unique in the world. We see the first poetic steps of John Shaw Neilson, that poet with no education, almost no eyesight, who as an itinerant labourer recited his poems to fellow workers for them to copy, whom many compare to the symbolist poets of France, but who probably never read them. He was maverick, unique, delicate and strangely robust as well.

There's David Unaipon, claimed to be the first Aborigine to write books in English (though this is arguable), but who certainly brought indigenous tales to a broader audience. His tales are superb poetic renderings of the stories of his people. It's the age of that symbolist-modernist Christopher Brennan, who wrote *livres composés* as great as anything written in the same period elsewhere in the world. An intellectual and academic, he took his knowledge of languages to Australian poetry, and without having to include overtly Australian referents made his readers see that what was being achieved in Europe was also being achieved close at hand.

This is the birth period of the great war poet Leon Gellert, who within twenty-two years of his birth date would be on his way to the trenches of Europe. His poetry stands up there with that of Sassoon and Owen. This is the age of the radical and unique Lesbia Harford, whose poetry of ambivalent sexuality, working-class values and tilted syntax would open the doors to modernism in so many ways. Zora Cross is in there as well: modern love that has the urge of Meredith's brilliant 'Modern Love' sequence, but with a feminist drive and a sensibility borne out of the destruction and madness of global war.

CHARLES TOMPSON

Ode V. to Sylvia

Hast thou not seen some captive bird
   Impatient flit within the wire,
And seek the bliss of liberty,
   With anxious fond desire?

Or hast thou not beheld, in chains,
   Some poor unhappy pris'ner pine?
E'en such a wretched slave am I,
   E'en such hard fetters mine.

But yet from these I differ too,
   For they would cast their chains away,
While I exult to wear the badge
   Of thy unpitying sway.

Then deign, fair nymph, one smile of love,
   One ray of ruddy hope impart!
O, give this life the pow'r to live,
   And heal the wounded heart!

'FRANK THE POET' (Francis MacNamara)

Labouring with the Hoe

I was convicted by the laws
Of England's hostile crown,
Conveyed across those swelling seas
In slavery's fetters bound.
For ever banished from that shore
Where love and friendship grow

That loss of freedom to deplore
And work the labouring hoe.

Despised, rejected and oppressed
In tattered rags I'm clad,
What anguish fills my aching breast
And almost drives me mad,
When I hear the settler's threatening voice
Say, 'Arise, to labour go;
Take scourging, convicts for your choice
Or work the labouring hoe.'

Growing weary from compulsive toil
Beneath the noontide sun,
While drops of sweat bedew the soil
My task remains undone.
I'm flogged for wilful negligence
Or the tyrants call it so,
Ah, what a doleful recompense
For labouring with the hoe.

Behold lofty woodbine hills
Where the rose in the morning shines,
Those crystal brooks that do distil
And mingle through those vines –
There seems to me no pleasure gained,
They but augment my woe
Whilst here an outcast doomed to live
And work the labouring hoe.

You generous sons of Erin's isle
Whose heart for glory burns,
Pity a wretched exile who

His long-lost country mourns;
Restore me, Heaven to liberty
Whilst I lie here below
Untie that clue of bondage
And release me from the hoe.

Farewell to Tasmania

Farewell Tasmania's Isle!
        I bid adieu
The possum and the kangaroo.
Farmers' Glory! Prisoners' Hell!
        Land of Buggers!
        Fare ye well.

CHARLES HARPUR

A Flight of Wild Ducks

Far up the River – hark! 'tis the loud shock
Deadened by distance, of some Fowler's gun:
And as into the stillness of the scene
It wastes now with a dull vibratory boom,
Look where, fast widening up at either end
Out of the sinuous valley of the waters,
And o'er the intervenient forest, – up
Against the open heaven, a long dark *line*
Comes hitherward stretching – a vast Flight of Ducks!
Following the windings of the vale, and still
Enlarging lengthwise, and in places too
Oft breaking into solitary dots,
How swiftly onward comes it – till at length,

The River, reaching through a group of hills,
Off leads it, – out of sight. But not for long:
For, wheeling ever with the water's course,
Here into sudden view it comes again
Sweeping and swarming round the nearest point!
And first now, a swift airy rush is heard
Approaching momently; – then all at once
There passes a keen-cutting, gusty tumult
Of strenuous pinions, with a streaming mass
Of instantaneous skiey streaks; each streak
Evolving with a lateral flirt, and thence
Entangling as it were, – so rapidly
A thousand wings outpointingly dispread
In passing tiers, seem, looked at from beneath,
With rushing intermixtures to involve
Each other as they beat. Thus seen o'erhead
Even while we speak – ere we have spoken – lo!
The living cloud is onward many a rood,
Tracking as 'twere in the smooth stream below
The multifarious shadow of itself.
Far coming – present – and far gone at once!
The senses vainly struggle to retain
The impression of an Image (as the same)
So swift and manifold: For now again
A long dark *line* upon the utmost verge
Of the horizon, steeping still, it sinks
At length into the landscape; where yet seen
Though dimly, with a wide and scattering sweep
It fetches eastward, and in column so
Dapples along the steep face of the ridge
There banking the turned River. Now it drops
Below the fringing oaks – but to arise

Once more, with a quick circling gleam, as touched
By the slant sunshine, and then disappear
As instantaneously, – there settling down
Upon the reedy bosom of the water.

A Mid-Summer Noon in the Australian Forest

Not a bird disturbs the air,
There is quiet everywhere;
Over plains and over woods
What a mighty stillness broods.

Even the grasshoppers keep
Where the coolest shadows sleep;
Even the busy ants are found
Resting in their pebbled mound;
Even the locust clingeth now
In silence to the barky bough:
And over hills and over plains
Quiet, vast and slumbrous, reigns.

Only there's a drowsy humming
From yon warm lagoon slow coming:
'Tis the dragon-hornet – see!
All bedaubed resplendently
With yellow on a tawny ground –
Each rich spot nor square nor round,
But rudely heart-shaped, as it were
The blurred and hasty impress there,

Of a vermeil-crusted seal
Dusted o'er with golden meal:
Only there's a droning where

Yon bright beetle gleams the air –
Gleams it in its droning flight
With a slanting track of light,
Till rising in the sunshine higher,
Its shards flame out like gems on fire.

  Every other thing is still,
Save the ever wakeful rill,
Whose cool murmur only throws
A cooler comfort round Repose;
Or some ripple in the sea
Of leafy boughs, where, lazily,
Tired Summer, in her forest bower
Turning with the noontide hour,
Heaves a slumbrous breath, ere she
Once more slumbers peacefully.

O 'tis easeful here to lie
Hidden from Noon's scorching eye,
In this grassy cool recess
Musing thus of Quietness.

CAROLINE CARLETON

On the Suicide of a Young Lady

No priestly requiem is heard,
  Hushed is the voice of prayer,
She lies in a dishonoured grave –
  The suicide lies there!

And did no funeral hymn arise?
  Hark to the pitying wall

That bursts from every mother's heart,
   Who hears that dreadful tale.

And prayer is there – but mutter's deep,
   By brothers with clench'd fists;
'The brand of Cain be on his brow,
   Wander he where he lists!'

O God of heaven! powerless to aid
   Are all our human laws!
Infinite judge of right! to thee
   We leave the victim's cause.

CAROLINE LEAKEY

The Prisoners' Hospital, Van Diemen's Land

O PRISON-HOUSE of sighing!
   Where the weary and the worn,
The long-pent and the dying,
   Lie friendless and forlorn;
Where sickness preys on weariness,
   And prey they both on life;
The mother weeps in dreariness,
   And pines the lonely wife.

Where tender babe and wasted child
   Look eagerly around,
And wonder why the face that smiled,
   Can nowhere *now* be found.
Where on the sickly little one
   Rests no kind eye of love;
Its pleading moan there heark'neth none,
   Save God, who dwells above.

Meet old and young together,
  Each their numbered days to fill;
One grudging still the other,
  And all fretting at God's will.
The widow mourns her widowhood.
  All childless and alone;
The old man dies in solitude,
  None near to call his own.

The piercing shriek of madness,
  And the hollow face of care,
Meet tears and sighs of sadness,
  And the wailings of despair,
Where the captive exile hasteth,
  And striveth to be free,
From the bitterness he tasteth
  Of sin's deep misery.

The restless cry for morning,
  The weary pine for night,
But darkness nor the dawning
  Cometh e'er to them aright.
Where Time, so heavy dragg'd with strife
  On wheels of grief moves slow;
Bearing the wretched on through life,
  Up paths of human woe.

O'er the dead there is no weeping,
  By the dying none to pray,
That Death's dark shade o'er creeping,
  Be illumined by Love's ray.
But cold, they watch each other die,
  Still shuddering to see

Yon ruthless hand close up each eye,
As theirs must closèd be.

Oh! ere Death's heavy bolt be drawn
Upon life's gate for ever,
And deeps of black perdition yawn
Beneath their souls for ever,
Thou who sweet mercy lov'st to show,
Look down! forgive – relent!
Haste, Lord, ere sealèd this worst woe,
On earth's long banishment.

ANONYMOUS

The Wild Colonial Boy

There was a wild colonial boy, Jack Donahoe by name,
Of poor but honest parents he was born in Castlemaine.
He was his father's dearest hope, his mother's pride and joy.
O, fondly did his parents love their Wild Colonial Boy.

Chorus:
So ride with me, my hearties, we'll cross the mountains high.
Together we will plunder, together we will die.
We'll wander through the valleys and gallop o'er the plains,
For we scorn to live in slavery, bound down with iron chains!

He was scarcely sixteen years of age when he left his father's home,
A convict to Australia, across the seas to roam.
They put him in the Iron Gang in the Government employ,
But ne'er an iron on earth could hold the Wild Colonial Boy.

And when they sentenced him to hang to end his wild career,
With a loud shout of defiance bold Donahue broke clear.

He robbed those wealthy squatters, their stock he did destroy,
But never a trap in the land could catch the Wild Colonial Boy.

Then one day when he was cruising near the broad Nepean's side,
From out the thick Bringelly bush the horse police did ride.
'Die or resign, Jack Donahoe!' they shouted in their joy.
'I'll fight this night with all my might!' cried the Wild Colonial Boy.

He fought six rounds with the horse police before the fatal ball,
Which pierced his heart with cruel smart, caused Donahoe to fall.
And then he closed his mournful eyes, his pistol an empty toy,
Crying: 'Parents dear, O say a prayer for the Wild Colonial Boy.'

ELIZABETH DEBORAH BROCKMAN

On Receiving From England a Bunch of Dried Wild Flowers

Pale Ghosts! of fragrant things that grew among
The woods and valleys of my native land,
Phantoms of flowers I played with long ago:
Here are the scented violets I sought
In their cool nooks of verdure, and the bells
That fringed the mountain crag with loveliest blue;
Here are the flushing clusters of the May,
The dainty primrose on its slender stem;
And the forget-me-not – all faint and pale
As those dim memories of home that haunt
The exile's wistful heart in banishment.

I look around and see
A thousand gayer tints; the wilderness
Is bright with gorgeous rainbow colouring

Of flowers that have no dear familiar names.
I see them closing ere the dews of night
Have touched their waxen leaflets: close they fold
Their tender blossoms through the darkened hours.
And will not open, though the fractious winds
Should wrestle with their roots and strain their stems.
They waken not until the softer airs,
Breathed from the rosy lips of early morn,
Come whispering, 'lo! the lordly sun is nigh.'

But in my hand these frail memorials
Lie closely pressed; a slight electric link,
By which thought over-passes time and space,
To other hands that plucked them: other hands
That never more to any touch of mine
Shall thrill responsive. Blessed be those hands
With prosperous labours, fruitful through long years,
Of all life's truest, tenderest charities.

J. BRENCHLEY

Odorous Melbourne

Odorous Melbourne, city of stinks!
What fragrance o'erhovers thy cesspools and sinks; –
I have smelt many smells, but the richest *per se*,
May justly be claim'd, luscious Melbourne, by thee.
When the sun has gone down, and the wind's in the west,
And the night-air is heavy, by closeness opprest,
From thy fam'd open drains, a soft essence is thrown,
An odour delightful, uniquely thine own.
  Odorous Melbourne – delectable Melbourne!
  Odoriferous Melbourne – sweet Stinkomalee!

Cologne may boast proudly – that sanctified town
Of the forty odd stinks that enhance its renown;
But thine has a raciness rivall'd by none,
Like all the full forty commingled in one.
And though time-honour'd odours pervade the Fleet Ditch,
With its full-flavour'd mud and perfumeries rich,
Let them boast as they may: to this creed I incline,
It is not a patch on these brave drains of thine.
  Odorous Melbourne – delectable Melbourne!
  Odoriferous Melbourne – soft Stinkomalee!

ADAM LINDSAY GORDON

The Sick Stockrider

Hold hard, Ned! Lift me down once more, and lay me in the
    shade.
  Old man, you've had your work cut out to guide
Both horses, and to hold me in the saddle when I sway'd,
  All through the hot, slow, sleepy, silent ride.
The dawn at 'Moorabinda' was a mist rack dull and dense,
  The sunrise was a sullen, sluggish lamp;
I was dozing in the gateway at Arbuthnot's bound'ry fence,
  I was dreaming on the Limestone cattle camp.
We crossed the creek at Carricksford, and sharply through the
    haze,
  And suddenly the sun shot flaming forth;
To southward lay 'Katâwa', with the sandpeaks all ablaze,
  And the flush'd fields of Glen Lomond lay to north.
Now westward winds the bridle path that leads to Lindisfarm,
  And yonder looms the double-headed Bluff;

From the far side of the first hill, when the skies are clear and
calm,
You can see Sylvester's woolshed fair enough.
Five miles we used to call it from our homestead to the place
Where the big tree spans the roadway like an arch;
'Twas here we ran the dingo down that gave us such a chase
Eight years ago – or was it nine? – last March.

'Twas merry in the glowing morn, among the gleaming grass,
To wander as we've wandered many a mile,
And blow the cool tobacco cloud, and watch the white wreaths
pass,
Sitting loosely in the saddle all the while.
'Twas merry 'mid the blackwoods, when we spied the station
roofs,
To wheel the wild scrub cattle at the yard,
With a running fire of stockwhips and a fiery run of hoofs;
Oh! the hardest day was never then too hard!

Ay! we had a glorious gallop after 'Starlight' and his gang,
When they bolted from Sylvester's on the flat;
How the sun-dried reed-beds crackled, how the flint-strewn
ranges rang
To the strokes of 'Mountaineer' and 'Acrobat'.
Hard behind them in the timber, harder still across the heath,
Close beside them through the tea-tree scrub we dash'd;
And the golden-tinted fern leaves, how they rustled
underneath!
And the honeysuckle osiers, how they crash'd!

We led the hunt throughout, Ned, on the chestnut and the
grey,

And the troopers were three hundred yards behind,
While we emptied our six-shooters on the bushrangers at bay,
In the creek with stunted box-tree for a blind!
There you grappled with the leader, man to man and horse to horse,
And you roll'd together when the chestnut rear'd;
He blazed away and missed you in that shallow watercourse –
A narrow shave – his powder singed your beard!

In these hours when life is ebbing, how those days when life was young
Come back to us; how clearly I recall
Even the yarns Jack Hall invented, and the songs Jem Roper sung;
And where are now Jem Roper and Jack Hall?

Ay! nearly all our comrades of the old colonial school,
Our ancient boon companions, Ned, are gone;
Hard livers for the most part, somewhat reckless as a rule,
It seems that you and I are left alone.

There was Hughes, who got in trouble through that business with the cards,
It matters little what became of him;
But a steer ripp'd up MacPherson in the Cooraminta yards,
And Sullivan was drown'd at Sink-or-swim;

And Mostyn – poor Frank Mostyn – died at last a fearful wreck,
In 'the horrors', at the Upper Wandinong,
And Carisbrooke, the rider, at the Horsefall broke his neck,
Faith! the wonder was he saved his neck so long!
Ah! those days and nights we squandered at the Logans' in the glen –
The Logans, man and wife, have long been dead.

Elsie's tallest girl seems taller than your little Elsie then;
And Ethel is a woman grown and wed.

I've had my share of pastime, and I've done my share of toil,
And life is short – the longest life a span;
I care not now to tarry for the corn or for the oil,
Or for the wine that maketh glad the heart of man.
For good undone and gifts misspent and resolutions vain,
'Tis somewhat late to trouble. This I know –
I should live the same life over, if I had to live again;
And the chances are I go where most men go.

The deep blue skies wax dusky, and the tall green trees grow dim,
The sward beneath me seems to heave and fall;
And sickly, smoky shadows through the sleepy sunlight swim,
And on the very sun's face weave their pall.
Let me slumber in the hollow where the wattle blossoms wave,
With never stone or rail to fence my bed;
Should the sturdy station children pull the bush flowers on my grave,
I may chance to hear them romping overhead.

I don't suppose I shall, though, for I feel like sleeping sound,
That sleep they say is doubtful. True; but yet
At least it makes no difference to the dead man underground
What the living men remember or forget.
Enigmas that perplex us is the world's unequal strife
The future may ignore or may reveal,
YET SOME, AS WEAK AS WATER, NED! TO MAKE THE BEST OF LIFE,
Have been, TO FACE THE WORST AS TRUE AS STEEL.

GEORGE GORDON McCRAE

Life's a Cigar

'Life's a cigar': the wasting body glows;
The head turns white as Kosciusko's snows;
And, with the last soul-fragrance still in air,
The ashes slowly sink in soft repose.

HENRY KENDALL

Aboriginal Death-Song

Feet of the flying, and fierce
  Tops of the sharp-headed spear,
Hard by the thickets that pierce,
  Lo! they are nimble and near.

Women are we, and the wives
  Strong Arrawatta hath won;
Weary because of our lives,
  Sick of the face of the sun.

Koola, our love and our light,
  What have they done unto you?
Man of the star-reaching sight,
  Dipped in the fire and the dew.

Black-headed snakes in the grass
  Struck at the fleet-footed lord –
Still is his voice at the pass,
  Soundless his step at the ford.

Far by the forested glen,
  Starkly he lies in the rain;

Kings of the council of men
  Shout for their leader in vain.

Yea, and the fish-river clear
  Never shall blacken below
Spear and the shadow of spear,
  Bow and the shadow of bow.

Hunter and climber of trees,
  Now doth his tomahawk rust,
(Dread of the cunning wild bees),
  Hidden in hillocks of dust.

We, who were followed and bound,
  Dashed under foot by the foe,
Sit with our eyes to the ground,
  Faint from the brand and the blow.

Dumb with the sorrow that kills,
  Sorrow for brother and chief,
Terror of thundering hills,
  Having no hope in our grief,

Seeing the fathers are far
  Seeking the spoils of the dead
Left on the path of the war,
  Matted and mangled and red.

Bell-birds

By channels of coolness the echoes are calling,
And down the dim gorges I hear the creek falling:
It lives in the mountain where moss and the sedges

Touch with their beauty the banks and the ledges.
Through brakes of the cedar and sycamore bowers
Struggles the light that is love to the flowers;
And, softer than slumber, and sweeter than singing,
The notes of the bell-birds are running and ringing.

The silver-voiced bell-birds, the darlings of daytime!
They sing in September their songs of the May-time;
When shadows wax strong and the thunder-bolts hurtle,
They hide with their fear in the leaves of the myrtle;
When rain and the sunbeams shine mingled together,
They start up like fairies that follow fair weather;
And straightway the hues of their feathers unfolden
Are the green and the purple, the blue and the golden.

October, the maiden of bright yellow tresses,
Loiters for love in these cool wildernesses;
Loiters, knee-deep, in the grasses, to listen,
Where dripping rocks gleam and the leafy pools glisten:
Then is the time when the water-moons splendid
Break with their gold, and are scattered or blended
Over the creeks, till the woodlands have warning
Of songs of the bell-bird and wings of the Morning.

Welcome as waters unkissed by the summers
Are the voices of bell-birds to thirsty far-comers.
When fiery December sets foot in the forest,
And the need of the wayfarer presses the sorest,
Pent in the ridges for ever and ever
The bell-birds direct him to spring and to river,
With ring and with ripple, like runnels whose torrents
Are toned by the pebbles and leaves in the currents.

Often I sit, looking back to a childhood,
Mixt with the sights and the sounds of the wildwood,
Longing for power and the sweetness to fashion,
Lyrics with beats like the heart-beats of Passion; –
Songs interwoven of lights and of laughters
Borrowed from bell-birds in far forest-rafters;
So I might keep in the city and alleys
The beauty and strength of the deep mountain valleys:
Charming to slumber the pain of my losses
With glimpses of creeks and a vision of mosses.

ADA CAMBRIDGE

An Old Doll

Low on her little stool she sits
  To make a nursing lap,
And cares for nothing but the form
  Her little arms enwrap.

With hairless skull that gapes apart,
  A broken plaster ball,
One chipped glass eye that squints askew,
  And ne'er a nose at all –

No raddle left on grimy cheek,
  No mouth that one can see –
It scarce discloses, at a glance,
  What it was meant to be.

But something in the simple scheme
  As it extends below

(It is the 'tidy' from my chair
    That she is rumpling so) –

A certain folding of the stuff
    That winds the thing about
(But still permits the sawdust gore
    To trickle down and out) –

The way it curves around her waist,
    On little knees outspread –
Implies a body frail and dear,
    Whence one infers a head.

She rocks the scarecrow to and fro,
    With croonings soft and deep,
A lullaby designed to hush
    The bunch of rags to sleep.

I ask what rubbish has she there.
    'My dolly,' she replies,
But tone and smile and gesture say,
    'My angel from the skies.'

Ineffable the look of love
    Cast on the hideous blur
That somehow means a precious face,
    Most beautiful, to her.

The deftness and the tenderness
    Of her caressing hands . . . . . .
How can she possibly divine
    For what the creature stands?

Herself a nurseling, that has seen
    The summers and the snows

Of scarce five years of baby life.
    And yet she knows – she knows.

Just as a puppy of the pack
    Knows unheard huntsman's call,
And knows it is a running hound
    Before it learns to crawl.

Just as she knew, when hardly born,
    The breast unseen before,
And knew – how well! – before they touched,
    What milk and mouth were for.

So! by some mystic extra-sense
    Denied to eyes and ears,
Her spirit communes with its own
    Beyond the veil of years.

She hears unechoing footsteps run
    On floors she never trod,
Sees lineaments invisible
    As is the face of God –

Forms she can recognise and greet,
    Though wholly hid from me.
Alas! a treasure that is not,
    And that may never be.

The majesty of motherhood
    Sits on her baby brow;
Before her little three-legged throne
    My grizzled head must bow.

That dingy bundle in her arms
    Symbols immortal things –

A heritage, by right divine,
    Beyond the claims of kings.

Fashion

See those resplendent creatures, as they glide
    O'er scarlet carpet, between footmen tall,
    From sumptuous carriage to effulgent hall –
A dazzling vision in their pomp and pride!
See that choice supper – needless – cast aside –
    Though worth a thousand fortunes, counting all,
    To them for whom no crumb of it will fall –
The starved and homeless in the street outside.

Some day the little great god will decree
    That overmuch connotes the underbred,
    That pampered body means an empty head,
And wealth displayed the last vulgarity.
When selfish greed becomes a social sin
The world's regeneration may begin.

MARCUS CLARKE

In a Lady's Album

(Written in the Album of Mrs. H.G. Turner, of Melbourne)

What can I write in thee, O dainty book,
  About whose daintiness quaint perfume lingers –
Into whose pages dainty ladies look,
  And turn thy dainty leaves with daintier fingers?

Fitter my ruder muse for ruder song,
  My scrawling quill to coarser paper matches,

My voice, in laughter raised too loud and long,
  Is hoarse and cracked with singing tavern-catches.

No melodies have I for ladies' ear,
  No roundelays for jocund lads and lasses, –
But only brawlings born of bitter beer,
  And chorused with the clink and clash of glasses.

So tell thy mistress, pretty friend, for me
  I cannot do her 'hest for all her frowning,
While dust and ink are but polluting thee,
  And vile tobacco smoke thy leaves embrowning.

Thou breathest purity and humble worth –
  The simple jest, the light laugh following after,
I will not jar upon thy modest mirth
  With harsher jest, or with less gentle laughter.

So some poor tavern-hunter steeped in wine,
  With staggering footsteps thro' the streets returning,
Seeing, through gathering glooms, a sweet light shine
  From household lamp in happy window burning,

May pause an instant in the wind and rain,
  To gaze on that sweet scene of love and duty,
But turns into the wild wet night again,
  Lest his sad presence mar its holy beauty.

MARY HANNAY FOOTT

Where the Pelican Builds

The horses were ready, the rails were down,
  But the riders lingered still, –
    One had a parting word to say,
  And one had his pipe to fill.
Then they mounted, one with a granted prayer,
  And one with a grief unguessed.
    'We are going' they said, as they rode away –
  'Where the pelican builds her nest!'

They had told us of pastures wide and green,
  To be sought past the sunset's glow;
    Of rifts in the ranges by opal lit;
  And gold 'neath the river's flow.
And thirst and hunger were banished words
  When they spoke of that unknown West;
    No drought they dreaded, no flood they feared,
  Where the pelican builds her nest!

The creek at the ford was but fetlock deep
  When we watched them crossing there;
    The rains have replenished it thrice since then
  And thrice has the rock lain bare.
But the waters of Hope have flowed and fled,
  And never from blue hill's breast
    Come back – by the sun and the sand devoured –
Where the pelican builds her nest!

ANONYMOUS

Botany Bay

Farewell to old England for ever,
Farewell to my rum culls as well,
Farewell to the well-known Old Bailey,
Where I used for to cut such a swell.

Chorus Singing, too-ral, li-ooral, li-addity,
Singing, too-ral, li-ooral, li-ay.
Singing, too-ral, li-ooral, li-addity,
Singing, too-ral, li-ooral, li-ay.

There's the captain as is our commander,
There's the bo'sun and all the ship's crew,
There's the first- and the second-class passengers,
Knows what we poor convicts goes through.

'Tain't leaving old England we care about,
'Tain't cos we misspells wot we knows,
But because all we light-fingered gentry
Hops round with a log on our toes.

For fourteen long years I have ser-vi-ed,
And for fourteen long years and a day,
For meeting a bloke in the area,
And sneaking his ticker away.

Oh had I the wings of a turtle-dove,
I'd soar on my pinions so high,
Slap bang to the arms of my Polly love,
And in her sweet presence I'd die.

Now, all my young Dook-ies and Duch-ess-es,
Take warning from what I've to say –
Mind all is your own as you touch-es-es,
Or you'll meet us in Botany Bay.

LOUISA LAWSON

A Child's Question

O, why do you weep mother, why do you weep
For baby that fell in the summer to sleep?
You say that you prayed, when she lingered in pain,
That God in His mercy would take her again.
He heeded your prayer, and a beautiful sleep
Stole over our darling; then why do you weep?
You tell how the angels sang pæans of love
To welcome her home to the mansions above,
Where lovingly over her spirit they keep
A bright watch forever; then why do you weep?
And have you not told us again and again
That we will yet see her set free from all pain,
Beyond the bright sun where no dark shadows creep?
Then why do you weep, mother? Why do you weep?

A Mother's Answer

You ask me, dear child, why thus sadly I weep
For baby the angels have taken to keep;
Altho' she is safe, and for ever at rest,
A yearning to see her will rise in my breast.
I pray and endeavour to quell it in vain,
But stronger it comes and yet stronger again,

Till all the bright thoughts of her happier lot
Are lost in this one – my baby is not.
And while I thus yearn so intensely to see
This child that the angels are keeping for me,
I doubt for the time where her spirit has flown –
If the love e'en of angels can fully atone
For the loss of a mother's, mysterious and deep.
I own that thought sinful, yet owning it – weep.

DOUGLAS B. W. SLADEN

Under the Wattle

A Rondel

'Why should not wattle do
  For mistletoe?'
Asked one – they were but two –
  Where wattles grow.

He was her lover, too,
  Who urged her so –
'Why should not wattle do
  For mistletoe?'

A rose-cheek rosier grew;
  Rose-lips breathed low;
'Since it is here, and *you*,
  I hardly know
Why wattle should not do.'

VICTOR J. DALEY

St Francis II

I learnt the language of the birds,
  A new St Francis I would be;
But, when I understood their words –
  The birds were preaching unto me.

Dreams

I have been dreaming all a summer day
Of rare and dainty poems I would write;
Love-lyrics delicate as lilac-scent,
Soft idylls woven of wind, and flower, and stream,
And songs and sonnets carven in fine gold.

The day is fading and the dusk is cold;
Out of the skies has gone the opal gleam,
Out of my heart has passed the high intent
Into the shadow of the falling night –
Must all my dreams in darkness pass away?

I have been dreaming all a summer day:
Shall I go dreaming so until Life's light
Fades in Death's dusk, and all my days are spent?
Ah, what am I the dreamer but a dream!
The day is fading and the dusk is cold.

My songs and sonnets carven in fine gold
Have faded from me with the last day-beam
That purple lustre to the sea-line lent,
And flushed the clouds with rose and chrysolite;
So days and dreams in darkness pass away.

I have been dreaming all a summer day
Of songs and sonnets carven in fine gold;
But all my dreams in darkness pass away;
The day is fading, and the dusk is cold.

ANONYMOUS

Click Go the Shears

Out on the board the old shearer stands,
Grasping his shears in his long, bony hands;
Fixed is his gaze on a bare-bellied yeo,
Glory if he gets her, won't he make the 'ringer' go!

Click go the shears boys, click, click, click;
Wide is his blow and his hands move quick,
The ringer looks round and is beaten by a blow,
And curses the old snagger with the bare-bellied yeo.

In the middle of the floor, in his cane-bottomed chair
Is the boss of the board, with eyes everywhere;
Notes well each fleece as it comes to the screen;
Paying strict attention if it's taken off clean.

The colonial experience man, he is there, of course,
With his shiny leggin's, just got off his horse;
Casting round his eye, like a real connoisseur,
Whistling the old tune, 'I'm the Perfect Lure'.

The tar-boy is there, awaiting in demand,
With his blackened tar-pot, and his tarry hand,
Sees one old sheep with a cut upon its back,
Here's what he's waiting for, 'Tar here, Jack!'

Shearing is all over and we've all got our cheques.
Roll up your swag boys, we're off on the tracks;
The first pub we come to, it's there we'll have a spree,
And everyone that comes along, it's 'Have a drink with
  me!'

Down by the bar the old shearer stands,
Grasping his glass in his thin bony hands;
Fixed is his gaze on a green-painted keg,
Glory, he'll get down on it, ere he stirs a peg.

There we leave him standing, shouting for all hands,
Whilst all around him, every drinker stands:
His eyes are on the cask, which is now lowering fast,
He works hard, he drinks hard, and goes to hell at last!

W. T. GOODGE

The Great Australian Adjective

A sunburnt bloody stockman stood,
And in a dismal bloody mood,
  Apostrophized his bloody cuddy:
'This bloody moke's no bloody good,
He doesn't earn his bloody food.
  Bloody! Bloody! Bloody!'

He jumped across his bloody horse
And galloped off of bloody course,
  The road was wet and bloody muddy.
He road up hill, down bloody dale,
The wind, it blew a bloody gale.
  Bloody! Bloody! Bloody!

He came up to a bloody creek;
The bloody horse was bloody weak;
   The creek was full and bloody floody.
He said, 'This moke must sink or swim,
The same for me as bloody him:
   Bloody! Bloody! Bloody!'

He plunged into the bloody creek:
The horse it gave a bloody shriek:
   The stockman's face a bloody study,
Ejaculating as they sank,
Before they reached the bloody bank:
   'Bloody! Bloody! Bloody!'

'THE BOULDER BARD' ('WILLY-WILLY')

Ode to West Australia

Land of Forrests, fleas and flies,
Blighted hopes and blighted eyes,
Art thou hell in earth's disguise,
            Westralia?

Art thou some volcanic blast
By volcanoes spurned, outcast?
Art unfinished – made the last
            Westralia?

Wert thou once the chosen land
Where Adam broke God's one command?
That He in wrath changed thee to sand,
            Westralia!

Land of politicians silly,
Home of wind and willy-willy,
Land of blanket, tent and billy,
Westralia.

Home of brokers, bummers, clerks,
Nest of sharpers, mining sharks,
Dried up lakes and desert parks,
Westralia!

Land of humpies, brothels, inns,
Old bag huts and empty tins,
Land of blackest, grievous sins
Westralia.

A. B. PATERSON

Man from Ironbark

It was the man from Ironbark who struck the Sydney town,
He wandered over street and park, he wandered up and down.
He loitered here, he loitered there, till he was like to drop,
Until at last in sheer despair he sought a barber's shop.
''Ere! shave my beard and whiskers off, I'll be a man of mark,
I'll go and do the Sydney toff up home in Ironbark.'

The barber man was small and flash, as barbers mostly are,
He wore a strike-your-fancy sash, he smoked a huge cigar:
He was a humorist of note and keen at repartee,
He laid the odds and kept a 'tote', whatever that may be,
And when he saw our friend arrive, he whispered 'Here's a
lark!
Just watch me catch him all alive, this man from Ironbark.'

There were some gilded youths that sat along the barber's wall.
Their eyes were dull, their heads were flat, they had no brains
at all;
To them the barber passed the wink, his dexter eyelid shut,
'I'll make this bloomin' yokel think his bloomin' throat is cut.'
And as he soaped and rubbed it in he made a rude remark:
'I s'pose the flats is pretty green up there in Ironbark.'

A grunt was all reply he got; he shaved the bushman's chin,
Then made the water boiling hot and dipped the razor in.
He raised his hand, his brow grew black, he paused awhile to
gloat,
Then slashed the red-hot razor-back across his victim's throat;
Upon the newly shaven skin it made a livid mark –
No doubt it fairly took him in – the man from Ironbark.

He fetched a wild up-country yell might wake the dead to hear,
And though his throat, he knew full well, was cut from ear to
ear,
He struggled gamely to his feet, and faced the murd'rous foe:
'You've done for me! you dog, I'm beat! one hit before I go!
I only wish I had a knife, you blessed murdering shark!
But you'll remember all your life, the man from Ironbark.'

He lifted up his hairy paw, with one tremendous clout
He landed on the barber's jaw, and knocked the barber out.
He set to work with tooth and nail, he made the place a wreck;
He grabbed the nearest gilded youth, and tried to break his
neck.
And all the while his throat he held to save his vital spark,
And 'Murder! Bloody Murder!' yelled the man from Ironbark.

A peeler man who heard the din came in to see the show;

He tried to run the bushman in, but he refused to go.
And when at last the barber spoke, and said, ''Twas all in
fun –
''Twas just a little harmless joke, a trifle overdone.'
'A joke!' he cried, 'By George, that's fine; a lively sort of lark;
I'd like to catch that murdering swine some night in Ironbark.'

And now while round the shearing floor the list'ning shearers
gape,
He tells the story o'er and o'er, and brags of his escape.
'Them barber chaps what keeps a tote, By George, I've had
enough,
One tried to cut my bloomin' throat, but thank the Lord it's
tough.'
And whether he's believed or no, there's one thing to remark,
That flowing beards are all the go way up in Ironbark.

ARTHUR BAYLDON

Crabs

(Written on the Queensland Beach)

Poisonous, bloated, crab-like shapes
Crawl in gangs around these capes –
Stopping here and feeding there;
Listening, crawling everywhere;
Searching every rotten weed
With a frothing wild-eyed greed;
Fighting o'er a lump of scurf,
Or a red boil of the earth;
Thrusting up their writhing claws
To their grinning, fiend-like maws.
And these horrid creatures wet

With a thick unwholesome sweat
Have most hideous banquets here
On the poor drowned marineer.
Down they hurry eagerly,
Chittering all the way with glee;
They have smelt the tainted air
From that body festering there.
How they twitch their claws and pry
Into each distorted eye;
How they spit on him with spite
As their nippers pinch and bite;
How they strip him clean and bare,
Leaving not a morsel there,
Till they're gorged and all squat near
Fleshless remnants with a leer.
When the billows near them roll,
Each will scoop himself a hole
In the mudbank and therein
Sleep like an embodied sin.

In the world so crass and blind
Human crabs feed on their kind –
All that fall into their power;
Glutted creatures that devour
Skulking near their dismal holes,
They sniff out poor wretched souls
Thrown by life's unpitying sea
On the beach of misery.

MARY GILMORE

Fourteen Poor Men

Fourteen poor men,
And each hung down,
Straight as a log
From his toes to his crown.

Fourteen men –
Chinamen they were,
Hanging on the trees
By their pigtailed hair.

Honest poor men,
But the diggers said, Nay!
So they strung them all up,
On a fine summer's day.

There they were hanging
As we came by,
Grown-ups on the front seat,
On the back seat I.

That was Lambing Flat.
And still I can see
The straight up and down
Of each on his tree.

Nurse No Long Grief

O, could we weep,
  And weeping bring relief!

But life asks more than tears
  And falling leaf.

Though year by year
  Tears fall and leaves are shed,
Spring bids new sap arise
  And blood run red.

Nurse no long grief,
  Lest thy heart flower no more;
Grief builds no barns; its plough
  Rusts at the door.

Remembrance

Keep me, within thine heart,
One chamber set apart.

There, though I never come,
Yet will I know it home.

There where no hand but mine
May lift the veil – or thine –

Keep me, within thine heart,
One chamber set apart.

The Myall in Prison

Lone, lone and lone I stand,
With none to hear my cry.
As the black feet of the night
Go walking down the sky.

The stars they seem but dust
Under those passing feet,
As they, for an instant's space,
Flicker and flame, and fleet.

So, on my heart, my grief
Hangs with the weight of doom,
And the black feet of its night
Go walking through my room.

BARCROFT BOAKE

Where the Dead Men Lie

Out on the wastes of the Never Never –
   That's where the dead men lie!
There where the heat-waves dance for ever –
   That's where the dead men lie!
That's where the Earth's loved sons are keeping
Endless Tryst: not the west wind sweeping
Feverish pinions can wake their sleeping –
   Out where the dead men lie!

Where brown Summer and Death have mated –
   That's where the dead men lie!
Loving with fiery lust unsated –
   That's where the dead men lie!
Out where the grinning skulls bleach whitely
Under the saltbush sparkling brightly;
Out where the wild dogs chorus nightly –
   That's where the dead men lie!

Deep in the yellow, flowing river –

That's where the dead men lie!
Under the banks where the shadows quiver –
That's where the dead men lie!
Where the platypus twists and doubles,
Leaving a train of tiny bubbles;
Rid at last of their earthly troubles –
That's where the dead men lie!

East and backward pale faces turning –
That's how the dead men lie!
Gaunt arms stretched with a voiceless yearning –
That's how the dead men lie!
Oft in the fragrant hush of nooning
Hearing again their mother's crooning
Wrapt for aye in a dreamful swooning –
That's how the dead men lie!

Only the hand of Night can free them –
That's when the dead men fly!
Only the frightened cattle see them –
See the dead men go by!
Cloven hoofs beating out one measure,
Bidding the stockmen know no leisure –
That's when the dead men take their pleasure!
That's when the dead men fly!

Ask, too, the never-sleeping drover:
He sees the dead pass by;
Hearing them call to their friends – the plover,
Hearing the dead men cry;
Seeing their faces stealing, stealing,
Hearing their laughter, pealing, pealing,

Watching their grey forms wheeling, wheeling
  Round where the cattle lie!

Strangled by thirst and fierce privation –
  That's how the dead men die!
Out on Moneygrub's farthest station –
  That's how the dead men die!
Hardfaced greybeards, youngsters callow;
Some mounds cared for, some left fallow;
Some deep down, yet others shallow;
  Some having but the sky.

Moneygrub, as he sips his claret,
  Looks with complacent eye
Down at his watch-chain, eighteen carat –
  There, in his club, hard by:
Recks not that every link is stamped with
Names of men whose limbs are cramped with
Too long lying in grave mould, cramped with
  Death where the dead men lie.

BERNARD O'DOWD

Australia

Last sea-thing dredged by sailor Time from Space,
Are you a drift Sargasso, where the West
In halcyon calm rebuilds her fatal nest?
Or Delos of a coming Sun-God's race?
Are you for Light, and trimmed, with oil in place,
Or but a Will o' Wisp on marshy quest?
A new demesne for Mammon to infest?
Or lurks millennial Eden 'neath your face?

The cenotaphs of species dead elsewhere
That in your limits leap and swim and fly,
Or trail uncanny harp-strings from your trees,
Mix omens with the auguries that dare
To plant the Cross upon your forehead sky,
A virgin helpmate Ocean at your knees.

ANONYMOUS

Two Aboriginal Songs

I

Korindabria-ah, korindabria-ah, bogarona-ah, bogarona-ah. Iwariniango, iwaringdo, iwariniang, iwaringdo, iwariniang, iwaringdo, iwariniang, iwaringdo, iwaringime. Iwaringiang, iwaringdo-oh, ilanenienow, coombagongniengowe, ilanenienow, coombagongiengowe-eh, ilanenienowe combagoniengowe-eh, ilanenienimme.

II

Buddha-buddharo, nianga, boomelana-ah, bulleranga, crobinea, narnmala-ah, yibbilwaadjo nianga, boomelana-ah, a, boomelana, buddha-buddharo, nianga, boomelana, buddharo nianga, boomelana, bulleranga-ah, crobinea-ah, narnmala, yibbilwaadjo, nianga, croilanume, a, croilanga-ah, yibbilwaadjo, nianga, croilanga-ah, yibbilwaadjo, nianga croilanga, coondheranea, tabiabina, boorganmala, yibbilwaadjo, nianga, croilanoome.

'VIATOR' (CHARLES W. ANDREE HAYWARD)

Along the Road to Cue

(Dedicated, without permission, to the Goldfields carriers)

1.

The race for gold that charms the bold
  Finds toil for man and beast,
And they, who left the East of old,
  Are daily streaming East.
The whips that crack along the track
  Are strong – the horses too;
And strong the words the teamsters use
  Along the road to Cue;
The words they use
To mark their views
  Along the road to Cue.

2.

O, fierce beats down the sun o'erhead,
  High poised in cloudless skies;
Thick lies the dust beneath our tread,
  And thicker swarm the flies;
But flies and heat and dust and thirst,
  And nags that pull askew,
They each and all get soundly cursed
  Along the road to Cue,
Bad, worse, and worst,
They all get cursed
  Along the road to Cue.

3.
I've known some travellers look askance,
  And others fume and fret,
I've seen the passing camels glance
  Betoken pained regret,
He cannot make his protest heard –
  Unlike the cockatoo,
Who shrieking flies from many a word
  Along the road to Cue,
The horse-power words
That shock the birds
  Along the road to Cue.

4.
Thames bargemen hide resourceful lips
  Behind their blackened pipes,
So do the mates of sailing ships
  That fly the Stars and Stripes –
I've heard them both of old, and each
  Can objurate 'a few',
But loftier heights than that they reach
  Along the road to Cue,
Choice gems of speech
Beyond our reach
  Along the road to Cue.

5.
I've heard bluff costers bless their mokes
  In soft, enraptured tones,
I know the way the gangers coax
  The men who lift the stones,
And yet I somehow fancy both

Could learn a thing or two –
Some up-to-date appropriate oath –
Along the road to Cue,
Some brand-new oath
Of native growth
Fresh from the mints of Cue!

6.
'Tis sad that wit should waste its fire,
And rhetoric spend its force
Upon the unresponsive wire,
The unreflecting horse!
The waste (per hour) of motive power,
If all I say be true,
Would surely drive ten head of stamps
To crush the quartz at Cue,
Ten head of stamps
To waken camps
Between Day Dawn and Cue.

7.
In truth I never knew before
(For all the songs I've sung)
One-half the wealth of verbal store
That marks our English tongue.
So don't decline this wreath of mine,
'Tis honest merit's due,
Knights of the lash, who earn your cash
Along the road to Cue,
Who ply the lash
With 'blank' and 'dash'
Along the road to Cue.

HENRY LAWSON

Middleton's Rouseabout

Tall and freckled and sandy,
  Face of a country lout;
This was the picture of Andy,
  Middleton's Rouseabout.

Type of a coming nation
  In the land of cattle and sheep;
Worked on Middleton's station
  'Pound a week and his keep.

On Middleton's wide dominions
  Plied the stockwhip and shears;
Hadn't any opinions,
  Hadn't any 'idears'.

Swiftly the years went over,
  Liquor and drought prevailed;
Middleton went as a drover,
  After his station had failed.

Type of a careless nation,
  Men who are soon played out,
Middleton was: – and his station
  Was bought by the Rouseabout.

Flourishing beard and sandy,
  Tall and robust and stout;
This is the picture of Andy,
  Middleton's Rouseabout.

Now on his own dominions
  Works with his overseers;
Hasn't any opinions,
  Hasn't any idears.

The Old Jimmy Woodser

The old Jimmy Woodser comes into the bar,
    Unwelcomed, unnoticed, unknown,
Too old and too odd to be drunk with, by far;
And he glides to the end where the lunch baskets are
    And they say that he tipples alone.

His frock-coat is green and the nap is no more,
    And the style of his hat is at rest.
He wears the peaked collar our grandfathers wore,
The black-ribboned tie that was legal of yore,
    And the coat buttoned over his breast.

When first he came in, for a moment I thought
    That my vision or wits were astray;
For a picture and page out of Dickens he brought,
'Twas an old file dropped in from the Chancery Court
    To a wine-vault just over the way.

But I dreamed as he tasted his bitters to-night,
    And the lights in the bar-room grew dim,
That the shades of the friends of that other day's light,
And of girls that were bright in our grandfathers' sight,
    Lifted shadowy glasses to him.

And I opened the door as the old man passed out,
    With his short, shuffling step and bowed head;

And I sighed, for I felt as I turned me about,
An odd sense of respect – born of whisky no doubt –
For the life that was fifty years dead.

And I thought – there are times when our memory trends
Through the future, as 'twere, on its own –
That I, out of date ere my pilgrimage ends,
In a new fashioned bar to dead loves and dead friends
Might drink like the old man alone:
While they whisper, 'He boozes alone.'

'E' (MARY FULLERTON)

Flesh

I have seen a gum-tree,
Scarred by the blaze
Of the pioneer axe,
Mend after long days;
Lip to lip shut
Of the separate bark,
Till the gape of the wound
Was a vanishing mark.

I have seen in the hunt
The pulse of rent flesh;
Seen the fingers of Time
Unite it afresh.
I have heard a man's cry
As the teeth of the mill
Bit marrow and bone –
To hurt, not to kill.

Oh, strong is the flesh
To cure and defend:
'Tis but the stopt heart
That Time cannot mend.

Lovers

To be unloved brings sweet relief:
The strong adoring eyes
Play the eternal thief
With the soul's fit disguise.

He will not sleep, and let be drawn
The screen of thy soul's ark;
They keep, those lidless eyes,
Thy sanctuary stark.

God, when he made each separate
Unfashioned his own act,
Giving the lover eyes,
So his love's soul be sacked.

To be unloved gives sweet relief;
The one integrity
Of soul is to be lone,
Inviolate, and free.

Modern Poets

Shall they not praise the cogs,
Praise the pistons and wheels,
And still be poets

To whom appeals

The recurring morn,
The immortal primrose,
And the scent-laden eve
In the marketable corn?

Yea, your footsteps can chime
With the myriad feet,
Finding rhythm and rhyme
On the asphalted street.

There is poetry there
In the whirl and the spin
For the makers of rhyme
Who shall dare to come in.

Life, and struggle and moil,
Day and day in the rough,
Poets knowing not these
Have not knowledge enough.

When the hour swings around
Come and barter and buy;
Come away, come away,
From green earth and blue sky.

CHRISTOPHER BRENNAN

Sweet Silence after Bells!

Sweet silence after bells!
deep in the enamour'd ear
soft incantation dwells.

Filling the rapt still sphere
a liquid crystal swims,
precarious yet clear.

Those metal quiring hymns
shaped ether so succinct:
a while, or it dislimns,

the silence, wanly prinkt
with forms of lingering notes,
inhabits, close, distinct;

and night, the angel, floats
on wings of blessing spread
o'er all the gather'd cotes

where meditation, wed
with love, in gold-lit cells,
absorbs the heaven that shed

sweet silence after bells.

[She is the Night: All Horror is of Her . . .]

She is the night: all horror is of her
heap'd, shapeless, on the unclaim'd chaotic marsh
or huddled on the looming sepulchre
where the incult and scanty herb is harsh.

She is the night: all terror is of her
when the distemper'd dark begins to boil
with wavering face of larve and oily blur
of pallor on her suffocating coil.

Or majesty is hers, when marble gloom
supports her, calm, with glittering signs severe
and grandeur of metallic roof of doom,
far in the windows of our broken sphere.

Or she can be all pale, under no moon
or star, with veiling of the glamour cloud,
all pale, as were the fainting secret soon
to be exhaled, bride-robed in clinging shroud.

For she is night, and knows each wooing mood:
and her warm breasts are near in the charm'd air
of summer eve, and lovingly delude
the aching brow that craves their tender care.

The wooing night: all nuptials are of her;
and she the musky golden cloud that hangs
on maiden blood that burns, a boding stir
shot thro' with flashes of alluring pangs,

far off, in creeks that slept unvisited
or moved so smoothly that no ripple creas'd
their mirror'd slip of blue, till that sweet dread
melted the air and soft sighs stole, releas'd;

and she the shame of brides, veiling the white
of bosoms that for sharp fulfilment yearn;
she is the obscure centre of delight
and steals the kiss, the kiss she would return

deepen'd with all the abysm that under speech
moves shudderingly, or as that gulf is known
to set the astonied spouses each from each
across the futile sea of sighs, alone.

All mystery, and all love, beyond our ken,
she woos us, mournful till we find her fair:
and gods and stars and songs and souls of men
are the sparse jewels in her scatter'd hair.

1908

The droning tram swings westward: shrill
the wire sings overhead, and chill
midwinter draughts rattle the glass
that shows the dusking way I pass
to yon four-turreted square tower
that still exalts the golden hour
where youth, initiate once, endears
a treasure richer with the years.

Dim-seen, the upper stories fleet
along the twisting shabby street;
beneath, the shop-fronts' cover'd ways
bask in their lampions' orange blaze,
or stare phantasmal, weirdly new,
in the electrics' ghastly blue:
and, up and down, I see them go,
along the windows pleas'd and slow
but hurrying where the darkness falls,
the city's drift of pavement thralls
whom the poor pleasures of the street
lure from their niggard homes, to meet
and mix, unknown, and feel the bright
banality 'twixt them and night:
so, in my youth, I saw them flit
where their delusive dream was lit;

so now I see them, and can read
the urge of their unwitting need
one with my own, however dark,
and questing towards one mother-ark.

But, past the gin-shop's ochrous flare,
sudden, a gap of quiet air
and gather'd dark, where, set a pace
beyond the pavement's coiling race
and mask'd by bulk of sober leaves,
the plain obtruncate chancel heaves,
whose lancet-windows faintly show
suffusion of a ruddy glow,
the lamp of adoration, dim
and rich with unction kept for Him
whom Bethlehem's manger first made warm,
the sweetest god in human form,
love's prisoner in the Eucharist,
man's pleading, patient amorist:
and there the sacring laver stands
where I was brought in pious hands,
a chrisom-child, that I might be
accepted of that company
who, thro' their journeying, behold
beyond the apparent heavens, controll'd
to likeness of a candid rose,
ascending where the gold heart glows,
cirque within cirque, the blessed host,
their kin, their comfort, and their boast.

With them I walk'd in love and awe
till I was ware of that grim maw
and lazar-pit that reek'd beneath:

what outcast howlings these? what teeth
gnashing in vain? and was that bliss
whose counter-hemisphere was this?
and could it be, when times fulfill'd
had made the tally of either guild,
that this mid-world, dredg'd clean in both,
should no more bar their gruesome troth?
So from beneath that choiring tent
I stepp'd, and tho' my spirit's bent
was dark to me as yet, I sought
a sphere appeas'd and undistraught;
and found viaticum and goal
in that hard atom of the soul,
that final grain of deathless mind,
which Satan's watch-fiends shall not find
nor the seven mills of darkness bruise,
for all permission to abuse;
stubborn, yet, if one seek aright,
translucent all within and bright
with sheen that hath no paradigm,
not where our proud Golcondas brim,
tho' sky and sea and leaf and flower,
in each rare mood of virtual power,
sleep in their gems' excepted day:
and so, nor long, the guarded ray
broke on my eagerness, who brought
the lucid diamond-probe of thought
and, driving it behind, the extreme
blind vehemence of travailing dream
against the inhibitory shell:
and found, no grim eternal cell
and presence of the shrouded Norn,

but Eden, clad in nuptial morn,
young, fair, and radiant with delight
remorse nor sickness shall requite.

Yes, Eden was my own, my bride;
whatever malices denied,
faithful and found again, nor long
absent from aura of wooing song:
but promis'd only, while the sun
must travel yet thro' times undone;
and life must guard the prize of youth,
and thought must steward into truth
the mines of magian ore divined
in rich Cipangos of the mind:
and I, that made my high attempt
no bliss whence any were exempt,
their fellow-pilgrim, I must greet
these listless captives of the street,
these fragments of an orphan'd drift
whose dower was our mother's thrift,
and, tho' they know it not, have care
of what would be their loving prayer
if skill bestow'd might help them heed
their craving for the simple meed
to be together in the light
when loneliness and dark incite:
long is the way till we are met
when Eden pays her hoarded debt
and we are orb'd in her, and she
hath still'd her hungering to be,
with plenitude beyond impeach,
single, distinct, and whole in each:

and many an evening hour shall bring
the dark crowd's dreary loitering
to me who pass and see the tale
of all my striving, bliss or bale,
dated from either spire that strives
clear of the shoal of shiftless lives,
and promise, in all years' despite,
fidelity to old delight.

Because She Would Ask Me Why I Loved Her

If questioning could make us wise
no eyes would ever gaze in eyes;
if all our tale were told in speech
no mouths would wander each to each.

Were spirits free from mortal mesh
and love not bound in hearts of flesh
no aching breast would yearn to meet
and find their ecstasy complete.

For who is there that lives and knows
the secret powers by which he grows?
Were knowledge all, what were our need
to thrill and faint and sweetly bleed?

Then seek not, sweet, the *If* and *Why*
I love you now until I die:
For I must love because I live
And life in me is what you give.

JOHN LE GAY BRERETON

The Silver Gull

With strong slow stroke
Oaring her way against the breeze
Above the blustering waves that shoulder and smoke
The silver gull moves on with strenuous ease;
Then sidelong shoots on high
With sudden cry
Of rapture in the wind's imperious will
And that sweet whirling dream
Of blending purpose;
She glides, a fancied shape of air, down that invisible
stream.

I lie on the warm sea-beach
And out to the wandering heart
Of feathered life in the beating air I reach
Arms that beseech
– Arms of my soul that in the living air
As answer to my prayer
Are wings of ecstasy;
And on the fierce quest silently I start
Above the envious crowding of the sea.

Delirium of delight!
Caught by the wind, I strain
In glorious throes of fight.
Finding the uttermost pleasure
That love can force from pain,
Naked I strive, and take
From poverty all her treasure,

Living for life's own sake.

O sister seabird, hearken, I call to thee!
Sister! my life and thine
Still intertwine,
And not till side by side
Equal and glad and free
Down the invisible stream we twain may glide,
Shall you or I seek rest
On weathered ledge or reef or feathered nest.

Wider the shelter of my grand wings outspread
Encloses earth and sea
And thee, unconscious wandering heart – and thee.
I am forgotten: but thou art still my care
Who have known thy life and know thy way is mine,
For over the waves thou lovest I too have sped
Where now at my heart they shine;
For I am the world-encircling eddying vast of air.

In me is the manifold urge,
The shedding of leaves, the upward push of the seed,
Of all the life upon earth
The scramble and fury and fret,
The ceaseless monotonous chant of eternal surge,
The pangs of change and of triumph in death and birth,
The ache of unending need
Lest we should have peace and forget.

And mine is the torrent of hate,
Growling black flood with a seething foam of red,
And the insolent pomp of the ape in a robe of state,
And the sliding silence of guile;

And mine is the eager meeting of souls that are newly
 wed
– Throb, throb, O passionate heart!
Heed not the impotent hands that would fain defile
The shrine of the god who for sake of the One still
 moulds the many apart.

I am the spirit of joy set free,
Knowing no limits, for further than thought can reach
And as far as love can bless
I hold exultant reign.
I am I, unbodied, supreme,
The spirit of joy.

O sister, warm wind-wrestling bird, we two
Are there like flying flakes against the blue.

JOHN SHAW NEILSON

Love's Coming

Quietly as rosebuds
 Talk to the thin air,
Love came so lightly
 I knew not he was there.

Quietly as lovers
 Creep at the middle moon,
Softly as players tremble
 In the tears of a tune;

Quietly as lilies
 Their faint vows declare

Came the shy pilgrim:
  I knew not he was there.

Quietly as tears fall
  On a wild sin,
Softly as griefs call
  In a violin;

Without hail or tempest,
  Blue sword or flame,
Love came so lightly
  I knew not that he came.

The Crane is My Neighbour

The bird is my neighbour, a whimsical fellow and dim;
There is in the lake a nobility falling on him.

The bird is a noble, he turns to the sky for a theme,
And the ripples are thoughts coming out to the edge of a
  dream.

The bird is both ancient and excellent, sober and wise,
But he never could spend all the love that is sent for his
  eyes.

He bleats no instruction, he is not an arrogant drummer;
His gown is simplicity – blue as the smoke of the summer.

How patient he is as he puts out his wings for the blue!
His eyes are as old as the twilight, and calm as the dew.

The bird is my neighbour, he leaves not a claim for a sigh,

He moves as the guest of the sunlight – he roams in the
 sky.

The bird is a noble, he turns to the sky for a theme,
And the ripples are thoughts coming out to the edge of a
 dream.

The Orange Tree

The young girl stood beside me. I
 Saw not what her young eyes could see:
– A light, she said, not of the sky
 Lives somewhere in the Orange Tree.

– Is it, I said, of east or west?
 The heartbeat of a luminous boy
Who with his faltering flute confessed
 Only the edges of his joy?

Was he, I said, borne to the blue
 In a mad escapade of Spring
Ere he could make a fond adieu
 To his love in the blossoming?

– Listen! the young girl said. There calls
 No voice, no music beats on me;
But it is almost sound: it falls
 This evening on the Orange Tree.

– Does he, I said, so fear the Spring
 Ere the white sap too far can climb?
See in the full gold evening
 All happenings of the olden time?

Is he so goaded by the green?
  Does the compulsion of the dew
Make him unknowable but keen
  Asking with beauty of the blue?

– Listen! the young girl said. For all
  Your hapless talk you fail to see
There is a light, a step, a call,
  This evening on the Orange Tree.

– Is it, I said, a waste of love
  Imperishably old in pain,
Moving as an affrighted dove
  Under the sunlight or the rain?

Is it a fluttering heart that gave
  Too willingly and was reviled?
Is it the stammering at a grave,
  The last word of a little child?

– Silence! the young girl said. Oh, why,
  Why will you talk to weary me?
Plague me no longer now, for I
  Am listening like the Orange Tree.

DAVID UNAIPON

Narrinyeri Saying

Like children at play we begin Life's journey,
Push our frail bark into the stream of Time,
That flows from snow-capped Mountain.
With no care; Singing and laughing as our boat glides

Upon the tide wending its way through steep
rocky banks,
And meadows with bushes and plants all abloom,
and sweet fragrent flowers.
Until we arrive in the Great Ocean where we are
baffled and tossed by angry waves.
Onward and onward.
For three score years and ten.
Then we are cast forlorn and shipwrecked
upon the shore of a strange land.

Song of the Platypus

Give me more Grubs as the water ripples.
And make for me bread of the Nardoo seed.
Do this often and often as the sun does rise; And I shall gather
in the shade of night.
The food thou shalt throw into the water hunting place of
mine.
Because I am hiding all day fearing that someone may call up
the Lightning Thunder and Rain.

The Song of Hungarrda

Bright, consuming Spirit. No power on earth so great as
Thee,
First-born child of the Goddess of Birth and Light,
Thy habitation betwixt heaven and earth within a veil of
clouds dark as night.
Accompanied by furious wind and lashing rain and hail.
Riding

majestically upon the storm, flashing at intervals, illuminating the
abode of man.

Thine anger and thy power thou revealest to us. Sometimes in a
streak of light, which leaps upon a great towering rock, which stood
impregnable and unchallenged in its birth-place when the earth was
formed, and hurls it in fragments down the mountain-side, striking
terror into man and beast alike.

Thus in wonder I am lost. No mortal mind can conceive. No
mortal tongue express in language intelligible. Heaven-born Spark,
I cannot see nor feel thee. Thou art concealed mysteriously wrapped
within the fibre and bark of tree and bush and shrubs.

Why dost thou condescend to dwell within a piece of stick?

As I roam from place to place for enjoyment or search of food,

My soul is filled with gratitude and love for thee.

And conscious, too, of thine all pervading spirit presence.

It seems so strange that thou wilt not hear or reveal thyself nor
bestow a blessing unless I pray.

But to plead is not enough to bring thee forth and cause thy
glowing smiles to flicker over my frame.

But must strive and wrestle with this piece of stick – pressing and
twirling into another stick with all the power I possess, to release

the bonds that bind thee fast.

Then shall thy living spark leap forth in contact with grass and twig.

Thy flame leaps upward like waves that press and roll,

Radiant sister of the Day, I cannot live without thee. For when at

twilight and in the depth of midnight; before the morning dawns,
the mist hangs over the valley like death's cold shroud, And
dewdrops chill the atmosphere. Ingee Too Ma.

Then like thy bright Mother shining from afar,

Thy beaming smiles and glowing energy radiates into this frail body.

Transfusing life, health, comfort, and happiness too.

C. J. DENNIS

The Mooch of Life

This ev'nin' I was sittin' wiv Doreen,
Peaceful an' 'appy wiv the day's work done,
Watchin', be'ind the orchard's bonzer green,
The flamin' wonder uv the settin' sun.

Another day gone by; another night
Creepin' along to douse Day's golden light;
Another dawnin' when the night is gone,
To live an' love – an' so life mooches on.

Times I 'ave thought, when things was goin' crook,
When 'Ope turned nark an' Love forgot to smile,
Of somethin' I once seen in some ole book
Where an ole sore-'ead arsts, 'Is life worf w'ile?'

But in that stillness, as the day grows dim,
An' I am sittin' there wiv 'er an' 'im –
  My wife, my son! an' strength in me to strive,
  I only know – it's good to be alive!

Yeh live, yeh love, yeh learn; an' when yeh come
  To square the ledger in some thortful hour,
The everlastin' answer to the sum
  Must alwus be, 'Where's sense in gittin' sour?'

Fer when yeh've come to weigh the good an' bad –
The gladness wiv the sadness you 'ave 'ad –
  Then 'im 'oo's faith in 'uman goodness fails
  Fergits to put 'is liver in the scales.

Livin' an' lovin'; learnin' day be day;
  Pausin' a minute in the barmy strife
To find that 'elpin' others on the way
  Is gold coined fer your profit – sich is life.

I've studied books wiv yearnings to improve,
To 'eave meself out of me lowly groove,
  An' 'ere is orl the change I ever got:
  ''Ark at yer 'eart, an' you kin learn the lot.'

I gives it in – that wisdom o' the mind –
  I wasn't built to play no lofty part.
Orl such is welkim to the joys they find;
  I only know the wisdom o' the 'eart.

An' ever it 'as taught me, day be day,
The one same lesson in the same ole way:
  'Look fer yer profits in the 'earts o' friends,
  Fer 'atin' never paid no dividends.'

Life's wot yeh make it; an' the bloke 'oo tries
To grab the shinin' stars frum out the skies
  Goes crook on life, an' calls the world a cheat,
  An' tramples on the daisies at 'is feet.

But when the moon comes creepin' o'er the hill,
  An' when the mopoke calls along the creek,
I takes me cup o' joy an' drinks me fill,
  An' arsts meself wot better could I seek.

An' ev'ry song I 'ear the thrushes sing
That everlastin' message seems to bring;
  An' ev'ry wind that whispers in the trees
  Gives me the tip there ain't no joys like these:

Livin' an' lovin'; wand'rin' on yer way;
  Reapin' the 'arvest uv a kind deed done;
An' watchin', in the sundown uv yer day,
  Yerself again, grown nobler in yer son.

Knowin' that ev'ry coin o' kindness spent
Bears interest in yer 'eart at cent per cent;
  Measurin' wisdom by the peace it brings
  To simple minds that values simple things.

An' when I take a look along the way
  That I 'ave trod, it seems the man knows best,
Who's met wiv slabs uv sorrer in 'is day,
  When 'e is truly rich an' truly blest.

An' I am rich, becos me eyes 'ave seen
The lovelight in the eyes of my Doreen;
  An' I am blest, becos me feet 'ave trod
  A land 'oo's fields reflect the smile o' God.

Livin' an' lovin'; learnin' to fergive
  The deeds an' words of some un'appy bloke
Who's missed the bus – so 'ave I come to live,
  An' take the 'ole mad world as 'arf a joke.

* * * *

Sittin' at ev'nin' in this sunset-land,
Wiv 'Er in all the World to 'old me 'and,
  A son, to bear me name when I am gone. . . .
  Livin' an' lovin' – so life mooches on.

HUGH McCRAE

Camden Magpie

(To Zoë Crookston)

Ho! Ho! The fine fellow
Topped on the willow –
Dipping his black and white
Into the yellow.

How mightn't Hokusai,
This summer morning,
Clap you in magical
Net without warning! –

Ink on his finger-nail,
Cleverly wiggled:
Dokoro – Tsukari!
– What thought you jiggled –

He'd have you, he'd hold you,
This Japanese wizard,

So fast by the feather,
So fast by the gizzard,

That it wouldn't be you
On the Bassingthwaighte fence,
Or in Adam's yard,
Not by any pretence.

And it wouldn't be you
Piratically sailing
To Thunderbolt's Rock
Across the high paling –

Only your atomy,
Soon out of focus, I
Watch – and then turn to
'Magpie' – signed Hokusai.

FREDERICK SPENCER BURNELL

A Mangrove Swamp

Look how the slow fat bubbles break in rings,
As though a man were stifling underneath.
The black stagnating water by no breath
Is stirred, a mirror for all evil things.

The long roots writhing upward from the mud,
Like fingers crooked in lust or pain or greed,
Have pendent tresses of putrescent weed,
Like dead men's hair clogged stiff with their own blood.

No light of flowers nor songs of birds dispel
The breathless, stealthy silence of the place.

Only a ripple o'erspreads the water's face
At times, like soundless, dreadful mirth in hell.

Only the grey mists come and go beneath
The pallid shadows of the sickly moon;
Only dead voices in the night breeze croon
A drear and melancholy masque of death.

E. J. RUPERT ATKINSON

The Stock Exchange

Through the stench and smoke of pipe and stale cigar –
Black coats, black hats, and raucous tones, bleared eyes,
Quick, past them – hold your breath! Yet in this guise
Here throbs the nation's heart! Iron, coal, and tar,
Goldfields, farms, foundries, and all earth at par,
Pour forth their wealth, like blood, to vitalise
These very walls, these very men, their lies,
Their houses, parks, and cities, near and far.

Today the world's romance is centred here.
This is the nation's heart – its arteries
Flood from this spot, and turn and twist and veer.
Here sluggish prudes and leech-like rakes, at ease,
Sap the land's life with schemes effete, austere –
As sure and tardy as their own disease.

'FURNLEY MAURICE' (FRANK WILMOT)

To a Telegraph Pole

The lanes are full of young men swallowing beer,
Some serious women ludicrously dressed
Watch autocars snort through the crush, in fear.
A railway train pants like a mammoth oppressed;
On a wind-gust
The swelling and failing moan of the street trams
Sounds through the stifling incense of the dust.
The wrecker signs flash out their blazoned shams,
Leading to doom who trust.

* * * *

I saw you in your slender whiteness there;
I put my hand upon your painted side;
You quivered in a sudden mountain air
And I was back to where your friends abide.
The brown ferns sway,
And your long rustling fingers of soft green
Plash in the light and give the light away
Perfumed and tinted to small things I've seen
That seldom touch pure day.

For you are joyous, beautiful, unbowed;
A thousand violets cluster at your feet;
The lark has lent her music to a cloud
So she might make your coronet fittingly sweet,
And you, I swear,
Were never dragged across these splendid hills,
Nor heard the lash thud on a sullen steer;

The low, amazing light that slowly fills
These groves saw not your bier.

Tenderly moves the dusk along the ways,
There's water falling through a phantom light,
A pungent smell of greenwood in a blaze
Whose frantic flame stabs at the coming night.
Unfold the packs!

Tomorrow comes rolling in behind the moon,
The rabbits are out the 'possums hunch their backs;
No songs to-night, we must be breaking soon
Along the morning tracks.

The forest silences are gathering,
Mute is the thrush, the cricket in the grass,
A brown leaf falls, flutters a frightened wing,
Into the gloom the folded ranges pass,
Sleep, and all's well!
Amid the ferns, maybe, there moves a ghost,
A gleaming axe; a portent; who can tell?
You are amongst the creatures God loves most –
I know you never fell.

* * * *

Somewhere in a faint world away from here
Or there; in this or some forgotten time
Pale autocars pant through a crush in fear,
The railway trains smash out a metal rhyme.
On a wind-gust
The swelling and failing moan of the street trams
Sounds through a veiling incense of the dust;
The will-o'-the-wisps glimmer their blazoned shams
To ruin folk who trust.

FREDERIC MANNING

Grotesque

These are the damned circles Dante trod,
Terrible in hopelessness,
But even skulls have their humour,
An eyeless and sardonic mockery:
And we,
Sitting with streaming eyes in the acrid smoke,
That murks our foul, damp billet,
Chant bitterly, with raucous voices
As a choir of frogs
In hideous irony, our patriotic songs.

Leaves

A frail and tenuous mist lingers on baffled and intricate
branches;
Little gilt leaves are still, for quietness holds every bough;
Pools in the muddy road slumber, reflecting indifferent stars;
Steeped in the loveliness of moonlight is earth, and the valleys,
Brimmed up with quiet shadow, with a mist of sleep.

But afar on the horizon rise great pulses of light,
The hammering of guns, wrestling, locked in conflict
Like brute, stone gods of old struggling confusedly;
Then overhead purrs a shell, and our heavies
Answer, with sudden clapping bruits of sound,
Loosening our shells that stream whining and whimpering
precipitately,
Hounding through air athirst for blood.

And the little gilt leaves
Flicker in falling, like waifs and flakes of flame.

The Trenches

Endless lanes sunken in the clay,
Bays, and traverses, fringed with wasted herbage,
Seed-pods of blue scabious, and some lingering blooms;
And the sky, seen as from a well,
Brilliant with frosty stars.
We stumble, cursing, on the slippery duck-boards,
Goaded like the damned by some invisible wrath,
A will stronger than weariness, stronger than animal fear,
Implacable and monotonous.

Here a shaft, slanting, and below
A dusty and flickering light from one feeble candle
And prone figures sleeping uneasily,
Murmuring,
And men who cannot sleep,
With faces impassive as masks,
Bright, feverish eyes, and drawn lips,
Sad, pitiless, terrible faces,
Each an incarnate curse.

Here in a bay, a helmed sentry
Silent and motionless, watching while two sleep,
And he sees before him
With indifferent eyes the blasted and torn land
Peopled with stiff prone forms, stupidly rigid,
As tho' they had not been men.

Dead are the lips where love laughed or sang,
The hands of youth eager to lay hold of life,
Eyes that have laughed to eyes,
And these were begotten,
O love, and lived lightly, and burnt
With a lust of a man's first strength: ere they were rent,
Almost at unawares, savagely; and strewn
In bloody fragments, to be the carrion
Of rats and crows.

And the sentry moves not, searching
Night for menace with weary eyes.

BRIAN VREPONT

The Net Menders

I came upon them by a strip of sea,
In a drizzle of rain mending their fishing-net,
Four swift brown hands, and lean with industry,
Shuttling the thin twine skillfully in-out, repairing the fret.
Of rock-jag, shark-tooth and thresh;
He, tense as a mackerel, strong and agile,
Sea-eyed and grim as a rock, turned, and his smile
Was as the wonder of sunshine on sea-rock,
His fingers harping the net-mesh;
She on the sea-side, facing the land, took stock
Of me leisurely nearing, through half-shut eyes.
'Defence,' I thought: but her mouth relaxed, went sweet
And soft as a sea-flower, her hands' enterprise
On the sea-side of the breaks in the net
Rippling the strings of the two-sided harp o' the sea,

And I thought, 'Here is where sea-melodies meet,
Mending the breakage of earth-sea fret,'
And the strange great grace if simplicity came on me.

If they had angers in them, these two by the sea,
Not in the two days dwelt with them,
Watching the shuttle flying, the flat corks tied,
And the strong boat pitch-caulked for battle with the sea,
Was flaw apparent in the gem;
Their poverty, too real for pride to hide,
Gave them no envy, not even in the lamp-light
And shadows of our talk,
Not when the net was trailed and netted naught
Save weed, nor when I spoke, that unforgettable night
We fought the tide, and drifted home star-caught,
And I spoke of the hawk
Now in the dark vanished, that all day long
Circled and soared and plunged innocence;
'Cruel life!' I cried,
But my cry crossed over the woman's song,
Over the zither of the boat cutting the brine, and died,
And the man said, 'It is life,'
And the boat gritted the waiting sand
With the sound of a cleansing knife,
And we slept, at life's command.

'WILLIAM BAYLEBRIDGE' (WILLIAM BLOCKSIDGE)

Moreton Miles (LIV)

Wherever I go, I do no wrong;
My love it burns the same:
So tribes who move the camp along
Carry the guarded flame.

Wherever I go my heart I leave
With my true Love alone:
I gave it as I vowed to give
For others keeping none.

I ask of her like bushmen told
By travellers of the rain –
Of overlanding mates of old,
If stirring yet or slain.

Life's Testament (VI)

The brain, the blood, the busy thews
That quickened in the primal ooze
Support me yet; till ice shall grip
The heart of Earth, no strength they'll lose.

They take my thought, they laugh, they run –
Ere megatherial moons, begun;
And shall, till they shall drop within
The shattering whirlwinds of the sun.

In subtle and essential ways,
Rich with innumerable days,

To mould, to charge, to impel me still,
Each through my broadest being plays.

They surged to this hour, this transfuse –
The brain, the blood, the busy thews;
That act of mine the ultimate stars
Shall look on sprang in primal ooze.

NIKOS KALLINIKOS

[The Heavens and the Stars Proclaim . . .]

The heavens and the stars proclaim,
   the moon is also willing
to say each pound we have will ne'er
   add up to make a shilling.

DOROTHEA MACKELLAR

My Country

The love of field and coppice,
  Of green and shaded lanes,
Of ordered woods and gardens
  Is running in your veins.
Strong love of grey-blue distance
  Brown streams and soft, dim skies –
I know but cannot share it,
  My love is otherwise.

I love a sunburnt country,
  A land of sweeping plains,
Of ragged mountain ranges,
  Of droughts and flooding rains.
I love her far horizons,
  I love her jewel-sea,
Her beauty and her terror –
  The wide brown land for me!

The stark white ring-barked forests,
  All tragic to the moon,
The sapphire-misted mountains,
  The hot gold hush of noon.
Green tangle of the brushes,
  Where lithe lianas coil,
And orchids deck the tree tops
  And ferns the warm dark soil.

Core of my heart, my country!
  Her pitiless blue sky,

When sick at heart, around us,
  We see the cattle die –
But then the grey clouds gather,
  And we can bless again
The drumming of an army,
  The steady, soaking rain.

Core of my heart, my country!
  Land of the Rainbow Gold,
For flood and fire and famine,
  She pays us back three-fold.
Over the thirsty paddocks,
  Watch, after many days,
The filmy veil of greenness
That thickens as we gaze . . .

An opal-hearted country,
  A wilful, lavish land –
All you who have not loved her,
  You will not understand –
Though earth holds many splendours,
  Wherever I may die,
I know to what brown country
  My homing thoughts will fly.

EDWARD VANCE PALMER

The Farmer Remembers the Somme

Will they never fade or pass!
  The mud, and the misty figures endlessly coming
In file through the foul morass,
And the grey flood-water lipping the reeds and grass,

And the steel wings drumming.

The hills are bright in the sun:
There's nothing changed or marred in the well-known places:
When work for the day is done
There's talk, and quiet laughter, and gleams of fun
On the old folks' faces.

I have returned to these:
The farm, and the kindly bush, and the young calves lowing:
But all that my mind sees
Is a quaking bog in a mist – stark, snapped trees,
And the dark Somme flowing.

These are My People

The men I know have rough tongues, and hard, bitter faces,
Their laughter comes swiftly, but there's harshness in its ring,
They've spent their days with bent backs in bleak, unlovely places,
In mill, and trench, and coal-pit: at work or soldering.

Their talk is all of prize-fights, and women, and race-horses,
And dark passions gather when the drink is in their blood,
Their minds are like the deep beds of sluggish watercourses,
But strange flowers blossom there like lilies in the mud.

They bear the brand of wrecked hopes and loveless toil and sorrow,
Ironic gods have shaped them to the metal beasts they tend,
There'll be little care for beauty in the world they build to-morrow,
But these are my people, and I'm with them to the end.

ZORA BERNICE MAY CROSS

from: Love Sonnets

X

And then came Science with her torch red-lit
And cosmic marvels round her glowing head –
The primal cell, the worm, the quadruped –
Striving to make each to the other fit.
Tongue-trumpeting her own unchallenged wit,
She offered me the woof of Wisdom's thread,
And Truth and Purity that hourly tread
The paths where sages in their wonder sit.

And still I smiled and kissed you with a sob.
My lips on yours, I heard, high up above
Love's feet ring laughter on the starry sod
And felt the echo through our bosoms throb.
Belovèd, Science ends in our pure love
Which shares alone the secrets of our God.

XV

Love, you have brought to me my perfect soul,
More sweet than earthly things, more precious rare,
Hiding its fragrance in my loosened hair
And folding up my body like a scroll.
O, lie with me all night, and let the roll
Of Rapture's waves wash over us, as, bare
Of anything save Love, we haply share
The joys of our first parents' chaste control.

My Love, my piece of Heaven God has spilled
Upon my outstretched hands, O, kiss me yet.

Here, lying close to you, I feel – I know,
My being, even now, is charged and filled
With light and bliss it never will forget
Though æons over my cold corpse should flow.

from: Sonnets of Motherhood

VIII

Make me the melody of meeting palms,
The roundelay of little running feet.
Strike me a measure to a trembling sweet
Of the mouth's laughter and the fingers' psalms.
I know of music in the ocean calms –
A siren singing where the long tides meet.
I know of lyrics in the leaf's long beat,
But the child-chant is symphony of balms.

Sing it to me. O, sing it to my blood . . .
Through chord and fibre of my being run
The liquid quavers, and the pause and turn
Of every note in its seraphic flood.
Sing on that anthem of the sea and sun
And the deep dreams that in your being yearn.

XXVII

O, not alone I weave this miracle
Of glowing spirit from my body's zone.
With every moment of the life unknown
You feed the glory of a growing cell.
All day I think of you, and night must tell
Dreams of my dreams unto your heart alone;

So, seeing you, I take you, O my own,
Into my child where first you wrought Life's spell.

Dearest, as much as I, you breathe in pain,
Breeding yourself – your very soul from me
By look and sign, soft word and action strong,
And all you longed for in its form regain.
I am a humble haven where we three,
Father and child and mother, make a song.

LESBIA HARFORD

Periodicity

My friend declares
Being woman and virgin she
Takes small account of periodicity

And she is right.
Her days are calmly spent
For her sex-function is irrelevant.

But I whose life
Is monthly broken in twain
Must seek some sort of meaning in my pain.

Women, I say,
Are beautiful in change,
Remote, immortal, like the moon they range.

Or call my pain
A skirmish in the whole
Tremendous conflict between body and soul.

Meaning must lie,
Some beauty surely dwell
In the fierce depths and uttermost pits of hell.

Yet still I seek,
Month after month in vain,
Meaning and beauty in recurrent pain.

Pruning Flowering Gums

One summer day, along the street,
Men pruned the gums
To make them neat.
The tender branches, white with flowers,
Lay in the sun
For hours and hours,
And every hour they grew more sweet,
More honey-like
Until the street
Smelt like a hive, withouten bees.
But still the gardeners
Lopped the trees.

Then came the children out of school,
Noisy and separate
As their rule
Of being is. The spangled trees
Gave them one heart:
Such power to please
Had all the flowering branches strown
Around for them
To make their own.

Then such a murmuring arose
As made the ears
Confirm the nose
And give the lie to eyes. For hours
Child bees hummed
In the honey flowers.

They gathered sprigs and armfuls. Some
Ran with their fragrant
Burdens home,
And still returned; and after them
Would drag great boughs.

Some stripped a stem
Of rosy flowers and played with these.
Never such love
Had earthly trees
As these young creatures gave. By night,
The treasured sprays
Of their delight
Were garnered every one. The street
Looked, as the council liked it, neat.

Learning Geography

They have a few little hours
To study the world –
Its lovely absence of clouds,
Or the thunderbolts hurled
By hidden powers –

All the soft shapes of the vales,
And the trees of the north,

They dream of a minute, no longer,
No longer – then forth
Ere the year fails

To cities where carnival glows
Or the furnace is bright.
So is measured or leisured
According as teachers dispose
Their cosmic delight.

PETER HOPEGOOD

Dithyramb in Retrospect

I was carried to a font.
Stranger fingers marked my front.
    Significant, no doubt, the rite
    that day was day and night was night:
    yet it could not make me see.
    Lifeless was that sorcery.

Then I sought a font in Toil,
smeared my sweaty brow with Soil.
    Still by fingers strange 'twas done,
    though the fingers were my own.

Then I sought a font in Fire;
leapt I Armageddon's pyre.
    Iron set on me his hand:
    but 'twas still a stranger brand.

Then a passion smote my heart
with a devastating dart.

Still I could in nowise see.
Darkness ever compassed me.

With my pain I face the Sky
when my planet there must ply . . .
and the fingers of the Wind
touch me with my Very Wand,
Straightaway know I power to see
what the light has hid from me.
By the Wind that walks the Night
I am baptized into sight.

LEON GELLERT

A Night Attack

Be still. The bleeding night is in suspense
Of watchful agony and coloured thought,
And every beating vein and trembling sense,
Long-tired with time, is pitched and overwrought.
And for the eye, the darkness holds strange forms,
Soft movements in the leaves, and wicked glows
That wait and peer. The whole black landscape swarms
With shapes of white and grey that no one knows;
And for the ear, a sound, a pause, a breath,
A distant hurried footstep moving fast.
The hand has touched the slimy face of death.
The mind is raking at the ragged past.
. . . . A sound of rifles rattles from the south,
And startled orders move from mouth to mouth.

May 24, 1915

The Attack at Dawn

'At every cost,' they said, 'it must be done.'
They told us in the early afternoon.
We sit and wait the coming of the sun.
We sit in groups, – grey groups that watch the moon.

We stretch our legs and murmur half in sleep,
And touch the tips of bayonets and yawn.
Our hands are cold. They strangely grow and creep,
Tugging at ends of straps. We wait the dawn!

Some men come stumbling past in single file.
And scrape the trench's side and scatter sand.
They trip and curse and go. Perhaps we smile.
We wait the dawn! . . . The dawn is close at hand!

A gentle rustling runs along the line.
'At every cost,' they said, 'it must be done.'
A hundred eyes are staring for the sign.
It's coming! Look! . . . Our God's own laughing sun!

May, 1915

The Diggers

The diggers are digging, and digging deep,
They're digging and singing,
And I'm asleep.
They're digging and singing, and swiftly they're
swinging
The flying earth as it falls in a heap.
And some of it scatters and falls on my head;

But the diggers dig on. They can only dig.
They can only sing, and their eyes are big.
Their eyes are big and heavy as lead.
They dig and they sing and they think I'm dead.

The diggers are digging, and filling the hole.
They're sighing and sighing.
They pray for my soul.
I hear what they say, and from where I am lying,
I hear a new corporal calling the roll.
But the diggers dig on and fill in my bed.
The diggers dig on, and they sweat and they sweat.
They sigh and they sigh, and their eyes are wet.
The brown earth clatters and covers my head;
Then I laugh and I laugh, for they think I'm dead.

July, 1915

Blind!

A red-roofed house is shining to the skies:
A house red-roofed and brilliant in the wind:
A house of colour filled with wandering eyes:
And all the eyes are blind.

A gentle sound of moving fills each room:
A sound of hands, – dumb hands that touch and pry:
A sound of fingers feeling in a tomb
Before they close and die.

A hundred windows face long rows of flowers –
Long rows of flowers, and flowers that sway and dance

Where lidded eyes can gaze for hours and hours;
  Blue eyes that shut in France.

The Hospital for the Blind
December 25, 1915

LEONARD MANN

The Earth

Minute made visible and heard,
  Fact born of space by lust of time,
The aftermath of the first word,
  Mote dried from a drift of slime;

Earth, 'tis enough to know but this,
  You give such beauty to our eyes
And all our senses, here love is
  And the dream-stuff of Paradise.

Your rise in night and your blood decline
  Sentries nor scientists behold.
No lovers pray of you divine
  Heat for a loved one's heart grown cold.

Yet in illimitable law
  Guessed at by symbols, you may be
Lovely as Venus whom you saw
  This night above your darkening sea.

And where a world has come alive
  May not your littleness be host,
Food of the spirit, the soul's hive,
Home and haven of Holy Ghost?

twentieth century

For those born in the twentieth century, the century of world wars and the nuclear bomb, of the Holocaust and the Vietnam War, of the Great Depression and the Cuban Missile Crisis, of the Stolen Generation and nuclear-weapons testing on the Montebellos and at Maralinga, it has been an apocalyptic era. At no other time in world history did the end seem so inevitably near. In a century of political extremes, of allegiances to fascism or communism or the 'middle way', political and ethical subtexts proliferated.

This is the realm of the modern poet. Quite frequently, though, the poems of this era were imagistic and observational. Often they were differentiating: what *is* Australian? Many poets seem to remain in denial and appear untouched by history, untouched by reality, while others speak of such issues in every poem. Most poets are a mixture of both. Celebrations of modernity, of progressive thinking, inform our best poets, but doubt is in there as well. A celebration of the natural environment often goes hand in hand with a lament for the damaged and the lost.

Australia's first parliament opened in 1901 and it didn't take long to pass the Immigration Restriction Act (1901), which resulted in the 'White Australia' policy. This sad point in time created a binary of conflict in the ensuing century as poets (and others) fought against the strictures placed on what constituted Australia. It is a wide-ranging journey from the classicist Augustan renderings of old-world Europe in A. D. Hope, and their complex and troubled engagement with modern Australia, through Kenneth Slessor's invigorations of language – utilising the full range of modernist techniques of the individual versus the mass, the primal and chthonic nature of the country ('South' and 'North') versus the constructed organism of the city (almost as living entity), personal alienation and the new language of technology – to the pastoral renderings with a metaphysical touch of mid-century (and later) poets such as David Campbell, to the lay-philosophical and musical utterances of Gwen Harwood, or the investigations of nature and belonging and dispossession in the activist poetics of Judith Wright. In Jas H. Duke, in Π.O., in the slam and performance poetry of Miles Merrill, a crossing of the political strictures and containments of language and culture is made.

Out of threat, danger and bleakness come the positives of language itself, of the drive towards poetry. It's the age of the new Romanticism, which by the end of the century will have led to the linguistic innovations of Peter Minter, Michael Brennan, and M. T. C. Cronin. The poets born in the early part of the century who make their mark by its middle are essential in understanding the picture of a contemporary poetry that can readily encompass the radical sexual politics of Gabrielle Everall and the lyrical hybridisations of Jaya Savige. We might look to Grace Perry, Rosemary Dobson and Dorothy Hewett for a range of voices that share an impulse to investigation and clarification, particularly of the female experience, and a desire to tap into many different sources for inspiration.

One of the crisis-points of the modern in Australia was the Ern Malley hoax. It is true that it gave levity to those opposed to the abstractions and 'indulgences' of the modern, of the rampant free verse and free ways outside the rules and regulations, but in many ways it was also a clarification, a point where visual art and sound finally erupted in poetry, creating a new set of rules that had long been observed in the automatic writings of the European Surrealists, the Dadaists before them, and the French symbolists before them.

Ironically, more than the great modernist Slessor, it was in the nationalistic and jingoistic Jindyworobaks, for all their appropriating and usage of indigenous myth and presence, that the streak of Ern Malley might be found. In the verse of place, undercurrents of dream and chthonic imagery come up out of the very *body* of the poems, and the borrowings reflect the techniques of McAuley and Stewart in their pillaging of Shakespeare and mosquito-extermination manuals, as much as anything else. The anonymity of the hoax, the revelation of it as a construct, and the ensuing trial for obscenity of Max Harris and the Angry Penguins have become as much part of poetry as the Ern Malley poems themselves.

In what is by and large an urban country, the pastoral world is celebrated and yet examined closely. The pastoral and anti-pastoral live hand in hand. Les Murray, with his book *The People's Other World*, invigorates the language of post-settler culture, and opens new ways of reading their presence. John Tranter brings New York to Sydney, and his deeply intelligent urban ironies resonate all the way back to his rural origins. The influence of Asian poetry, aesthetically and stylistically, the concentrations of American and British Imagism from the early part of the twentieth century, and the rendering of the 'bush', the natural world, into 'nature' poetry, strengthens as the century progresses. Indigenous culture is celebrated and celebrates the land. And it resists. And lays claim to the land that has been stolen.

In essence, against a backdrop of horror, Australian poets have looked to understand where they are, what they have and what has been lost, and, most importantly, how poetry might talk about this or even replace the lost. It has become a major world poetry because it has reached out to the world, but it has grown in its own directions out of 'isolation', or a concept of isolation.

E. G. MOLL

Beware the Cuckoo

BEWARE the cuckoo, though she bring
Authentic tidings of the spring,
And though her voice among the trees
Transport you to the Hebrides!

I saw her come one sunny day,
And pause awhile and fly away,
And I knew where she took her rest
There was a honeyeater's nest.

Later I came again and found
Three dead fledgelings on the ground,
And red ants busy in a throng
At throats that had been made for song.

But in the low nest in the tree
The cuckoo chick sat cosily,
And seemed, to my unhappy sight,
A grey and monstrous appetite.

Beware the cuckoo! By what name
You call her, she is still the same.
And, if you must admire her art,
Keep a wing over your heart.

KENNETH SLESSOR

Beach Burial

Softly and humbly to the Gulf of Arabs
The convoys of dead sailors come;
At night they sway and wander in the waters far under,
But morning rolls them in the foam.

Between the sob and clubbing of the gunfire
Someone, it seems, has time for this,
To pluck them from the shallows and bury them in burrows
And tread the sand upon their nakedness;

And each cross, the driven stake of tidewood,
Bears the last signature of men,
Written with such perplexity, with such bewildered pity,
The words choke as they begin –

'*Unknown seaman*' – the ghostly pencil
Wavers and fades, the purple drips,
The breath of the wet season has washed their inscriptions
As blue as drowned men's lips,

Dead seaman, gone in search of the same landfall,
Whether as enemies they fought,
Or fought with us, or neither; the sand joins them together,
Enlisted on the other front.

El Alamein.

Five Bells

Time that is moved by little fidget wheels
Is not my Time, the flood that does not flow.
Between the double and the single bell
Of a ship's hour, between a round of bells
From the dark warship riding there below,
I have lived many lives, and this one life
Of Joe, long dead, who lives between five bells.

Deep and dissolving verticals of light
Ferry the falls of moonshine down. Five bells
Coldly rung out in a machine's voice. Night and water
Pour to one rip of darkness, the Harbour floats
In air, the Cross hangs upside-down in water.

Why do I think of you, dead man, why thieve
These profitless lodgings from the flukes of thought
Anchored in Time? You have gone from earth,
Gone even from the meaning of a name;
Yet something's there, yet something forms its lips
And hits and cries against the ports of space,
Beating their sides to make its fury heard.

Are you shouting at me, dead man, squeezing your face
In agonies of speech on speechless panes?
Cry louder, beat the windows, bawl your name!

But I hear nothing, nothing . . . only bells,
Five bells, the bumpkin calculus of Time.
Your echoes die, your voice is dowsed by Life,
There's not a mouth can fly the pygmy strait –
Nothing except the memory of some bones

Long shoved away, and sucked away, in mud;
And unimportant things you might have done,
Or once I thought you did; but you forgot,
And all have now forgotten – looks and words
And slops of beer; your coat with buttons off,
Your gaunt chin and pricked eye, and raging tales
Of Irish kings and English perfidy,
And dirtier perfidy of publicans
Groaning to God from Darlinghurst.

Five bells.

Then I saw the road, I heard the thunder
Tumble, and felt the talons of the rain
The night we came to Moorebank in slab-dark,
So dark you bore no body, had no face,
But a sheer voice that rattled out of air
(As now you'd cry if I could break the glass),
A voice that spoke beside me in the bush,
Loud for a breath or bitten off by wind,
Of Milton, melons, and the Rights of Man,
And blowing flutes, and how Tahitian girls
Are brown and angry-tongued, and Sydney girls
Are white and angry-tongued, or so you'd found.
But all I heard was words that didn't join
So Milton became melons, melons girls,
And fifty mouths, it seemed, were out that night,
And in each tree an Ear was bending down,
Or something had just run, gone behind grass,
When, blank and bone-white, like a maniac's thought,
The naphtha-flash of lightning slit the sky,
Knifing the dark with deathly photographs.
There's not so many with so poor a purse

Or fierce a need, must fare by night like that,
Five miles in darkness on a country track,
But when you do, that's what you think.

Five bells.

In Melbourne, your appetite had gone,
Your angers too; they had been leeched away
By the soft archery of summer rains
And the sponge-paws of wetness, the slow damp
That stuck the leaves of living, snailed the mind,
And showed your bones, that had been sharp with rage,
The sodden ecstasies of rectitude.
I thought of what you'd written in faint ink,
Your journal with the sawn-off lock, that stayed behind
With other things you left, all without use,
All without meaning now, except a sign
That someone had been living who now was dead:
'At Labassa. Room 6 x 8
On top of the tower; because of this, very dark
And cold in winter. Everything has been stowed
Into this room – 500 books all shapes
And colours, dealt across the floor
And over sills and on the laps of chairs;
Guns, photoes of many differant things
And differant curioes that I obtained . . . .'

In Sydney, by the spent aquarium-flare
Of penny gaslight on pink wallpaper,
We argued about blowing up the world,
But you were living backward, so each night
You crept a moment closer to the breast,
And they were living, all of them, those frames

And shapes of flesh that had perplexed your youth,
And most your father, the old man gone blind,
With fingers always round a fiddle's neck,
That graveyard mason whose fair monuments
And tablets cut with dreams of piety
Rest on the bosoms of a thousand men
Staked bone by bone, in quiet astonishment
At cargoes they had never thought to bear,
These funeral-cakes of sweet and sculptured stone.

Where have you gone? The tide is over you,
The turn of midnight water's over you,
As Time is over you, and mystery,
And memory, the flood that does not flow.
You have no suburb, like those easier dead
In private berths of dissolution laid –
The tide goes over, the waves ride over you
And let their shadows down like shining hair,
But they are Water; and the sea-pinks bend
Like lilies in your teeth, but they are Weed;
And you are only part of an Idea.
I felt the wet push its black thumb-balls in,
The night you died, I felt your eardrums crack,
And the short agony, the longer dream,
The Nothing that was neither long nor short;
But I was bound, and could not go that way,
But I was blind, and could not feel your hand.
If I could find an answer, could only find
Your meaning, or could say why you were here
Who now are gone, what purpose gave you breath
Or seized it back, might I not hear your voice?

I looked out of my window in the dark
At waves with diamond quills and combs of light
That arched their mackerel-backs and smacked the sand
In the moon's drench, that straight enormous glaze,
And ships far off asleep, and Harbour-buoys
Tossing their fireballs wearily each to each,
And tried to hear your voice, but all I heard
Was a boat's whistle, and the scraping squeal
Of seabird's voices far away, and bells,
Five bells. Five bells coldly ringing out.

Five bells.

Choker's Lane

In Choker's Lane, the doors appear
Like black and shining coffin-lids,
Whose fill of flesh, long buried here,
Familiar visiting forbids.

But sometimes, when their bells are twirled,
They'll show, like Hades, through the chink,
The green and watery gaslight world
Where girls have faces white as zinc.

And sometimes thieves go smoothly past,
Or pad by moonlight home again.
For even thieves come home at last,
Even the thieves of Choker's Lane.

And sometimes you can feel the breath
Of beasts decaying in their den –
The soft, unhurrying teeth of Death
With leather jaws come tasting men.

Then sunlight comes, the tradesmen nod.
   The pavement rings with careless feet,
And Choker's Lane – how very odd! –
   Is just an ordinary street.

Sleep

Do you give yourself to me utterly,
   Body and no-body, flesh and no-flesh,
Not as a fugitive, blindly or bitterly,
   But as a child might, with no other wish?
Yes, utterly.

Then I shall bear you down my estuary,
Carry you and ferry you to burial mysteriously,
Take you and receive you,
Consume you, engulf you,
In the huge cave, my belly, lave you
With huger waves continually.

And you shall cling and clamber there
And slumber there, in that dumb chamber,
Beat with my blood's beat, hear my heart move
Blindly in bones that ride above you,
Delve in my flesh, dissolved and bedded,
Through viewless valves embodied so –

Till daylight, the expulsion and awakening,
   The riving and the driving forth,
Life with remorseless forceps beckoning –
   Pangs and betrayal of harsh birth.

ROBERT DAVID FITZGERALD

The Wind at Your Door

(To Mary Gilmore)

My ancestor was called on to go out –
a medical man, and one such must by law
wait in attendance on the pampered knout
and lend his countenance to what he saw,
lest the pet, patting with too bared a claw,
be judged a clumsy pussy. Bitter and hard,
see, as I see him, in that jailhouse yard.

Or see my thought of him: though time may keep
elsewhere tradition or a portrait still,
I would not feel under his cloak of sleep
if beard there or smooth chin, just to fulfil
some canon of precision. Good or ill
his blood's my own; and scratching in his grave
could find me more than I might wish to have.

Let him then be much of the middle style
of height and colouring; let his hair be dark
and his eyes green; and for that slit, the smile
that seemed inhuman, have it cruel and stark,
but grant it could be too the ironic mark
of all caught in the system – who the most,
the doctor or the flesh twined round that post?

There was a high wind blowing on that day;
for one who would not watch, but looked aside,
said that when twice he turned it blew his way
splashes of blood and strips of human hide

shaken out from the lashes that were plied
by one right-handed, one left-handed tough,
sweating at this paid task, and skilled enough.

That wind blows to your door down all these years.
Have you not known it when some breath you drew
tasted of blood? Your comfort is in arrears
of just thanks to a savagery tamed in you
only as subtler fears may serve in lieu
of thong and noose – old savagery which has built
your world and laws out of the lives it split.

For what was jailyard widens and takes in
my country. Fifty paces of stamped earth
stretch; and grey walls retreat and grow so thin
that towns show through and clearings – new raw birth
which burst from handcuffs – and free hands go forth
to win tomorrow's harvest from a vast
ploughland – the fifty paces of that past.

But see it through a window barred across,
from cells this side, facing the outer gate
which shuts on freedom, opens on its loss
in a flat wall. Look left now through the grate
at buildings like more walls, roofed with grey slate
or hollowed in the thickness of laid stone
each side the court where the crowd stands this noon.

One there with the officials, thick of build,
not stout, say burly (so this obstinate man
ghosts in the eyes) is he whom enemies killed
(as I was taught) because the monopolist clan
found him a grit in their smooth-turning plan,

too loyally active on behalf of Bligh.
So he got lost; and history passed him by.

But now he buttons his long coat against
the biting gusts, or as a gesture of mind,
habitual; as if to keep him fenced
from stabs of slander sticking him from behind,
sped by the schemers never far to find
in faction, where approval from one source
damns in another clubroom as of course.

This man had Hunter's confidence, King's praise;
and settlers on the starving Hawkesbury banks
recalled through twilight drifting across their days
the doctor's fee of little more than thanks
so often; and how sent by their squeezed ranks
he put their case in London. I find I lack
the hateful paint to daub him wholly black.

Perhaps my life replies to his too much
through veiling generations dropped between.
My weakness here, resentments there, may touch
old motives and explain them, till I lean
to the forgiveness I must hope may clean
my own shortcomings; since no man can live
in his own sight if it will not forgive.

Certainly I must own him whether or not
it be my will. I was made understand
this much when once, marking a freehold lot,
my papers suddenly told me it was land
granted to Martin Mason. I felt his hand

heavily on my shoulder, and knew what coil
binds life to life through bodies, and soul to soil.

There, over to one corner, a bony group
of prisoners waits; and each shall be in turn
tied by his own arms in a human loop
about the post, with his back bared to learn
the price of seeking freedom. So they earn
three hundred rippling stripes apiece, as set
by the law's mathematics against the debt.

There are the Irish batch of Castle Hill,
rebels and mutineers, my countrymen
twice over: first, because of those to till
my birthplace first, hack roads, raise roofs; and then
because their older land time and again
enrolls me through my forbears; and I claim
as origin that threshold whence we came.

One sufferer had my surname, and thereto
'Maurice', which added up to history once;
an ignorant dolt, no doubt, for all that crew
was tenantry. The breed of clod and dunce
makes patriots and true men: could I announce
that Maurice as my kin I say aloud
I'd take his irons as heraldry, and be proud.

Maurice is at the post. Its music lulls,
one hundred lashes done. If backbone shows
then play the tune on buttocks! But feel his pulse;
that's what a doctor's for; and if it goes
lamely, then dose it with these purging blows –

which have not made him moan; though, writhing there,
'Let my neck be,' he says, 'and flog me fair.'

One hundred lashes more, then rest the flail.
What says the doctor now? 'This dog won't yelp;
he'll tire you out before you'll see him fail;
here's strength to spare; go on!' Ay, proud to pulp;
yet when you've done he'll walk without your help,
and knock down guards who'd carry him being bid,
and sing no song of where the pikes are hid.

It would be well if I could find, removed
through generations back – who knows how far? –
more than a surname's thickness as a proved
bridge with that man's foundations. I need some star
of courage from his firmament, a bar
against surrenders: faith. All trials are less
than rain-blacked wind tells of that old distress.

Yet I can live with Mason. What is told
and what my heart knows of his heart, can sort
much truth from falsehood, much there that I hold
good clearly or good clouded by report;
and for things bad, ill grows where ills resort:
they were bad times. None know what in his place
they might have done. I've my own faults to face.

JAMES PICOT

To the Rosella in the Poinsettia Tree

Beautiful bird, in as your wings as vivid
A tree, Rosella! Beautiful bird, I said:

'Your tent won't shelter you or love or me,
Red lad, these nine-o'-clocks, when Beauty looks
Pomp undue – indeed a ceremony
Too grand for the brown-eaten ribbed old livid
Wall behind of a tin factory!'

But the upward sun still burned them on
To tulip crimson from their poppy scarlet,
The poinsettia petals, till at almost
Noon, he glowed in turn behind each moon,
Lamp, leaf – the Wished-for-One – O, separate, crimson! –

For he seemed to burn each petal free,
Till but that Double Fire was to see –
And now there is but Light for Love to be!

A. D. HOPE

The Death of the Bird

For every bird there is this last migration:
Once more the cooling year kindles her heart;
With a warm passage to the summer station
Love pricks the course in lights across the chart.

Year after year a speck on the map, divided
By a whole hemisphere, summons her to come;

Season after season, sure and safely guided,
Going away she is also coming home.

And being home, memory becomes a passion
With which she feeds her brood and straws her nest,
Aware of ghosts that haunt the heart's possession
And exiled love mourning within the breast.

The sands are green with a mirage of valleys;
The palm-tree casts a shadow not its own;
Down the long architrave of temple or palace
Blows a cool air from moorland scraps of stone.

And day by day the whisper of love grows stronger;
The delicate voice, more urgent with despair,
Custom and fear constraining her no longer,
Drives her at last on the waste leagues of air.

A vanishing speck in those inane dominions,
Single and frail, uncertain of her place,
Alone in the bright host of her companions,
Lost in the blue unfriendliness of space,

She feels it close now, the appointed season:
The invisible thread is broken as she flies;
Suddenly, without warning, without reason,
The guiding spark of instinct winks and dies.

Try as she will, the trackless world delivers
No way, the wilderness of light no sign,
The immense and complex map of hills and rivers
Mocks her small wisdom with its vast design.

And darkness rises from the eastern valleys,
And the winds buffet her with their hungry breath,

And the great earth, with neither grief nor malice,
Receives the tiny burden of her death.

Australia

A Nation of trees, drab green and desolate grey
In the field uniform of modern wars,
Darkens her hills, those endless, outstretched paws
Of Sphinx demolished or stone lion worn away.

They call her a young country, but they lie:
She is the last of lands, the emptiest,
A woman beyond her change of life, a breast
Still tender but within the womb is dry.

Without songs, architecture, history:
The emotions and superstitions of younger lands,
Her rivers of water drown among inland sands,
The river of her immense stupidity

Floods her monotonous tribes from Cairns to Perth.
In them at last the ultimate men arrive
Whose boast is not: 'we live' but 'we survive',
A type who will inhabit the dying earth.

And her five cities, like five teeming sores,
Each drains her: a vast parasite robber-state
Where second hand Europeans pullulate
Timidly on the edge of alien shores.

Yet there are some like me turn gladly home
From the lush jungle of modern thought, to find

The Arabian desert of the human mind,
Hoping, if still from the deserts the prophets come,

Such savage and scarlet as no green hills dare
Springs in that waste, some spirit which escapes
The learned doubt, the chatter of cultured apes
Which is called civilization over there.

Hay Fever

Time, with his scythe honed fine,
Takes a pace forward, swings from the hips; the flesh
Crumples and falls in windrows curving away.
Waiting my turn as he swings – (Not yet, not mine!)
I recall the sound of the scythe on an earlier day:
Late spring in my boyhood; learning to mow with the men;
Eight of us moving together in echelon line,
Out of the lucerne patch and into the hay,
And I at the end on the left because I was fresh,
Because I was new to the game and young at the skill –
As though I were Time himself I remember it still.

The mild Tasmanian summer; the men are here
To mow for my minister father and make his hay.
They have brought a scythe for me. I hold it with pride.
The lucerne is up to my knee, the grass to my waist.
I set the blade into the grass as they taught me the way;
The still dewy stalks nod, tremble and tilt aside,
Cornflowers, lucerne and poppies, sugar-grass, summer-grass,
  laced
With red-stemmed dock; I feel the thin steel crunch

Through hollow-stalk milk thistle, self-sown oats and rye;
I snag on a fat-hen clump; chick weed falls in a bunch,
But sorrel scatters; dandelion casts up a golden eye,
To smell of cows chewing their cuds, the sweet hay-breath:
The boy with the scythe never thinks it the smell of death.

The boy with the scythe takes a stride forward, swings
From the hips, keeping place and pace, keeping time
By the sound of the scythes, by the swish and ripple, the sigh
Of the dying grass like an animal breathing, a rhyme
Falling pat on the ear that matches the steel as it sings
True through the tottering stems. Sweat runs into my eye,
How long to a break? How long can I hold out yet?
I nerve my arms to go on; I am running with, flooding with,
sweat.

How long ago was it? – Why, the scythe is as obsolete now
As arrows and bow. I have lived from one age to another;
And I have made hay while I could and the sun still shone,
Time drives a harvester now: he does not depend on the
weather.
Well, I have rolled in his hay, in my day, and now it is gone;
But I still have a barn stacked high with that good, dry mow,
Shrivelled and fragrant stems, the grass and the flowers together
And a thistle or two in the pile for the prick of remorse.
It is good for a man when he comes to the end of his course
In the barn of his brain to be able to romp like a boy in the
heap . . .
To lie still in well-cured hay . . . to drift into sleep.

HARRY HOOTON

Words

Words that have fallen from the lips are dead.
The reverberating murmurs from the branches out-thrust
With the waves' confused mutter in the wind are lost,
And words, wise and otherwise, alike are tossed
Carelessly aside. Oh, how the cool sweet trees
So irresponsive scatter their leaves upon the earth;
A million sounds and hues irrelevantly die.
They must make way for new things, let them die –
Leaves that have fallen from the trees are dead . . .
Words are the treasured corpses of the mind;
O'er the dust of withered words man's incantations fall,
Ghoulishly he gathers them, and stores them in his morgue;
Memories, theories and meanings are dust –
Words that have fallen from the lips are dead!

RONALD McCUAIG

Love Me and Never Leave Me

Love me, and never leave me,
Love, nor ever deceive me,
And I shall always bless you
If I may undress you:
    This I heard a lover say
    To his sweetheart where they lay.

He, though he did undress her,
Did not always bless her;
She, though she would not leave him,

Often did deceive him;
Yet they loved, and when they died
They were buried side by side.

ELIZABETH RIDDELL

News of a Baby

Welcome, baby, to the world of swords
And deadlier words.
We offer you a rough bed, and tears at morning,
And soon a playground
Bounded by ice and stones,
A buttonhole of thorns,
A kiss on war's corner.

We promise you, baby,
The stumble of fear in the heart,
The lurch of fear in the bones.

Painted upon your mother's cheek already
I see the dark effusion of your blood,
Bending already beside her patient chair the bandaged ghosts.
Welcome, baby, no dread thing will be omitted.
We are your eager hosts.

W. HART-SMITH

Limpets

remind me of cups
turned upside-down in saucers.
Their stony lips are glued
so that no one may read
the runes within.

Between flesh and crust
an area where friction is eased
with nacreous lubrication.

Drills of whelks,
the smothering of stars,
may empty me,
waves turn me right side up.
Then Death may read my cup.

Space

Columbus looks towards the New World,
the sea is flat and nothing breaks the rim
of the world's disc;
he takes the sphere with him.

Day into night the same, the only change
the living variation at the core
of this man's universe;
and silent on the silver ship he broods.

Red gouts of weed, and skimming fish, to crack

the stupefying emptiness of sea,
night, and the unimpassioned gaze of stars . . .

And God be praised for the compass, oaths
bawled in the fo'c'sle,
broken heads and wine,
song and guitars,

the tramp of boots,
the wash and whip of brine.

IAN MUDIE

Underground

Deep flows the flood,
deep under the land.
Dark is it, and blood
and eucalypt colour and scent it.
Deep flows the stream,
feeding the totem-roots,
deep through the time of dream
in Alcheringa.
Deep flows the river,
deep as our roots reach for it;
feeding us, angry and striving
against the blindness
ship-fed seas bring us
from colder waters.

HAL PORTER

Obverse

Man-and-axe, the two-edged curse,
hew a landscape in obverse;
these ring-barked ruptured arteries
seem nerve-white roots of unseen trees –

trees of a honey under-land
(leaves like a lory's wing outfanned)
where claret boughs are love-long weighed
by plums of plenty, fans of shade.

Butterflies spin nervous mesh
over mosses deep as flesh
whose fibres, up, are calcined weeds –
a waste wind-shot by shrapnel seeds.

Hills that furnace fever shakes
brim, reversed, with riesling lakes,
iced by the green corroded hopes
of fissured, charred and bare-back slopes.

Leather man (oh, hare-lean thighs)
seeks like crow, with summer eyes,
rose-water rain and creeks of frost
that his Medusa-land has lost.

ROLAND ROBINSON

Casuarina

The last, the long haired casuarina
stands upon the hillside where,
against the turquoise night of those first
yellow stars, she shakes her hair.

She shakes her hair out in her singing
of cliffs and caves and waterfalls,
and tribes who left the lichened sandstone
carved in gods and animals.

This is her country; honeyeaters
cry out its aboriginal name
where on her ridges still the spear-tall
lilies burn in flame and flame.

I listen, and our legend says not
more than this dark singing tree,
although her golden flowering lover
lies slain beside the winter sea.

JOHN BLIGHT

Flatworms

On rocky foreshores which picnickers avoid
in the hot weather, or shun when hard winds blow,
we know now, life is still enjoyed
under each heavy rock by the slug-like slow
flatworm, denizen of the rock-shelves of the sea.
But there are seasons he is wont to show

himself above, on surfaces of tide-exposed
decaying shale; a point I did not know
till after my first flatworm was disclosed
flowing – he moves by flowing, though it's slow
movement – over the sediment of mud
which in bay-water settles where the flow
of tides can't scour. Oozing like foul blood,
like a black tongue, wafer-thin, he roves promiscuously.

W. FLEXMORE HUDSON

Drought

Midsummer noon; and the timbered walls
start in the heat,
and the children sag listlessly over the desks
with bloodless faces oozing sweat
sipped by the stinging flies.
Outside the tall sun fades the shabby mallee,
and drives the ants deep underground;
the stony driftsand shrivels
the drab sparse plants:
there's not a cloud in all the sky to cast
a shadow on the tremulous plain.
Stirless the windmills, thirsty cattle standing
despondently about the empty tanks
stamping and tossing their heads
in torment of the flies from dawn to dark.
For ten parched days it has been like this
and, although I love the desert, I
have found myself
                    dreaming

of upright gums by a mountain creek
where the red boronia blooms,
where bell-birds chime through the morning mists,
and greenness can hide from the sun;
of rock-holes where the brumbies slink
like swift cloud-shadows from the gidgi-scrub
to drink when the moon is low.
And as I stoop to drink, I too,
just as I raise my cupped hands to my lips,
I am recalled to this drought-stricken plain
by the petulant question
of a summer-wearied child.

Bashō

Bashō, the ragged poet, the wanderer Bashō,
astride a sleepy horse at the edge of a rustling pond
where teal, at the splash of a salmon, sail for clumps of bamboo.

High on the opposite bank, a gusty pine is waving
across the noon-white snow of distant Fujisan,
pouring cascades of gold-dust, luminous, gentle as mist,
on blue sky, blue ripples, and morning glory bells.

And his horse is drowsing, drowsing – a dragonfly close to its ears! –
while Bashō, brushing the gold from its glossy mane, is smiling
that such a little thing as pollen clouding a wind
should outweigh the fifty sorrows, the disillusioned years.

REX INGAMELLS

The Golden Bird

I watched the new moon fly
behind a summit tree
to perch on an upper branch
and so look down at me.

Upon that very instant,
the glowing gully rang
with a kookaburra's laughter,
while frogs and crickets sang.

I was a dreamy lad,
walking the bush alone;
it was thirty years ago . . . .
In all that I have known,

the frogs have never croaked,
the crickets never chirred,
so blithely as on the night
when the moon was a laughing bird,

new moon, a golden bird,
perched high, with beak in air,
when I was a dreamy lad
and the bush was everywhere.

KENNETH MACKENZIE

Caesura

Sometimes at night when the heart stumbles and stops
a full second endless the endless steps
that lead me on through this time terrain
without edges and beautiful terrible
are gone never to proceed again.

Here is a moment of enormous trouble
when the kaleidoscope sets unalterable
and at once without meaning without motion
like a stalled aeroplane in the middle sky
ready to fall down into a waiting ocean.

Blackness rises. Am I now to die
and feel the steps no more and not see day
break out its answering smile of hail all's well
from east full round to east and hear the bird
whistle all creatures that on earth do dwell?

Not now. Old heart has stopped to think of a word
as someone in a dream by far too weird
to be unlikely feels a kiss and stops
to praise all heaven stumbling in all his senses . . .
and suddenly hears again the endless steps.

The Snake

Withdrawing from the amorous grasses
from the warm and luscious water
the snake is soul untouched by both
nor does the fire of day through which it passes
mark it or cling. Immaculate navigator
it carries death within its mouth.

Soul is the snake that moves at will
through all the nets of circumstance
like the wind that nothing stops
immortal movement in a world held still
by rigid anchors of intent or chance
and ropes of fear and stays of hopes.

It is the source of all dispassion
the voiceless life above communion
secret as the spring of wind
nor does it know the shames of self-confession
the weakness that enjoys love's coarse dominion
or the betrayals of the mind.

Soul is the snake the cool viator
sprung from a shadow on the grass
quick and intractable as breath
gone as it came like the everlasting water
reflecting God in immeasurable space –
and in its mouth carries death.

DOUGLAS STEWART

The Silkworms

All their lives in a box! What generations,
What centuries of masters, not meaning to be cruel
But needing their labour, taught these creatures such patience
That now though sunlight strikes on the eye's dark jewel
Or moonlight breathes on the wing they do not stir
But like the ghosts of moths crouch silent there.

Look it's a child's toy! There is no lid even,
They can climb, they can fly, and the whole world's their tree;
But hush, they say in themselves, we are in prison.
There is no word to tell them that they are free,
And they are not; ancestral voices bind them
In dream too deep for wind or word to find them.

Even in the young, each like a little dragon
Ramping and green upon his mulberry leaf,
So full of life, it seems, the voice has spoken:
They hide where there is food, where they are safe,
And the voice whispers, 'Spin the cocoon,
Sleep, sleep, you shall be wrapped in me soon.'

Now is their hour, when they wake from that long swoon;
Their pale curved wings are marked in a pattern of leaves,
Shadowy for trees, white for the dance of the moon;
And when on summer nights the buddleia gives
Its nectar like lilac wine for insects mating
They drink its fragrance and shiver, impatient with waiting,

They stir, they think they will go. Then they remember
It was forbidden, forbidden, ever to go out;
The Hands are on guard outside like claps of thunder,
The ancestral voice says Don't, and they do not.
Still the night calls them to unimaginable bliss
But there is terror around them, the vast, the abyss,

And here is the tribe that they know, in their known place,
They are gentle and kind together, they are safe for ever,
And all shall be answered at last when they embrace.
White moth moves closer to moth, lover to lover.
There is that pang of joy on the edge of dying –
Their soft wings whirr, they dream that they are flying.

DAVID CAMPBELL

from: Cocky's Calendar

Hawk and Hill

When from the still crystal of thought
My eyes look out and make report
Of hill and hovering hawk, I find
They do but give me back my mind.

The hawk, the hill, the loping hare,
The blue tree and the blue air,
O all the coloured world I see
And walk upon, are made by me.

First I would praise the world of sense;
Then praise that sweet Intelligence,
The hovering far-sighted love
That sees me and in whom I live.

Windy Gap

As I was going through Windy Gap
A hawk and a cloud hung over the map.

The land lay bare and the wind blew loud
And the hawk cried out from the heart of the cloud,

'Before I fold my wings in sleep
I'll pick the bones of your travelling sheep,

'For the leaves blow back and the wintry sun
Shows the tree's white skeleton.'

A magpie sat in the tree's high top
Singing a song on Windy Gap

That streamed far down to the plain below
Like a shaft of light from a high window.

From the bending tree he sang aloud,
And the sun shone out of the heart of the cloud

And it seemed to me as we travelled through
That my sheep were the notes that trumpet blew.

And so I sing this song of praise
For travelling sheep and blowing days.

JOHN MANIFOLD

The Tomb of Lt. John Learmonth, A.I.F.

'At the end on Crete he took to the hills, and said he'd fight it out with only a revolver. He was a great soldier . . .'
– One of his men in a letter

This is not sorrow, this is work: I build
A cairn of words over a silent man,
My friend John Learmonth whom the Germans killed.

There was no word of hero in his plan;
Verse should have been his love and peace his trade,
But history turned him to a partisan.

Far from the battle as his bones are laid
Crete will remember him. Remember well,
Mountains of Crete, the Second Field Brigade!

Say Crete, and there is little more to tell
Of muddle tall as treachery, despair
And black defeat resounding like a bell;

But bring the magnifying focus near
And in contempt of muddle and defeat
The old heroic virtues still appear.

Australian blood where hot and icy meet
(James Hogg and Lermontov were of his kin)
Lie still and fertilise the fields of Crete.

* * *

Schoolboy, I watched his ballading begin:
Billy and bullocky and billabong,
Our properties of childhood, all were in.

I heard the air though not the undersong,
The fierceness and resolve; but all the same
They're the tradition, and tradition's strong.

Swagman and bushranger die hard, die game,
Die fighting, like that wild colonial boy –
Jack Dowling, says the ballad, was his name.

He also spun his pistol like a toy,
Turned to the hills like wolf or kangaroo,
And faced destruction with a bitter joy.

His freedom gave him nothing else to do
But set his back against his family tree
And fight the better for the fact he knew

He was as good as dead. Because the sea
Was closed and the air dark and the land lost,
'They'll never capture me alive,' said he.

* * *

That's courage chemically pure, uncrossed
With sacrifice or duty or career,
Which counts and pays in ready coin the cost

Of holding course. Armies are not its sphere
Where all's contrived to achieve its counterfeit;
It swears with discipline, it's volunteer.

I could as hardly make a moral fit
Around it as around a lightning flash.
There is no moral, that's the point of it,

No moral. But I'm glad of this panache
That sparkles, as from flint, from us and steel,
True to no crown nor presidential sash

Nor flag nor fame. Let others mourn and feel
He died for nothing: nothings have their place.
While thus the kind and civilized conceal

This spring of unsuspected inward grace
And look on death as equals, I am filled
With queer affection for the human race.

JUDITH WRIGHT

At Cooloolah

The blue crane fishing in Cooloolah's twilight
has fished there longer than our centuries.
He is the certain heir of lake and evening,
and he will wear their colour till he dies,

but I'm a stranger, come of a conquering people.
I cannot share his calm, who watch his lake,
being unloved by all my eyes delight in,
and made uneasy, for an old murder's sake.

Those dark-skinned people who once named Cooloolah
knew that no land is lost or won by wars,
for earth is spirit: the invader's feet will tangle
in nets there and his blood be thinned by fears.

Riding at noon and ninety years ago,
my grandfather was beckoned by a ghost –
a black accoutred warrior armed for fighting,
who sank into bare plain, as now into time past.

White shores of sand, plumed reed and paperbark,
clear heavenly levels frequented by crane and swan –
I know that we are justified only by love,
but oppressed by arrogant guilt, have room for none.

And walking on clean sand among the prints
of bird and animal, I am challenged by a driftwood spear
thrust from the water; and, like my grandfather,
must quiet a heart accused by its own fear.

Naked Girl and Mirror

This is not I. I had no body once –
only what served my need to laugh and run
and stare at stars and tentatively dance
on the fringe of foam and wave and sand and sun.
Eyes loved, hands reached for me, but I was gone
on my own currents, quicksilver, thistledown.
Can I be trapped at last in that soft face?

I stare at you in fear, dark brimming eyes.
Why do you watch me with that immoderate plea –
'Look under these curled lashes, recognize
that you were always here; know me – be me.'
Smooth once-hermaphrodite shoulders, too tenderly
your long slope runs, above those sudden shy
curves furred with light that spring below your space.

No, I have been betrayed. If I had known
that this girl waited between a year and a year,
I'd not have chosen her bough to dance upon.
Betrayed, by that little darkness here, and here
this swelling softness and that frightened stare
from eyes I will not answer; shut out here
from my own self, by its new body's grace –

for I am betrayed by someone lovely. Yes,
I see you are lovely, hateful naked girl.
Your lips in the mirror tremble as I refuse
to know or claim you. Let me go – let me be gone.
You are half of some other who may never come.
Why should I tend you? You are not my own;
you seek that other – he will be your home.

Yet I pity your eyes in the mirror, misted with tears;
I lean to your kiss. I must serve you; I will obey.
Some day we may love. I may miss your going, some day,
though I shall always resent your dumb and fruitful years.
Your lovers shall learn better, and bitterly too,
if their arrogance dares to think I am part of you.

Request to a Year

If the year is meditating a suitable gift,
I should like it to be the attitude
of my great-great-grandmother,
legendary devotee of the arts,

who, having had eight children
and little opportunity for painting pictures,

sat one day on a high rock
beside a river in Switzerland

and from a difficult distance viewed
her second son, balanced on a small ice-floe,
drift down the current toward a waterfall
that struck rock-bottom eighty feet below,

while her second daughter, impeded,
no doubt, by the petticoats of the day,
stretched out a last-hope alpenstock
(which luckily later caught him on his way).

Nothing, it was evident, could be done;
and with the artist's isolating eye
my great-great-grandmother hastily sketched the scene.
The sketch survives to prove the story by.

Year, if you have no Mother's day present planned,
reach back and bring me the firmness of her hand.

Flying Fox on Barbed Wire

Little nightmare flying-fox
trapped on the cruel barbs of day
has no weapon but a wing
and a tiny scream.
Here's a patch of night, a thing
that looks by daylight like a hoax;
dawn wouldn't let it fly away
with its kin into a dream,
but stabbed with a pin its velvet hand
and hung it in a hostile land.

Imp from the world of upside-down,
here's some darkness in a bag
to foil your frightened needle-bite.
Now we can untie
from the staring stake of pain
your black claw on its velvet rag.
Scramble, silent, out of the light
and hang by your feet in the kind-leaved tree.
Gargoyle, thief, forget your grief
and go to your country night; and we,
accomplice to day's enemy,
too must forget
that we and the Devil ever met.

HAROLD STEWART

The Leaf-makers

There was an ancient craftsman once, who made
From silk-green, semi-transparent jade
The likeness of a glossy mulberry leaf;
Minutely carved in delicate relief,
Its map of veins and lucid arteries
Seemed to flow with the green blood of trees.
On this his ingenuity had spent
Years of intricate patience, to indent
Around its profile every nick and notch,
And even use, for a rain-discoloured blotch,
Markings with which the mineral was laced –
Perfect in imperfection, thus defaced.
Before the Prince of Sung the man displayed
His portrait of a leaf. When it was laid

With fresh mulberry leaves to rival it,
A silk-worm, curious with hunger, bit
The jade configuration, tip to stem.
It could not tell his handiwork from them.
The Prince of Sung unwittingly allowed
Wonder to change his face, and so endowed
The artist with a pension and his praise
For skill that could outwit an insect's gaze.
Hearing of which, Lieh Tzŭ countered, 'Now,
If it should take as long as that for Tao
To make a single bud unfold with care
Its crinkled wing into the harsh spring air,
Seldom would trees have anything to wear.'

VAL VALLIS

Shipwright

He is a builder of ships. I watched him at work
In the late afternoon, fashioning each plank
With a sculptor's care – this flare, that sweep of frame
And gunwale line. A jeweller's eye he has,
Matching the perfection of one beech plank to another,
Judging the sea-width of his sun-dried pine.

And he has scanned the flight of gulls to learn
New grace of curve, some secret of wind-power
That opening sails might sing on sunlit flight.

He has honoured the pines and beeches of the forest,
As Phidias honoured some white quarried stone;
By transmutation reassuring Time
That men still live who toil for labour's beauty.

The Mooring Buoy

Neither old age nor winter snowed your head,
Florid-faced politician of the sea,
Now left, now right inclined, with ebb and flow,
Demanding ships to seek your ministry.

Puffed up with self-esteem until you float
A swollen toad, secure in safer seas
Than those of ships the tides are proud to bear,
You dole to bird and hull your charities.

Vain, no doubt, of your essential service,
And all the attention to your coat of red,
Have you wondered what the gulls are really thinking
As they pile their blushing honours on your head?

JACK DAVIS

Death of a Tree

The power saw screamed,
Then turned to a muttering.
She leaned forward,
fell.
A sad abruptness
in the limpness of foliage,
in the final folding of limbs.
I placed my hand on what was left:
one hundred years of graceful beauty ended,
and the underside of leaves pale
blended with the morning rain.
Better for her to have been overpowered

by wind or storm.
That would have been a battle,
a fitter end for such a forest giant
than this ignoble inevitability
because man was involved.
Man is pain.
I walked away and left her,
saddened,
aware of my loss.
Yet – still,
part of the gain.

Mining Company's Hymn

The Government is my shepherd,
I shall not want.
They let me search in the Aboriginal reserves
which leads me to many riches
for taxation sake.
Though I wallow in the valley of wealth I will fear no weevil
because my money is safe in the bank
vaults of the land,
and my Government will always comfort me.
They will always protect me,
from the Aborigines there and claims there.
So I can then take wealth whenever I have a need to
and my bank account will grow ever more.
Oh! Surely wealth and materialism will shorten the
days of my life, but I will dwell safely protected
by Government for ever.

Rottnest

These rocks placed here by man
to form a bridgewater
The sea's age typified
by algae clinging to the stone
The Indian Ocean limitless
breathing might and power
even on this day of calm
I look across at Rottnest
in the far off haze
where my people
breathed their last sigh
for home the mainland
to them the distant blue
What did they do
but stand within the paths
of cloven hooves
their only crime
to fight for what was rightly theirs
To them the island was a place of souls
departed down through
eons of time
but by a savage twist of fate
No flight of soul for them
But chained they waited
for their lot's conclusion
to be forever part of
the island of the dead

JAMES McAULEY

Holiday

Sunlight runs like fluid gold in the veins,
A soft hilarity upon hair and skin.
    A bird's momentary shadow stains
        The stone paths we walk in.

It is good not to do what we should do,
But something good we needn't do – like spin
    Straw into gold, or living into
        Surprises, as this thin

Voltage of pale sunshine may incite.
For loving is a game where both can win,
    And freedom to do nothing right
        Is the flower of discipline.

Self-portrait, Newcastle 1942

First day, by the open window,
He sits at a table to write,
And watches the coal-dust settle
Black on the paper's white.

Years of breathing this grime
Show black in the lungs of the dead
When autopsies are done;
So at least it is said.

Sunset over the steelworks
Bleeds a long rubric of war;

He thinks he knows, but doesn't,
The black print of the score.

He, like that sullied paper,
Has acquired no meaning yet.
He goes for long walks at night,
Or drinks with people he's met.

In sleeping panic he shatters
The glass of a window-pane.
What will he do with his life?
Jump three storeys down in the rain?

Something – guilt, tension, or outrage –
Keeps coming in nightmare shape.
Screams often startle the house:
He leaps up blind to escape.

By day he teaches the dullest
Intermediate class;
He gets on well with them, knowing
He too has a test to pass.

With friends he talks anarchism,
The philosophical kind,
But *Briefe an einen jungen*
Dichter speaks close to his mind.

Pietà

A year ago you came
Early into the light.
You lived a day and night,

Then died; no-one to blame.

Once only, with one hand,
Your mother in farewell
Touched you. I cannot tell,
I cannot understand

A thing so dark and deep,
So physical a loss:
One touch, and that was all

She had of you to keep.
Clean wounds, but terrible,
Are those made with the Cross.

W. S. FAIRBRIDGE

Consecration of the House

House, you are done . . .
                              And now before
The high contracting parties take
Final possession, let us stand
Silent for this occasion at the door,
Who here a lifelong compact make:
That you were not for trading planned,
Since barter wears the object poor,
But are henceforth our living stake
– And hereunto we set our hand.
  Be over us, be strong, be sure.

You may not keep from world alarms,
But from the daily wind and rain
Of guessed, or real, or of imagined wrong

Shadow us between your arms;
Be our sincere affection, and maintain
A corner here for art and song;
Yet no mere image of benumbing calms,
But a bold premiss, where the mind may gain
Purchase for adventurous journeys long.
  Be round us, and protect from harms.

A roof well timbered, hollow walls
Where the damp creep never comes,
Kiln-hardened joists no worm can bore;
Low sills where early daylight falls
Beneath wide eaves against the summer suns;
Huge cupboards, where a child might store
Surfeit of treasures; and no cramping halls,
But spacious and proportioned rooms;
A single, poured foundation, perfect to the core.
  Be our security against all calls.

Six orange trees, a lemon, and a passion vine.
All the lush living that endears
A home be yours: some asters for a show,
And roses by the wall to climb,
Hydrangeas fat as cauliflowers.
We who (how arduously!) have watched you grow,
We feel you in the very soil; and time
Shall tie your flesh with ours, your piers
And pipes intestinal, that anchor you below.
  Be through us, and prevent our fears.

Your windows face the north: the sun
At four o'clock leaps in;
By breakfast-time has swung so high

We lose him; till upon his downward run,
Swollen and yellow as a mandarin,
We catch his amber from the western sky.
Then when the night's dark web is spun,
Let your glass like a stationary comet gleam,
And lantern to our light supply.
  Be our sure welcome, and a wakeful beam.

Though we designed and built you, we
Will not outlive what we have done.
And if our children here succeed,
Our gain is now, and yours. Let this mortar be
Consecrate to death – a place where one
Gladly might wither to his glowing seed.
We serve you then in all humility
Who serve us, and by our sweat were won
When we had most need.
  Give us the obligations that make free.

House, you are done. . . . And nevermore
So painted, new, so arrogantly clean;
The tang of lime, the horrid clang
Of footsteps on the naked floor
Will fade to a serene
Patina of sounds and smells that hang
Like the reverberations of a shore
Of history: a hive where love has been,
And whence the future sprang.
  Be powerful above us all. Be sure.

'ERN MALLEY'

Dürer: Innsbruck, 1495

I had often, cowled in the slumberous heavy air,
Closed my inanimate lids to find it real,
As I knew it would be, the colourful spires
And painted roofs, the high snows glimpsed at the back,
All reversed in the quiet reflecting waters –
Not knowing then that Dürer perceived it too.
Now I find that once more I have shrunk
To an interloper, robber of dead men's dream,
I had read in books that art is not easy
But no one warned that the mind repeats
In its ignorance the vision of others. I am still
The black swan of trespass on alien waters.

Petit Testament

In the twenty-fifth year of my age
I find myself to be a dromedary
That has run short of water between
One oasis and the next mirage
And having despaired of ever
Making my obsessions intelligible
I am content at last to be
The sole clerk of my metamorphoses.
Begin here:

In the year 1943
I resigned to the living all collateral images
Reserving to myself a man's

Inalienable right to be sad
At his own funeral.
(Here the peacock blinks the eyes
of his multipennate tail.)
In the same year
I said to my love (who is living)
Dear we shall never be that verb
Perched on the sole Arabian Tree
Not having learnt in our green age to forget
The sins that flow between the hands and feet
(Here the Tree weeps gum tears
Which are also real: I tell you
These things are real)
So, I forced a parting
Scrubbing my few dingy words to brightness.

Where I have lived
The bed-bug sleeps in the seam, the cockroach
Inhabits the crack and the careful spider
Spins his aphorisms in the corner.
I have heard them shout in the street
The chiliasms of the Socialist Reich
And in the magazines I have read
The Popular Front-to-Back.
But where I have lived
Spain weeps in the gutters of Footscray
Guernica is the ticking of the clock
The nightmare has become real, not as belief
But in the scrub-typhus of Mubo.

It is something to be at last speaking
Though in this No-Man's-language appropriate

Only to No-Man's-Land.
Set this down too:
I have pursued rhyme, image, and metre,
Known all the clefts in which the foot may stick,
Stumbled often, stammered,
But in time the fading voice grows wise
And seizing the co-ordinate of all existence
Traces the inevitable graph
And in conclusion:
There is a moment when the pelvis
Explodes like a grenade. I
Who have lived in the shadow that each act
Casts on the next act now emerge
As loyal as the thistle that in session
Puffs its full seed upon the indicative air.
I have split the infinitive. Beyond is anything.

ROSEMARY DOBSON

In My End is My Beginning

Draw a circle round me thrice
Arm's radius to this piece of earth;
Here's my Tom Tiddler's Land of danger,
Hazardous path to Death from Birth.

In this small orb is compassed wonder,
Passion, despair, and state of grace.
I am that traveller who, returning,
Finds destination's starting-place.

For blood's my argument and reason,
And flesh audible, and heart

Will know the way if these should fail,
And head will bear a steady part.

Wit's the one weapon for my fending,
Who travels farthest journeys light,
Save that the mind has faggots stored
To kindle fire on darkest night.

No fares for ferrying. If you will,
Saint Christopher, be with me still.

Folding the Sheets

You and I will fold the sheets
Advancing towards each other
From Burma, from Lapland.

From India where the sheets have been washed in the river
And pounded upon stones:
Together we will match the corners.

From China where women on either side of the river
Have washed their pale cloth in the White Stone Shallows
'Under the shining moon.'

We meet as though in the formal steps of a dance
To fold the sheets together, put them to air
In wind, in sun over bushes, or by the fire.

We stretch and pull from one side and then the other –
Your turn. Now mine.
We fold them and put them away until they are needed.

A wish for all people when they lie down in bed –
Smooth linen, cool cotton, the fragrance and stir of herbs
And the faint but perceptible scent of sweet clear water.

The Mirror

Jan Vermeer Speaks

Time that is always gone stays still
A moment in this quiet room.
Nothing exists but what we know,
The mirror gathers in the world,
Time and the world. And I shall hold
All summers in a stroke of gold.

Twilight, and one last fall of sun
That slants across the window-sill,
And, mirrored darkly in the glass
(Can paint attempt that unlit void?)
All night, oblivion, is stayed
Within the curtain's folded shade.

Upon the table bread and wine.
The earthen pitcher's perfect curve
Once spun upon the potter's wheel
Is pivot of the turning world,
Still centre where my peace abides,
Round moon that draws all restless tides.

There, it is done. The vision fades
And Time moves on. Oh you who praise
This tangled, broken web of paint,
I paint reflections in a glass:

Who look on Truth with mortal sight
Are blinded in its blaze of light.

GWEN HARWOOD

Home of Mercy

By two and two the ruined girls are walking
at the neat margin of the convent grass
into the chapel, counted as they pass
by an old nun who silences their talking.

They smooth with roughened hands the clumsy dress
that hides their ripening bodies. Memories burn
like incense as towards plaster saints they turn
faces of mischievous children in distress.

They kneel: time for the spirit to begin
with prayer its sad recourse to dream and flight
from their intolerable weekday rigour.
Each morning they will launder, for their sin,
sheets soiled by other bodies, and at night
angels will wrestle them with brutish vigour.

Suburban Sonnet

She practises a fugue, though it can matter
to no one now if she plays well or not.
Beside her on the floor two children chatter,
then scream and fight. She hushes them. A pot
boils over. As she rushes to the stove
too late, a wave of nausea overpowers
subject and counter-subject. Zest and love

drain out with soapy water as she scours
the crusted milk. Her veins ache. Once she played
for Rubinstein, who yawned. The children caper
round a sprung mousetrap where a mouse lies dead.
When the soft corpse won't move they seem afraid.
She comforts them; and wraps it in a paper
featuring: *Tasty dishes from stale bread.*

Dialogue

If an angel came with one wish
I might say, deliver that child
who died before birth, into life.
Let me see what she might have become.
He would bring her into a room
fair skinned   the bones of her hands
would press on my shoulderblades
in our long embrace

we would sit
with the albums spread on our knees:
now here are your brothers   and here
your sister   here the old house
among trees and espaliered almonds.
– But where am I?

Ah my dear
I have only one picture

here
in my head   I saw you lying
still folded   one moment   forever
your head bent down to your heart
eyes closed on unspeakable wisdom

your delicate frog-pale fingers
spread
apart as if you were playing
a woodwind instrument.
– My name?
It was never given.
– Where is my grave?
in my head   I suppose
the hospital burnt you.
– Was I beautiful?
To me.
– Do you mourn for me every day?
Not at all   it is more than thirty years
I am feeling the coolness of age
the perspectives of memory change.
Pearlskull   what lifts you here
from night-drift to solemn ripeness?
Mushroom dome? Gourd plumpness?
The frog in my pot of basil?
– It is none of these, but a rhythm
the bones of my fingers   dactylic
rhetoric smashed from your memory.
Forget me again.
Had I lived
no rhythm would be the same
nor my brothers and sister feast
in the world's eternal house.

Overhead   wings of cloud
burning   and under my feet
stones marked with demons' teeth.

OODGEROO NOONUCCAL (KATH WALKER)

Municipal Gum

Gumtree in the city street,
Hard bitumen around your feet,
Rather you should be
In the cool world of leafy forest halls
And wild bird calls.
Here you seem to me
Like that poor cart-horse
Castrated, broken, a thing wronged,
Strapped and buckled, its hell prolonged,
Whose hung head and listless mien express
Its hopelessness.
Municipal gum, it is dolorous
To see you thus
Set in your black grass of bitumen –
O fellow citizen,
What have they done to us?

Namatjira

Aboriginal man, you walked with pride,
And painted with joy the countryside.
Original man, your fame grew fast,
Men pointed you out as you went past.

But vain the honour and tributes paid,
For you strangled in rules the white men made;
You broke no law of your own wild clan
Which says, 'Share all with your fellow-man.'

What did their loud acclaim avail
Who gave you honour, then gave you jail?
Namatjira, they boomed your art,
They called you genius, then broke your heart.

Gooboora, the Silent Pool

For Grannie Sunflower Last of the Noonuccals

Gooboora, Gooboora, the Water of Fear
That awed the Noonuccals once numerous here,
The Bunyip is gone from your bone-strewn bed,
And the clans departed to drift with the dead.

Once in the far time before the whites came
How light were their hearts in the dance and the game!
Gooboora, Gooboora, to think that today
A whole happy tribe are all vanished away!

What mystery lurks by the Water of Fear,
And what is the secret still lingering here?
For birds hasten by as in days of old,
No wild thing will drink of your waters cold.

Gooboora, Gooboora, still here you remain,
But where are my people I look for in vain?
They are gone from the hill, they are gone from the shore,
And the place of the Silent Pool knows them no more.

But I think they still gather when daylight is done
And stand round the pool at the setting of sun,
A shadowy band that is now without care,
Fearing no longer the Thing in its lair.

Old Death has passed by you but took the dark throng;
Now lost is the Noonuccal language and song.
Gooboora, Gooboora, it makes the heart sore
That you should be here but my people no more!

COLIN THIELE

Radiation Victim

Beneath your cooling coverlet you lie,
The unseen fire still burning in your flesh,
Yet all humanity may pass you by
Unheeded while you melt before its flame,
And the slim needles of its secret rays drive
Inwards to incinerate your name.
God, that we should see you slowly burn alive!

This is the stealthy modern way to die:
To take the passive metal in your grip
And unaware set all your hand on fire.
Walk down the street or work your innocent bench,
While the unfelt heat burns slowly to the bone
With flame that no man's artifice can quench.

A fine ghastliness this is to end our days:
An ancient incandescence fanned and freed
To leap the air invisibly until
Each mortal breast, ignited and ablaze,
Shrinks to its blackened ashes silently.
And a strange compassion has macabre birth
Now that the unseen fire may stalk and scorch
Its darting probe through the wide round Earth,
May thrust its flame against our cringing flesh
And make mankind its hideous secret torch.

NAN McDONALD

The Hawk

I came out in the morning
And he was there –
The pale hawk, alone
On the lightning-blasted tree.
The fierce and burning air
Struck at my lifted face –
I had not thought to see him
Again in this place.

Ash-grey on the grey wood,
White on the hot white sky,
A ghost he seemed, from the years
When the deep forest stood
Around that one stark tree
(A child, I saw them die
Felled as the city spread),
But he turned, and down his long
Curved wing the shadow darkened,
Showed him alive and strong.

He turned his flat, cruel head
And looked out on the land,
The baking roofs of the suburb,
The dusty streets, and beyond,
The paddocks bleached with drought,
The shimmering glare of sand
In the dry bed of the creek,
The dreadful blackened miles,
The twisted iron and rubble

Where there were towns last week.

He did not open his beak,
He made no cry,
But I looked in his savage eye,
I heard him speak.

'You thought the hawk had fled
And dared no more come near?
That you had driven me out
As you drove beyond your city
The famine, the fear?
It has been a long time,' he said,
'But I am here.'

DIMITRIS TSALOUMAS

The Harbour

I arrived late one summer evening.
From a far parapet of hills
I'd seen the harbour and the ship
and window-panes ablaze
with the setting sun.
I was glad, for it had been
a long, lonely tramp.

I approached the town when dusk
was thickening to night
but saw no lights come on,
heard no dogs bark in the lanes.
Maybe there were no windows
or they'd been shut, made fast
against the flooding dark.

Yet I plodded on as though against
receding currents, drawn to
some centre, perhaps a boisterous inn
where there'd be supper waiting
and the warmth of straw.

But in the lurid light of the torch
I sat alone waiting,
thinking of the garden in heaven
and how it must be on the lawns
of that unending spring
with neither age nor fear nor hunger,
nor loneliness.

Is there nobody there to tend
on a belated guest?

The torch reshuffled the shadows
and flickered one that bent
over the long trestle-table.
He sat, a gentle and thoughtful man,
his voice soft with sadness.
Nobody lives in this town, friend,
he said. There is no town at all.

You must be dreaming, I cried. I saw
the sun setting, the ship
in the harbour. What crude deception
is this? What childish prank?

He looked perplexed. Our truth,
he said with distant patience,
our truth is in another's fiction.
We are incapable of dreaming.

And suddenly he rose, his voice
a stagger of flame straining
to flee its candle in the draughts
of some wintry island shrine.
The ship ferries no passengers,
he said, carries no cargo. This town
is of no substance to the living.

GEOFFREY DUTTON

Burning Off

for Sam

We let fire rip, we blacken the pale-gold acres,
But being farmers, we do it cautiously,
Sneaking first by the red clods of the firebreak
With our back-burn, cautiously watching it with water,
Drawing safe rings around our sacred trees.

Then inside the windward fence, mooed at by the neighbour's
cows,
We drag the bouncing rake with its flaring straw bundle
And little wisps of flame snuggle into the stubble
Not yet revealing their true hunger. For fire
Is passionate of all plants, and becomes them,
Furious as creepers, sullen as thistles,
And sows its seed like bees on the wind.

Just now the flames run forward like children
In spurts and zigzags, not staying to argue
With the indomitable green of summer-loving weeds
Left standing proudly, horrible horehound, splendid artichoke.

This fire may be a child, but it does not tell its secrets,
How if it jumped the firebreak it would grow up a giant
Leaping from treetops, exploding the safest green.

For fire incorporates all the elements,
It makes air visible and angry,
It advances lashing like rain, there's a shield of shimmer
Before it streaming like a fish-shop window,
Its black clouds loom full as thunderstorms.

It flushes out earth's secrets, some of them terrible,
As once a black tomcat with its fur on fire
Sprang over two firebreaks and lit the neighbour's paddock.
Now a quail rockets lurchingly off
Pursued by a slanting goshawk,
And four shrewd whistling eagles hang high
Waiting for delicacies, grilled mouse or lizard.

It is all over, Earth exhausted sighs
In little volcanoes of smoking dung.
Fire seems to be a barren passion, uniting all,
Leaving nothing behind to fill the absence of all colour.

But watch the tractor going home across the blackness,
That instant trail the evidence of unharmed earth
Ready for rain, and the first, most vivid green
Springing electric from the paddock's night.

DOROTHY HEWETT

Country Idyll

A glittering girl went out one day
On a dappled horse through the meadow hay,
And the quail rose clumsily, freckled brown,
In the morning light he rose up high
and then dropped down.
And 'Sweet, sweet, we all must die'
Sang the glittering girl on the louring sky.

O she rode down to the gliding river
And the water covered her face forever,
And she prayed on horseback all of the way,
Crying, 'This is the judge of all the days,
this is the master day.'
And the sun rose up in a dusty haze,
And the plover sank in his song of praise.

O the girl went out on the gladsome water,
And the farmer searched for that whore, his daughter.
He smashed the haycocks, rattled the barn.
He said he'd find where the slut was laid
if he wrecked the farm.
While her lovers squatted in dust and played
Two-up under the peppermint shade.

And the river hid that she'd never been married,
And the river hid the child she carried
From the tea-cup tongues of the town.
It hid her breasts and her round high belly
as she floated down.

But her lovers never came out to see,
Playing two-up under the peppermint tree.

Psyche's Husband

He is the Monster-husband who comes
to Psyche in the darkness of her wish-palace.
Robert Duncan: The Truth & Life of Myth

In the darkness of the myth-palace I sit waiting
the feast is laid the tapers lit   the musak plays
the crow sharpens & taps a beak on the iron cradle
along the marble halls I can hear paws dragging
a giant shadow falls
the baby cries with the wind in its christening robes
& the beast is upon me
the stink from its snout   its sad pig eyes
its fur ripples along my skin
kiss me   it sobs   melodious-voiced   *kiss me*

I run shrieking through the palace
as I snatch up the child the crow pecks at my wrists
the carpet lifts with the draughts under the doors
the air-conditioner   humming   is set up high
I look back only once
there is a toad with a horned head
sadly plopping down the stairs behind me
kiss me   it croaks   *kiss me*
the crow drinks my blood on the doormat
that spells   WELCOME

now I live in the woodcutter's cottage
nodding in the peaceful kingdom
sometimes I hear the crow squawking
as it scans the canopy of leaves above my head
the toad squats & snaps in the marshes
the glamorous roar of the beast hums under my feet

my son with the beast's snout   the toad's horn
& the crow's claw snuffles for acorns
along the floor of the rain-forest
kiss me   he snorts   *kiss me.*

Yealering in the Mind

corrugated towns
smelling of saltlake water
old men in dirty flannels
with a growth of bristle
blue heelers nosing behind them
the iron rattles
as the train goes through
sundown swims in a giant ball
a smother of dust

the Co-op manager
waters the sugar gum saplings
in pools of dark
outside the cool drink shop
the blacks and the poor whites gather
the silos shine
silvered in moonlight
the wheat ears glow

on spindly legs with wings
and a cardboard crown
the old woman
perched on a spring cart
steers a crooked wheel rut
                    out of town . . .

NANCY KEESING

Revelation

Observe this man, he is an engineer;
Notice his useful hands; his eyes are keen.
He has spent his life in the designing
And service – and faithful love – of the machine.

All joy for him existed in smooth surface,
Music was in the purr of a good flywheel,
A satisfactory evening's conversation
Concerned the nice efficiency of steel.

We can assume that it was business that forced him
To drive down the Windsor road at the end of the day
When, for an hour, the landscape is sharply focussed
Before night smooths each long contour away.

With every mile the mountains close on the traveller
Who, with a sudden, a wholly astonishing vision
Finds they are part of a plan, an entire conception
Terrifying in its harmony and precision.

His sight, being trained only to see essentials,
Can strip the trees from the hills and the moss from the boulders

Revealing the ultimate anatomy,
Spreading away from the plateau's stony shoulders.

A mind that had thought too long in terms of blueprint
Discovered affinity with the slopes and the plain,
Losing itself in technical admiration
Of this enormous provision for stress and strain. . . .

Perhaps he came again, I cannot tell you;
But this I know, his eyes proclaim a change.
He can touch his machines, but has no comfort from them,
The oily wheels are meaningless and strange.

Not that he views the world as a machine;
Nevertheless, he is an engineer
And, having known perfection for an hour,
Lives all his hours in beauty – and in fear.

One could expect that. Hoping to find solutions
In man's small science and his vast defeat,
While in strength thus sought, and tested by the ages,
Rest in the earth, absolute and complete.

ERIC ROLLS

Sheaf Tosser

The lone crow caws from the tall dead gum:
Caw. Caw. Caw-diddle-daw.
And judges the stack with one bleared eye
Then turns the other to fix its lie:
Caw. Caw. Caw-diddle-daw.
There are four tiers of sheaves on the waggon yet
And one more loaded is standing by;

My arms are aching and I'm dripping sweat
But the sun is three axe-handles in the sky
And I must toss sheaves till dark.

It is fourteen feet from the ground to the eaves:
Caw. Caw. Caw-diddle-daw.
And two feet six to the third roof row;
Six feet high stands the load below:
Caw. Caw. Caw-diddle-daw.
Teen feet six now must I pitch,
Into the centre of the stack I throw
To the turner and the short-handled fork with which
He thrusts sheaves to the builder in endless flow,
Butts out and long-side down.

There are twenty-five crows on the old dry gum:
Caw. Caw. Caw-diddle-daw.
Thirteen on one branch and twelve on the other
And each one calls as long as his brother:
Caw. Caw. Caw-diddle-daw.
My hands are blistered, my sore lips crack
And I wonder whether the turner would smother
If a hard throw knocked him off the stack
In a slide of hay; but there'd come another
And I'd still toss sheaves.

There are thousands of crows on the gaunt white gum:
Caw. Caw. Caw-diddle-daw.
The reds are pale in the western sky
And the stack is more than sixty feet high:
Caw. Caw. Caw-diddle-daw.
My fork grows heavy as the light grows dim.
There are five sheaves left but I've fear of a whim

That one of the crows has an evil eye
And the five sheaves left will be there when I die
For each bird's forgotten how to fly
Till he drives out my soul with the force of his cry:
Caw. Caw. Caw. Caw.
Caw. Caw. Caw. Caw.

DAVID ROWBOTHAM

First Man Lost in Space

I took in death
with your goodbye.
What then have I
to fear of death?

I live with death
as with a star.
It isn't far
to go with death
when death, the fear
that floats the earth,
stars empty forth.
The earth dies here,
the seas, not I.
I mourn the earth.
And I mourn death
its birth goodbye.

You buried me
with one red roar.
Don't grieve more
the given. See,

as I see now,
the atom's urn
in which you turn
the seaborne prow
and craft of earth
about, for fear,
in seas of death,
so empty here . . .

What is it bears
my craft to birth,
my ark of earth
away from yours? –
the thing I seem,
the time I have,
the light you gave,
the launch of dream.
And a great star
is standing by.
I have gone through
the kingdom's eye.

I go before –
before the gods grew,
to where none knew
creation, nor,
trailing the plume
of ice and fire,
the rose desire.
Another bloom
shall summon me,
shall save us all,

and the past be
perpetual . . .

VINCENT BUCKLEY

Secret Policeman

Pledge me: I had the hangman for a father
And for my mother the immortal State;
My playground was the yard beside the lime-pit,
My play-songs the after-cries of hate.

Admire me: I fill those shining boots,
I am soul expanded to a uniform;
A hired world glitters at my senses,
The smell of blood keeps my blood-stream warm.

Pity me: from a world ruddy with flame
I am tugged in dreams to the first cave again,
And in that humid soil and atmosphere
Lie down each night beside the murdered men.

The dead eyes point the way to go,
The dead hands presage me in air.
I run on shifting pavements, by fired walls
Falling, and weighted lamp-posts everywhere.

FRANCIS WEBB

Cap and Bells

Tonight the stars are yellow sparks
Dashed out from the moon's hot steel;
And for me, now, no menace lurks

In this darkness crannied by lights; nor do I feel
A trace of the old loneliness here in this crowded train;
While, far below me, each naked light trails a sabre
Of blue steel over the grave great peace of the harbour.

To know this peace is to have outgrown
Thoughts of despair, of some driving crank of fate,
Of corroded tissues in the bleak shell of a town:
Darkness, lights, happiness – all are right,
All bear messages of the hidden heart;
And for me always the grave great peace is stronger
In flaring colours, and a laugh, and a careless singer.

Die in the blood and salt of your thoughts; and die
When the columns of your sun are thrust aside and broken;
But I have chosen the little, obscure way
In the dim, shouting vortex; I have taken
A fool's power in his cap and bells
And know that in my time the haggard Prince will discover
A blunt shell of Yorick, that laughs for ever and ever.

Pneumo-encephalograph

Tight scrimmage of blankets in the dark;
Nerve-fluxions, flints coupling for the spark;
Today's guilt and tomorrow's blent;
Passion and peace trussed together, impotent;
Dilute potage of light
Dripping through glass to the desk where you sit and write;
Hour stalking lame hour. . . .
May my every bone and vessel confess the power

To loathe suffering in you
As in myself, that arcane simmering brew.

Only come to this cabin of art:
Crack hardy, take off clothes, and play your part.
Contraband enters your brain;
Puckered guerrilla faces patrol the vein;
The spore of oxygen passes
Skidding over old inclines and crevasses,
Hunting an ancient sore,
Foxhole of impulse in a minute cosmic war.
Concordat of nature and desire
Was revoked in you; but fire clashes with fire.

Let me ask, while you are still,
What in you marshalled this improbable will:
Instruments supple as the flute,
Vigilant eyes, mouths that are almost mute,
X-rays scintillant as a flower,
Tossed in a corner the plumes of falsehood, power?
Only your suffering.
Of pain's amalgam with gold let some man sing
While, pale and fluent and rare
As the Holy Spirit, travels the bubble of air.

GRACE PERRY

Red Scarf

Next, please.
Will you come in?
Cracked shoes squeak across the vinyl floor,
and shining blue-grey squares reflect the dust,

loose-hanging trousers, and the long-tongued belt,
limp shirt and bold flamboyant scarf.
What can I say?
You do not feel so well today?
You will be better soon. Sometime, but not now.
Remove your shirt and let me see.
Open your mouth and breathe for me.
Your scarf discarded on my chair,
laughs in the antiseptic air;
laughs at the sterile ritual, the sad futility
of this naked acolyte who must seek
eternal life in me.
Skin hangs in folds upon your frame,
and languor slows
the rhythm of living that remains
like pale twilight rain dripping unseen
through forests shadowed where the sun has been.
Upon your forehead, sweat gleams faint and cold;
your flushed cheeks seem unreal.
I stand behind you, so I do not see
the depthless eyes, the wordless loud appeal
shrieking in black pools of pain
I am powerless to heal.
Rapid and shallow, stale air moves
through your frosted mouth,
hungry no more for news of summer
sprawling in the leaping grass.
I listen.
And soon a wind disturbs the sea,
and undulating, deadly weed
is rustling to me.
Can you not feel the sprouting death,

the blaze of splitting buds,
frenzied foam and strangled breath,
insistent penetration of the bone?
Listen carefully.
Within your darkness, I can hear the sound,
crumbling and falling in slow decay,
milk-white honeycomb eaten away.
How is the cough?
Blood again, bright as a tartan scarf
crumbled on my empty chair in a crimson laugh.
It will be better soon. Sometime, but not now.
I cannot restore the squandered years;
I offer only a limit of long days
of drowsy poppy magic
trailing moist fingers on your throbbing eyes,
softly untwining tentacles of pain
and sinuously inundating the convolutions of your brain.
I give euphoria in deep injection,
yohimbine and male hormone
so that your flaccid flesh may rise again,
a fullbodied root of fire,
blood and pain forgotten in the white flood of desire.
And yet, I cannot tell you these mysterious things,
for when I listen to your lungs,
it is your death who sings.
You will be better soon. Sometime, but not now.
You dress and go out,
and I hear your feet disturb the sunlight on the street.
Your scarf, forgotten on my chair,
flames in the antiseptic air.

BRUCE BEAVER

Ode XIII

Again a grue of cold surrounds
the house, contracts within it. An icy
hypodermic has snapped off in
the tendons of my neck. Frost burns my head.

Outside, the light is usual –
not stark but mild as an average sunny
morning but at about the level
of a human head the chopping air

lops the nerve-ends, slices the day.
Moon-pallid in a crystal cave
a giantess breathes over all
this highland park of southern countryside,

fills every heart with ice splinters.
Even the retired horse
next door, as ginger-dusty as
as coir mat sits down upon a threadbare

tarpaulin and does not trust its legs.
The cold is metaphysical.
It emanates invisibly
from grey Saturnian climes; the cave of the goddess

transmits without creating it.
A bastard of the moon, it jells
the very blood and cracks its huge
arthritic fingers like an inching glacier.

Even the magpies' glottal stops
have brittle overtones. The generous
bladders of the local dogs
react in spate entailing every second

tree and the bushes in between.
Yet still the sky presents itself,
ingenuous and vast, of blue
and merging white, an empty sepulchre.

Waiting on words, how squalid seems
my little talent's origins.
Likening them to the muddy chyme
and worm-run murk about the roots of flowers,

I wonder at such transformations:
dirt into fragile fleshy bloom,
dark into bright, slow seepage into
juicy sap and musky centred calyx.

It is the consciousness no flower
knows that keeps the head and heart
at loggerheads upon a stem
rooted in earthy essences, yet moving,

a walking tree alive with leaf
of verbiage, little tongue and lip sounds
muffled, half-stifled with a growth
of thought-usurping mental mistletoe.

And yet the moving, making act
continues intermittently.
The special seeing and the half-conscious
ordering of words into a chant

that changes consciousness in others –
for good or bad's the moral catch –
justifies most. Parentheses
compress like metal palms the doubting mind.

It's best to stay awake and open
to the inrush of stinging powers
that leave a residue of honey
after the intellect has smoked them out.

The blessing spirits are another
matter beyond the weight of matter.
They meet the psyche more than halfway
leaving it with a memory of song

to share with even the habitually
tone-deaf who feel the drumming rhythm
as native to them as the beating
of their blood, yet never dancing mad.

The hour and I are warm again.
The neck is flexible that was
constricted, and the present moment
surrounds the past like a flask about a vacuum.

Of pain and cold the memory
is less than the echo of these words
in the cave-womb of the giantess,
is lost in the glaze of green and golden noon.

PETER PORTER

Phar Lap in the Melbourne Museum

A masterpiece of the taxidermist's art,
Australia's top patrician stares
Gravely ahead at crowded emptiness.
As if alive, the lustre of dead hairs,
Lozenged liquid eyes, black nostrils
Gently flared, otter-satin coat declares
That death cannot visit in this thin perfection.

The democratic hero full of guile,
Noble, handsome, gentle Houyhnhnm
(In both paddock and St Leger difference is
Lost in the welter of money) – to see him win
Men sold farms, rode miles in floods,
Stole money, locked up wives, somehow got in:
First away, he led the field and easily won.

It was his simple excellence to be best.
Tough men owned him, their minds beset
By stakes, bookies' doubles, crooked jocks.
He soon became a byword, public asset,
A horse with a nation's soul upon his back –
Australia's Ark of the Covenant, set
Before the people, perfect, loved like God.

And like God to be betrayed by friends.
Sent to America, he died of poisoned food.
In Australia children cried to hear the news
(This Prince of Orange knew no bad or good).
It was, as people knew, a plot of life:

To live in strength, to excel and die too soon,
So they drained his body and they stuffed his skin.

Twenty years later on Sunday afternoons
You still can't see him for the rubbing crowds.
He shares with Bradman and Ned Kelly some
Of the dirty jokes you still don't say out loud.
It is Australian innocence to love
The naturally excessive and be proud
Of a big-boned chestnut gelding who ran fast.

An Exequy

In wet May, in the months of change,
In a country you wouldn't visit, strange
Dreams pursue me in my sleep,
Black creatures of the upper deep –
Though you are five months dead, I see
You in guilt's iconography,
Dear Wife, lost beast, beleaguered child,
The stranded monster with the mild
Appearance, whom small waves tease,
(Andromeda upon her knees
In orthodox deliverance)
And you alone of pure substance,
The unformed form of life, the earth
Which Piero's brushes brought to birth
For all to greet as myth, a thing
Out of the box of imagining.

This introduction serves to sing
Your mortal death as Bishop King

Once hymned in tetrametric rhyme
His young wife, lost before her time;
Though he lived on for many years
His poem each day fed new tears
To that unreaching spot, her grave,
His lines a baroque architrave
The Sunday poor with bottled flowers
Would by-pass in their mourning hours,
Esteeming ragged natural life
('Most dearly loved, most gentle wife'),
Yet, looking back when at the gate
And seeing grief in formal state
Upon a sculpted angel group,
Were glad that men of god could stoop
To give the dead a public stance
And freeze them in their mortal dance.

The words and faces proper to
My misery are private – you
Would never share your heart with those
Whose only talent's to suppose,
Nor from your final childish bed
Raise a remote confessing head –
The channels of our lives are blocked,
The hand is stopped upon the clock,
No one can say why hearts will break
And marriages are all opaque:
A map of loss, some posted cards,
The living house reduced to shards,
The abstract hell of memory,
The pointlessness of poetry –
These are the instances which tell

Of something which I know full well,
I owe a death to you – one day
The time will come for me to pay
When your slim shape from photographs
Stands at my door and gently asks
If I have any work to do
Or will I come to bed with you.
O scala enigmatica,
I'll climb up to that attic where
The curtain of your life was drawn
Some time between despair and dawn –
I'll never know with what halt steps
You mounted to this plain eclipse
But each stair now will station me
A black responsibility
And point me to that shut-down room,
'This be your due appointed tomb.'

I think of us in Italy:
Gin-and-chianti-fuelled, we
Move in a trance through Paradise,
Feeding at last our starving eyes,
Two people of the English blindness
Doing each masterpiece the kindness
Of discovering it – from Baldovinetti
To Venice's most obscure jetty.
A true unfortunate traveller, I
Depend upon your nurse's eye
To pick the altars where no Grinner
Puts us off our tourists' dinner
And in hotels to bandy words
With Genevan girls and talking birds,

To wear your feet out following me
To night's end and true amity,
And call my rational fear of flying
A paradigm of Holy Dying –
And, oh my love, I wish you were
Once more with me, at night somewhere
In narrow streets applauding wines,
The moon above the Apennines
As large as logic and the stars,
Most middle-aged of avatars,
As bright as when they shone for truth
Upon untried and avid youth.

The rooms and days we wandered through
Shrink in my mind to one – there you
Lie quite absorbed by peace – the calm
Which life could not provide is balm
In death. Unseen by me, you look
Past bed and stairs and half-read book
Eternally upon your home,
The end of pain, the left alone.
I have no friend, or intercessor,
No psychopomp or true confessor
But only you who know my heart
In every cramped and devious part –
Then take my hand and lead me out,
The sky is overcast by doubt,
The time has come, I listen for
Your words of comfort at the door,
O guide me through the shoals of fear –
'Fürchte dich nicht, ich bin bei dir.'

Max is Missing

The stars are there as mathematics is,
The very there of nothing to be proved.

And so we say that theorems rely
On axioms or proof by the absurd.

The stars outshine the tenses, kings on plinths,
And each enigma of the numerate,

While all along our mathematicians fear
They're stalking-horses of an abstract god,

And posit the suspicion there's no room
For rich historic tit-bits in their space –

The big and little of it, shrunk or spun,
A million needle-points, a 'Mono-Ange'.

Out of the corner of Philosophy's eye
A Mathematician's pinning on a post

Max is missing: ginger tabby cat
With white sabots – reward for his return.

The government of integers will wait
While our researcher searches for his cat,

The stars be patient, God donate his time –
A theorem is for Christmas, but a cat

Is for forever. Come home, Maximus,
The magnets on the fridge are slipping down.

The page is Luddite quite as stars are bright,
A ball-point and a brain out-twinkle them.

Should stars know Max is missing, would they guess
How little he must miss them where he is?

R. A. SIMPSON

Diver

Alone on the tower
I'm not confident.
The water is black
And distant.

I think of style
And raise my arms and aim,
Holding back the plunge.
It's mostly a game

That touches terror
Then terror goes –
I view my fingers,
My toes.

'Defiance, love and revolt
Make the diver dive
And prove, through dying,
He's alive,'
A voice preaches in my head . . .

And so I dive.

Water gulps me down,
Chilling me with its grip,
Then arms pine up and up
Like worship.

BRUCE DAWE

Elegy for Drowned Children

What does he do with them all, the old king:
Having such a shining haul of boys in his sure net,
How does he keep them happy, lead them to forget
The world above, the aching air, birds, spring?

Tender and solicitous must be his care
For these whom he takes down into his kingdom one by one
– Why else would they be taken out of the sweet sun,
Drowning towards him, water plaiting their hair?

Unless he loves them deeply how could he withstand
The voices of parents calling, calling like birds by the water's edge,
By swimming-pool, sand-bar, river-bank, rocky ledge,
The little heaps of clothes, the futures carefully planned?

Yet even an old acquisitive king must feel
Remorse poisoning his joy, since he allows
Particular boys each evening to arouse
From leaden-lidded sleep, softly to steal

Away to the whispering shore, there to plunge in,
And fluid as porpoises swim upward, upward through the
    dividing
Waters until, soon, each back home is striding
Over thresholds of welcome dream with wet and moonlit skin.

A Victorian Hangman Tells His Love

Dear one, forgive my appearing before you like this,
in a two-piece track-suit, welder's goggles
and a green cloth cap like some gross bee – this is the State's idea . . .
I would have come
arrayed like a bridegroom for these nuptials
knowing how often you have dreamed about this
moment of consummation in your cell.
If I must bind your arms now to your sides
with a leather strap and ask if you have anything to say
– these too are formalities I would dispense with:
I know your heart is too full at this moment
to say much and that the tranquilliser which I trust
you did not reject out of a stubborn pride
should by this time have eased your ache for speech, breath
and the other incidentals which distract us from our end.
Let us now walk a step. This noose
with which we're wed is something of an heirloom, the last three
members of our holy family were wed with it, the softwood beam
it hangs from like a lover's tree notched with their weight.
See now I slip it over your neck, the knot
under the left jaw, with a slip ring
to hold the knot in place . . . There. Perfect.
Allow me to adjust the canvas hood
which will enable you to anticipate the officially prescribed
    darkness
by some seconds.
The journalists are ready with the flash-bulbs of their eyes
raised to the simple altar, the doctor twitches like a stethoscope
– you have been given a clean bill of health, like any
modern bride.

With this spring of mine
from the trap, hitting the door lever, you will go forth
into a new life which I, alas, am not yet fit to share.
Be assured, you will sink into the generous pool of public
feeling
as gently as a leaf – accept your rôle, feel chosen.
You are this evening's headlines. Come, my love.

CHARLES HIGHAM

The War Museum at Nagasaki

Here are two helmets, stamped
With the marks of burning death,
A twisted toy in a case,
Its glass smoked by the breath
Of a passer-by;
Dim in the photograph
A dying patient's face
Smiling patiently;
Where the moment tramped
He holds a bitter staff.

A woman pauses now,
Fixing her face in the glass,
Squinting to read words
That summon up the crass
Immoment, silly facts:

The dates of birth and dying,
Name, height, the broken sherds
Of long-dead artefacts;

Broken is that bough;
The rest is useless lying.

Our pity, *their* regret
Are lost before the face
Of truth, the hollow bowl,
The twisted, worthless trace
Of broken wedding-rings.
Nothing, nothing can work,
Not love nor sorrow, yet,
One registers those things,
Throwing the dead a net
Across that foundering dark.

KEVIN GILBERT

Shame

And some say 'Shame' when we're talkin' up
And 'Shame' for the way we are
And 'Shame' cause we ain't got a big flash house
Or a steady job and a car.

Some call it 'Shame' when our kids they die
From colds or from sheer neglect
'Shame' when we live on the river banks
While collectin' our welfare cheques
'Shame' when we're blind from trachoma
'Shame' when we're crippled from blights

But I reckon the worstest shame is yours
You deny us human rights.

VIVIAN SMITH

Convolvulus

The tendrils shoot towards us through the green
of plums and lemons wearing a shawl of leaves.
We drag at a single twine and the vine
trembles and the whole garden heaves.

A liquid lattice work alive as eels –
less than a week to rope the ficus in.
It celebrates with flags and festoons
and waits for the next foray to begin.

Each flower opens from its chrysalis
such tiny trumpets twirling on their stems,
liqueur glasses balanced on the air,
flaring for bees, dreaming stratagems.

This is the time when nature starts to move
tangling with neglect and with repose.
The leaves are spreading like a waterfall.
They have designs on us and on the rose.

JENNIFER STRAUSS

Tending the Graves

There are days when the dead will have nothing to do with us –
In summer mostly, when a dry wind from the north
Gusts up just as you enter the cemetery gates
And the roses are overblown, the gum trees stripping,
And you know the flowers you've brought will wither fast
And are besides the wrong size for the holder

And you've forgotten scissors, and something to carry water.

It's not reproach. They have no need to tell us 'You
Have given away my books, taken another lover into my bed,
Made of my children something I do not approve' – all that
We can say for ourselves. It is absolute absence.
They are so engrossed by death they refuse even to haunt us.
We must tend the grave and walk away: unrewarded,
Unreproached, unforgiven: our feet heavy with life.

FAY ZWICKY

Bride Drinking from a Pool

(Arthur Boyd, 1960)

Who is she?
Dragonfly wraith,
white child tilted headlong
floating sus-
pended, blind pebble eyes
dive a dark hole.
why are her overblown
wingsleeves splayed
groping miasma's rim? Why
such swollen spider spatulates
for a puppet-hold on nightmare?
Whose is this haunting?

Who's watching this
plummeting sleeper?
Trapped between sky and water,
you're spotted by a shady duo:
inky crow's swivelling topaz eye

pimps for his babydoll cockatoo,
scared as a soul adrift, parrots
your bridal plunge down to the
reptile kingdom secret with
savage totems. The spectral hooks of
burned trunks grimace like sickles.

Bride,
        where is your epithalamium?
Your dove-mother mourns, falling and
fumbling, a barren tree stunned
into silence.
Why has the groom forsaken his dark one?
Why banished his flying fool?
Were you unclean?
Do you lie unreachable, fail to plant
joy in his bed?
Did your creeks and gullies dry
at his touch?
Did your spider clasp terrify?

Pitched from the cradle,
rocked with the motion of mourning,
the veiled pupa hovers inches above
her dark mirror, eyed by insouciant crow
flashing his cool, cocky drag-queen
in tow, fellow-travellers in flight.
Call it a bird's eye view, turfed out
to risky air to end hanging
headlong in a dead wood.

Bride-haunted,
your own face is thrown back

larval in the pool of exile. Without
hope of reward you reach down
to drink, trusting
to be fed.

DAVID MALOUF

At a School Athletics Day

Strollers of April green; white tent-poles hold
the sky, the crowd's breath catches
on the heel of a javelin thrower,
a boy as thick as two short planks who never
will learn to distinguish
between perfect past and past conditional.

I walk between hurdles fallen,
on a cinder track where sprinters kneel, with two
friends, my former students, freed
from blue serge to the daring
of corduroy and sideburns,
the faded blue-sky blue of washed-out jeans.

They argue: was Prince Hamlet hesitant
of murder lest the act
define him with its blood (he being for his taste
too narrowly defined
already by the too too sullied flesh);
or was he

(long shaft steady now)
caught, rat's foot and star,
in the metaphysical mousetrap, O so subtly
baited with death,

that his timid soul, nose twitching in the darkness,
sniffed and nibbled at?

Questions indeed for a clear spring day, sun breeding
desire like daffodils,
the dead in green troughs nudging
our heels. And was he
twenty – they mean like *them* –
or balding, short of breath, a curious reader between the lines
of documents and faces,
well-meaning, impassioned, vague, an eternal student pushing
thirty,
like *me*? So time breaks
on the skull's bleak promontory, idle fellows
exit underground, and April raises
questions, or daffodils, out of their end.

On the far side of the field the crowd's breath lifts
away over our head, steel
flies to nail its shadow in the grass.
Falling, not out of sight but where
two schoolboys in sneakers
run up snow-footed with a measuring tape.

CHRIS WALLACE-CRABBE

Chaos

My stars,
To have seen this,
To have seen it! he said, returning
From the flotsam in the funnel of the maelstrom,
From dark beasts growling in the gap of ages,

From the monster-mash of history, the meaningless sword-rust
As junky as the car-piles ruinous at a great town's edge,
From the double-dark on dark than which the middle of the
night seemed brighter,
From the black warp and the black woof, densely
interpenetrating, without weave at the last,
From the silence violated by no speech, where no words had
been spoken, even long before the present words were not
And had one word been spoken down there it would have
vibrated like the most radiant poem, hung down like the
heaviest tome of philosophy,
Where one cry or breath or one crayon line would have been
the creation of music and metaphysics, shape and society,
purpose and history and the tame heavy beasts of the
farmer's yard,
The very first word or gesture undoing the uncreation as a
thunderdrum or lightning-lance shatters the fat purple
of the summer night, laying the blest foundation stone or
starting a sole rusted clock in the ruined mansion of the
world.

My stars,
I have been there,
I have seen it, he said, returning
To the bright junk on the face of this our world.

Out to Lunch

The waiter
unscrewed
his arm
at the elbow

and strong
black coffee
poured out
of his thumb.

Melbourne

Not on the ocean, on a muted bay
Where the broad rays drift slowly over mud
And flathead loll on sand, a city bloats
Between the plains of water and of loam.
If surf beats, it is faint and far away;
If slogans blow around, we stay at home.

And, like the bay, our blood flows easily,
Not warm, not cold (in all things moderate),
Following our familiar tides. Elsewhere
Victims are bleeding, sun is beating down
On patriot, guerrilla, refugee.
We see the newsreels when we dine in town.

Ideas are grown in other gardens while
This chocolate soil throws up its harvest of
Imported and deciduous platitudes,
None of them flowering boldly or for long;
And we, the gardeners, securely smile,
Humming a bar or two of rusty song.

Old tunes are good enough, if sing we must;
Old images, revamped *ad nauseam*,
Will sate the burgher's eye and keep him quiet
As the great wheels run on. And should he seek

Variety, there's wind, there's heat, there's frost
To feed his conversation all the week.

Highway by highway, the remorseless cars
Strangle the city, put it out of pain,
Its limbs still kicking feebly on the hills.
Nobody cares. The artists sail at dawn
For brisker ports, or rot in public bars.
Though much has died there, little has been born.

RODNEY HALL

Mrs Macintosh

Mrs Macintosh so simply
has reduced the world's dilemmas
to her obsession, birdcage buying.
Exhibits fill her rooms:
some are miniature pagodas,
and one a jail of cells.
The smallest, made from a lost
girl's hand, is bones enmeshed
in silver wire. The largest,
as an anarchy of cleverness
and total snub to cage-convention,
is a cloud so frail and knobbled
it dangles crazily askew, high
against the inconvenience of a wall.

These, her eccentricities,
are cherished catalogued
and paraded for the delectation
of visiting evangelist

salesman or charity collector.
Her cages, Mrs Macintosh
is careful to point out, are empty.
Birds revolt her – frighten
her wrinkled eye with theirs
and mock her ways with harsh high
female voices; or sing so sweetly
they could almost lure her back
to join the world. Unbearable.
No, she guards her symbolism:
cages free of birds, pure capitivity
that's innocent of pain.

All day her hymns escape the house.

ANTIGONE KEFALA

The Alien

. . . at night I see it rising from the hollow tower
dripping with mist
this land we search for in each other's eyes
its surface steaming in the shafts of light
immersed in silence
waves that flow in me till I am filled with terror
till all the outlines of my face are lost
till all the magic of my eyes is sucked away
and I am naked
engulfed in tentacles of emptiness
dissolving

and now, I sense only these stone hands,
moving unseen, closer and closer to the grain.

Rocks shall sprout out of us and still
the light will flower everywhere impassive . . .

The Wanderer

The river
moved further away
in the heat of the road
shimmers of water
towards the horizon.

The salt
which they gave him at home
he would place on his tongue
to taste his own roots
and draw comfort.

The world
made of a matter that never
forgets, a symmetry so exact,
fatality at the heart
of each thing.

TOM SHAPCOTT

Chekhov's Mongoose

Dr Chekhov was infatuated. This is the story.
Returning from the Russian prison isle of Sakhalin
where he circulated ten thousand questionaires and noted
with his usual dispassion the appalling conditions,
he made his first foray beyond Russian soil
via the China Sea. In Ceylon he acquired a mongoose.

It was lithe, tame and affectionate. It was quick, this mongoose,
and the doctor spent the homeward voyage like a story
out of a children's adventure, laughing, mopping its soil
and the broken crockery, replacing the memories of Sakhalin
with this new-found love. Without leash or chain, without
    conditions
to restrict its freedom, his pet became famous, more noted

(in that shipboard idyll) than Chekhov was, more noted
than any rival souvenirs: Siamese cat, monkey. His mongoose
loved him. When it broke all the rules and conditions
of social behaviour it turned dark soulful eyes, like a Story
Book Princess, and melted him with a look. Not even Sakhalin
with all its woes and tragedy could dredge from the dark soil

of its soul such pathos. Caught in his own soil
where ardour mixed with rancour, the good doctor noted
how vulnerable he was, and relented. Sakhalin
eased gently from his mind, replaced by a mongoose
which cried when it was left alone. The story
does not end there. Life has a way of imposing conditions.

When Chekhov returned, nothing was changed. The conditions
he fled from in Moscow – a demanding family, lovers, the grim soil
he had turned into rich prose in each celebrated story –
now returned to chill him. 'When I come to visit', he noted,
'please be warned. I come with my pet mongoose
who is tamer than children, wilder than Sakhalin.'

His published report, THE ISLAND OF SAKHALIN,
caused a sensation, and calls to reform penal conditions.
Life became a whirlwind again and though his mongoose

was the season's novelty, on his new Estate on the dark soil
of Malikhovo, it ran off. Yes, it was found, but he noted
the broken plates, the damage, the way every least story

mixes charm with wreckage. Some say it's Chekhov's own story.
Moscow's Zoo was, well, provincial. It was not noted
for health or for hygiene. Until 1893 it possessed no mongoose.

RANDOLPH STOW

The Land's Meaning

for Sidney Nolan

The love of man is a weed of the waste places.
One many think of it as the spinifex of dry souls.

I have not, it is true, made the trek to the difficult country
where it is said to grow; but signs come back,
reports come back, of continuing exploration
in that terrain. And certain of our young men,
who turned in despair from the bar, upsetting a glass,
and swore: 'No more' (for the tin rooms stank of flyspray)
are sending word that the mastery of silence
alone is empire. What is God, they say,
but a man unwounded in his loneliness?

And the question (applauded, derided) falls like dust
on veranda and bar; and in pauses, when thinking ceases,
the footprints of the recently departed
march to the mind's horizons, and endure.

And often enough as we turn again, and laugh,
cloud, hide away the tracks with an acid word,
there is one or more gone past the door to stand

(wondering, debating) in the iron street,
and toss a coin, and pass, to the township's end,
where one-eyed 'Mat, eternal dealer in camels,
grins in the dusty yard like a split fruit.

But one who has returned, his eyes blurred maps
of landscapes still unmapped, gives this account:

'The third day, cockatoos dropped dead in the air.
Then the crows turned back, the camels knelt down and stayed
there,
and a skin-coloured surf of sandhills jumped the horizon
and swamped me. I was bushed for forty years.

'And I came to a bloke all alone like a kurrajong tree.
And I said to him: "Mate – I don't need to know your name –
Let me camp in your shade, let me sleep, till the sun goes down."'

On a Favourite Cat

Your house was a palace, full of arcane nooks
to discover and rediscover; all your life

a long imperialist adventure, where
kingdoms bowed down to your triumphal tail.

How can a little marble dish, abraded
by a rough tongue, so shake the heart? The fall

of sparrows is not man's concern: I took
no thought of what must leave me for your grave.

Under the mirabelle tree in my godson's garden,
be earth's pet now. What can I do? – but wish you

a matriarchy of blackbirds to teach you peaceable manners
and a Malplaquet of a mansion, to stalk and explore for ever.

GLEN PHILLIPS

Spring Burning

I stood thigh deep
in wild oats on
a roadside verge
of mine. This spring
greening had plumped them.
The full heads nodded
heavy on emerald fibre optic shafts
and swayed in the breath
that shook
the loose-leafed eucalypts.

And yes, summer
would come like a
brazen border-invader
soaring up the stalks
with a brief
rinse of gold
before husks become pale flags
fluttering
at the edge of farms.

Then we must think,
a falling spark
of conflagration
in this dry grass
could sweep for miles.

Better to act now!
A spring burning
would see us safe
all summer long.

But still I stood;
whichever way
I looked, the road
stretched on and on.

After all, this
was just another
growing oat crop.

It's hard to clear
the feral off
your property.

Then I felt spring
still burning
in me.

JUDITH RODRIGUEZ

Nu-plastik Fanfare Red

I declare myself:
I am painting my room red.
Because they haven't any
flat red suitable for interiors,
because their acres of colour-card
are snowy with daylight only,
because it will look like Danger! Explosives,
or would you prefer a basement cabaret?

a decent home where Italians moved in,
Como perhaps (yes, I've gilded the mirror)
or simply infernal –

I rejoice to be doing it
with quick-drying plastic,
for small area decoration.
I tear at the wall, brush speeding:
let's expand this limited stuff!
It dries impetuously in patches,
I at edges too late scrub; this is a fight.
I sought the conditions,
and the unbroken wall is yet to come.
Clear stretches screech into clots
streak into smokiness.
Botched job, this, my instant
hell! And no re-sale value, Dad;
cliché too. Well, too bad.

It's satisfying to note
this mix is right for pottery.
(Good glad shock of seeing
that red-figure vases *are*.
Not 4th-edition-earthy, but stab-colour,
new-vine, red-Attis-flower, the full howl.)
My inward amphora!

Even thus shyly to surface:
up we go red, flag-balloon,
broomstick-rocket!
Brandishing blood and fire, pumping
lungs external as leaves!
This is a red land, sour

with blood it has not shed,
money not lost, risks evaded,
blood it has forgotten, dried
in furnace airs that vainly
figure (since mines are doing well)
the fire. Torpor
of a disallowed abortion.

Why not a red room?

NORMAN TALBOT

The Uncommercial Traveller

I passed through the town
rapidly past midnight
under the townhall clock

rapidly but halfhunched
with pointed knots in my belly
kneetangling words, inward alien sounds

halfhunched against the glint
of a human look & shriek
townlong that I was there –

I looked if I remember
a Gobbo demon in my hopping lope
high spring by the trainlines

hopping up the walls across
the ridge of houseroof & down
imprinting my one split foot.

A fantail swung her laced sudden
hanging harmony in & out
over the nightswept grassheads

to my falsedawn orange glow & thump
where the river thickened brush
& the song never resolved –

because she saw me & crept
benighted at the grassroots
her feathers a damp sightless grey.

It was no wonder a rosella
hurled her quick wingcolours
forward between the trees

from my jolt & treeheaving leap,
her backhand curse vivid
at an angle of the hid moon –

nature is closed to the natural man
& my straight steel hobble
poisoned the town moonlight like a well.

PHILIP HAMMIAL

Exile

Before, when we lived in the room with the blown horse, flies
as thick as a whoop, we were as clear
as clear can be in our red
rubber hats. Seven
seats we had for to keep
our seven mothers neat, & when they were gone

that we'd have seven more we knew
for a fact, & the other fact was: blessed be
the medicine dabblers (whose constant menace
kept us warm). What harm

was there in that? Plenty,
they must have thought, who drove us out
with a yawn. But yowl
about that? – who would
have listened? So sequentially
is the way we've been, spooning
what we can & in general pulling no face
at the interrogators who are thrice weekly sent
to ply us, song
their only excuse. Abuse (we know it
when we hear it) about jolly
up, niggle fingers, playback furies, astonish
giggles, bloodpie dupes, dim duplicities . . . in
& out it goes, & up
& down, & around & around, & it won't
ever stop unless . . . somehow, somewhere
another room (o miracle
of miracles)as cosy
as our first – blown horse, flies
as thick as a whoop.

MUDROOROO

Blotched Country Boy

Would you believe that once I breathed
The country air of dreaming forth the big city
Highway straddled me, or I the highway

Take your pick and sing a country tune
I was a country boy – once, entire
Now patched blotches map my face
Free from country roads
This is the end of the highway
Sweating, junkie thoughts skin pops the needle
Veined desire hurts worse than country boots
Legs meant for striding
Stagger to the bossman
Remaindering grains of super glue
To fasten down my widebrimmed hat
In shade my face leans away from the sun
To talk of shattered hours through the day
Poverty trembles my lost country voice
As brain cells urge me to avoid the straights in suits
Pontificating in their nice clean city frames

I am a bed rented out by the hour
I am well sold out to the lowest bidder
I mumble a country lie for my feed
I stumble my dole cheque to the Master
Who sprinkles the powder of forgetfulness
Beneath my cowman's hat in scorn
I suck in phantasy like bulldust
Watching the vein pop up then implode
As cells overdrive into ecstasy
And I ride the range the Marlboro man
Or skid down the highway whole and entire

LES MURRAY

Widower in the Country

I'll get up soon, and leave my bed unmade.
I'll go outside and split off kindling wood
from the yellow-box log that lies beside the gate,
and the sun will be high, for I get up late now.

I'll drive my axe in the log and come back in
with my armful of wood, and pause to look across
the Christmas paddocks aching in the heat,
the windless trees, the nettles in the yard . . .
and then I'll go in, boil water and make tea.

This afternoon, I'll stand out on the hill
and watch my house away below, and how
the roof reflects the sun and makes my eyes
water and close on bright webbed visions smeared
on the dark of my thoughts to dance and fade away.
Then the sun will move on, and I will simply watch,
or work, or sleep. And evening will come on.

Getting near dark, I'll go home, light the lamp
and eat my corned-beef supper, sitting there
at the head of the table. Then I'll go to bed.
Last night I thought I dreamed – but when I woke
the screaming was only a possum ski-ing down
the iron roof on little moonlit claws.

The Grassfire Stanzas

August, and black centres expand on the afternoon paddock.
Dilating on a match in widening margins, they lift
a splintering murmur; they fume out of used-up grass
that's been walked, since summer, into infinite swirled licks.

The man imposing spring here swats with his branch,
    controlling it:
only small things may come to a head, in this settlement
    pattern.

Fretted with small flame, the aspiring islands leave
odd plumes behind. Smuts shower up every thermal
to float down long stairs. Aggregate smoke attracts a kestrel.

Eruption of darkness from far down under roots
is the aspect of these cores, on the undulating farmland;
dense black is withered into web, inside a low singing;
it is dried and loosened, on the surface; it is made weak.

The green feed that shelters beneath its taller death yearly
is unharmed, under new loaf soot. Arriving hawks teeter
and plunge continually, working over the hopping outskirts.

The blackenings are balanced, on a gradient of dryness
in the almost-still air, between dying thinly away
and stripping the whole countryside. Joining, they never gain
more than they lose. They spread away from their high
    moments.

The man carries smoke wrapped in bark, and keeps applying it
starting new circles. He is burning the passive ocean
around his ark of buildings and his lifeboat water.

It wasn't this man, but it was man, sing the agile
exclamatory birds, who taught them this rapt hunting
(strike! in the updrafts, snap! of hardwood pods).
Humans found the fire here. It is inherent. They learn,
wave after wave of them, how to touch the country.

Sterilizing reed distaffs, the fire edges on to a dam;
it circuits across a cow-track; new surf starts riding outward
and a nippy kestrel feeds from its foot, over cooling mergers.

It's the sun that is touched, and dies in expansion, mincing,
making the round dance, foretelling its future, driving
the frantic lives outwards. The sun that answers the bark tip
is discharged in many little songs, to forestall a symphony.

Cattle come, with stilted bounding calves. They look across the
ripple lines of heat, and shake their armed heads at them;
at random, then, they step over. Grazing smudged black
    country
they become the beasts of Tartarus. Wavering, moving out over
dung-smouldering ground still covered with its uncovering.

Bats' Ultrasound

Sleeping-bagged in a duplex wing
with fleas, in rock-cleft or building
radar bats are darkness in miniature,
their whole face one tufty crinkled ear
with weak eyes, fine teeth bared to sing.

Few are vampires. None flit through the mirror.
Where they flutter at evening's a queer
tonal hunting zone above highest C.

Insect prey at the peak of our hearing
drone re to their detailing tee:

ah, eyrie-ire, aero hour, eh?
O'er our ur-area (our era aye
ere your raw row) we air our array,
err, yaw, row wry – aura our orrery,
our eerie ü our ray, our arrow.

A rare ear, our aery Yahweh.

The Quality of Sprawl

Sprawl is the quality
of the man who cut down his Rolls-Royce
into a farm utility truck, and sprawl
is what the company lacked when it made repeated efforts
to buy the vehicle back and repair its image.

Sprawl is doing your farming by aeroplane, roughly,
or driving a hitchhiker that extra hundred miles home.
It is the rococo of being your own still centre.
It is never lighting cigars with ten-dollar notes:
that's idiot ostentation and murder of starving people.
Nor can it be bought with the ash of million-dollar deeds.

Sprawl lengthens the legs; it trains greyhounds on liver and beer.
Sprawl almost never says Why not? with palms comically raised
nor can it be dressed for, not even in running shoes worn
with mink and a nose ring. That is Society. That's Style.
Sprawl is more like the thirteenth banana in a dozen
or anyway the fourteenth.

Sprawl is Hank Stamper in *Never Give an Inch*
bisecting an obstructive official's desk with a chainsaw.
Not harming the official. Sprawl is never brutal
though it's often intransigent. Sprawl is never Simon de
    Montfort
at a town-storming: Kill them all! God will know his own.
Knowing the man's name this was said to might be sprawl.

Sprawl occurs in art. The fifteenth to twenty-first
lines in a sonnet, for example. And in certain paintings;
I have sprawl enough to have forgotten which paintings.
Turner's glorious *Burning of the Houses of Parliament*
comes to mind, a doubling bannered triumph of sprawl –
except, he didn't fire them.

Sprawl gets up the nose of many kinds of people
(every kind that comes in kinds) whose futures don't include it.
Some decry it as criminal presumption, silken-robed Pope
    Alexander
dividing the new world between Spain and Portugal.
If he smiled *in petto* afterwards, perhaps the thing did have
    sprawl.

Sprawl is really classless, though. It's John Christopher
    Frederick Murray
asleep in his neighbours' best bed in spurs and oilskins
but not having thrown up:
sprawl is never Calum who, drunk, along the hallways of our
    house,
reinvented the Festoon. Rather
it's Beatrice Miles going twelve hundred ditto in a taxi,
No Lewd Advances, No Hitting Animals, No Speeding,
on the proceeds of her two-bob-a-sonnet Shakespeare readings.

An image of my country. And would that it were more so.

No, sprawl is full-gloss murals on a council-house wall.
Sprawl leans on things. It is loose-limbed in its mind.
Reprimanded and dismissed
it listens with a grin and one boot up on the rail
of possibility. It may have to leave the Earth.
Being roughly Christian, it scratches the other cheek
and thinks it unlikely. Though people have been shot for
sprawl.

JAS H. DUKE

Positive Poem

I love my work
I love waking up every working day
I love the tram that carries me there
I love my time clock
I love the chair I sit in
I love my pens and pencils
I love the drawings that I do
I love the ones that have been rejected and torn up
I love the ones that have been kept
I love lunch time
I love clocking off too
I love working hard
I love not working at all
I really am in love

I love my boss (who tells me what to do)
I love the government (who pay me once a fortnight)
I love President Carter* (who threatens me with war)

I love the Russians (who give him someone to fight)
I love being alive in such stirring times
I love destruction
but don't get me wrong
I love quiet times too
I love both war and peace
I love everything that happens, has happened, is going to happen
if I didn't love everything I'd be unhappy
I don't want to be unhappy
you wouldn't want to be unhappy either

I really love being alive
When I'm dead I'm going to love being dead

*Written May 1980. *Substitute and any other suitable official American as necessary.*

J. S. HARRY

a quality of loss

'fire' they cried in the middle of the dance,
wheyfaced girls and weary men came pouring out
their faces rekindled by a vivid life
because it was a fire: a need – somebody's house
was burning up.
                                        It could have seemed that what he had
was burning in that house. It could have seemed he saw his days
on fire, and the leafless trees
stood away like fishbones in the dark.
His chairs were on the coals where the flames died
and the smoke trailed out
                    uncertain as a dog.

And 'fire' the dancers cried, again, as a latecoming wave
surged out;
they held him back
when he tried to go inside
the burning doorway of his golden house;
late one had asked, and he hadn't remembered,
what it was, of his life, that he'd lost
that he could
have brought out, if he'd had the time –
from the glowing bones of the liquid fire –
He'd long remember
something else how a dog might try
to re-take a haunch had and buried years before –
vague, a trace, the dimmest scent –
Late he circled
round the black down-dropping struts,
held, by their stares, as perfectly
as a bee, by a glass around a flower.

GEOFFREY LEHMANN

Pear Days in Queensland

Based on comments of Judith Wright and an article of James Wansfell

Days of pear-murder, nights of pear-madness we spent
Digging and burning the prickly pear,
Poisoning, crushing with rollers drawn by bullocks,
Standing in pubs and swapping pear yarns,
Scraping the spines off with knives,
Sponging our thorn wounds with mustard,
Scratched brown and purple with Condy's and gentian violet,

While beyond the pressure lamp's wavering circle
The pear massed its nightmare armies by moonlight
And peered with balloon green faces over pub railings.

We hacked, we poisoned, we crushed, but the pads
Just split and sprouted again.
A tree grew from a burned green ear.
Eating the yellow flowers and soft red fruit
A wandering cow scattered the seeds in her stools.
The pear flew in the stomachs of birds,
Breathed on the fur of bees,
A pad lived for three years hung in a room.

How could we fight what stuck to our boots and travelled
The red volcanic soil on our clothes and horses?
We sweated, were smeared with pear.
Pear cities covered millions and millions of acres,
Our horses galloped,
Pear leaves flying in all directions,
The roads just narrow green tunnels.
We climbed up trees to spot the heads
Of cattle amongst the plazas of cactus.
Our horses jumped and crashed in the pear,
As we tried to muster
A strange new race of small, dodging beasts
With horny palates and nimble gait.

We bred and we hacked in the great pear-loneliness,
Close neighbours cut off by the walls of thorns
That buried wire fences and boundaries,
Creeks and even hills lost,
No one quite knew where.
We walked the moonlit track to the privy

Striking with sticks at slits in the moonlight,
The small death-adders who swarmed among the cactus.
We cut and we slept,
Afraid of losing our one track out,
And stared at night from our verandas
Looking for neighbours' lights.

But we learned to live with these miles
Of green intestine digesting the world into pear.
We mashed the pads for feed,
Fermented them into alcohol
And extracted second grade dyes and oils.
We used the big yellow thorns for gramophone needles
And heard Enrico Caruso husky and faint
Sing from a thorn as we boiled in hot pear nights.

Then a moth came and Troy fell overnight.
The cactoblastis chewed through green cities,
And the arcades of pear collapsed.
We blinked at the sky
And a hemisphere of grassland tilting to the sea.
Our houses stood unpainted and rusty
In acres of pear-slime and melting branches.
And we waded through the slush
To shake the hands of forgotten neighbours.
Now the hillside is a honeycomb crumbling with fire
As in winter we burn the sugarcane
In blue indigo twilights blowing with orange smoke.
Our rivers and country daze us with largeness.
But at night we doze in mosquito nets
And smell ghost armies of cactus
In the heart of the rain forest,
New resistant strains sending out clouds of pollen.

KATE LLEWELLYN

Breasts

As I lean over to write
one breast warm as a breast from the sun
hangs over as if to read what I'm writing
these breasts always want to know everything
sometimes exploring the inside curve of my elbow
sometimes measuring a man's hand
lying as still as a pond
until he cannot feel he is holding anything
but water
then he dreams he is floating

in the morning my breast is refreshed
and wants to know something new
although it is soft it as also ambitious
we never speak
but I know my breast knows me more than I do
prying hanging over fences
observant as a neighbour
or eager as a woman wanting to gossip
they tell me nothing
but they say quite a lot about me

there is a dark blue river vein here
straggling down taking its time
to the little pale strawberry
picked too soon and left too long
in the punnet in a warm shop

when I lie
these breasts spread like spilt milk

and standing naked in the sea
float like figs
as you will realise
these are my body's curious fruit
wanting to know everything
always getting there first
strange as white beetroot
exotic as unicorns
useless as an out of order dishwasher
more of a nuisance than anything else

some men seem to think highly of them
peering and staring
what they don't know is the breast stares straight back
interested as a reporter

some love them
and invest them with glamour
but like life they are not glamorous
merely dangerous

JAN OWEN

Blue Bowl

This pedestal bowl against the light
shows a leftward tilt,
a yen toward some philosophy
other than fruit.
The obtuse angle makes me think
of a certain man:
what that cocked head had on its mind
was Kierkegaard not Zen.

I admire asymmetry luckily
but balance too.
So did my doctor when we were young,
lowering his stethoscope
with a little frown
then deftly tilting my left nipple back
to match its mate.
A purely aesthetic gesture
like my picking lint off his coat.
I remember we used to laugh a lot
at next to nothing.
Later I heard his marriage fell apart
and thought of that year
when we both felt
regular check-ups advisable.
Was it training or natural bent
that helped him keep things straight?

GEOFF PAGE

Inscription at Villers-Bretonneux

The dead at Villers-Bretonneux
rise gently on a slope towards
the sky. The land is trim – skylines

of ploughed earth and steeples; unfallen
rain still hanging in the air;
confusion smoothed away

and everything put back – the village
too (red brick/white sills) in nineteen
twenty, unchanged since. Headstones

speak a dry consensus. Just one
breaks free: 'Lives Lost, Hearts Broken –
And for What?' I think of the woman

and those she saddened by insisting –
the Melbourne clerk
who must have let it through.

Smalltown Memorials

No matter how small
Every town has one;
Maybe just the obelisk,
A few names inlaid;
More often full-scale granite,
Marble digger (arms reversed),
Long descending lists of dead:
Sometimes not even a town,
A thickening of houses
Or a few unlikely trees
Glimpsed on a back-road
Will have one.

1919, 1920:
All over the country;
Maybe a band, slow march;
Mayors, shire councils;
Relatives for whom
Print was already
Only print; mates
Come back, moving
Into unexpected days;

A ring of Fords and sulkies;
The toned-down bit
Of Billy Hughes from an
Ex-recruiting sergeant.
Unveiled;
Then seen each day –
Noticed once a year;
And then not always,
Everywhere.
The next bequeathed us
Parks and pools

But something in that first
Demanded stone.

ANDREW TAYLOR

The Gardener and His Garden: A Dialogue

Ignoring the dour alternatives of winter
I've planted a fleshy tropic which the sun
should never graze, lolloping if it can
under a canopy of trees much prized
and slaughtered for their furniture grain.
Transported here, on the salt-water edge
of summer, sun slanting like a flare
from the Grim Scythe, no matter
how I water it, it decides no for now.

I won't take that for an answer.
Like a middle-rank executive
it will mature, I determine,
and grow into its role. Elms have, poplars,

blackberries, the flu virus,
Paterson's curse. So shall this.

Transported like a felon to provide
some far-flung scion of a British stock
his dotty sense of what the tropics are
or might be, had he ever been
awash with crocodiles and curious bugs
and universal mozzies, we eke out
a post-colonial repertoire of roles:
exotica, noteworthy introduced
species, plant of the month, old-
fashioned but still of some appeal
then common stock, then weed.

Sand isn't enough, nor the plants
sand succours. I want
this world, and a world elsewhere
I want melaleuca and lawn, banksia
and basil. I want what I have
and the promise of what I can grow -
a desert and a tropic, a gardener's
absurdity, produced
at the point of a knife
at the tip of a hose.

We age
together, but more gracefully
than he, that stringy fool
with secateurs, twine, and a short memory.

Folds in the Map

Lucid as always
you guide us along the autobahn
until at Exit 43
the map falls apart.

Groping on the floor you fail
to tell me to turn.
Furious I find
no repentance on your face.

We overshoot by 80 k
miss our appointment
arrive to observe ducks tow
rippling arrows over the lake

and hear bells from the Romanesque
church tell us that the hour
is always late. Folds
in the map, you say

weakened the paper and we fell
through. A meal
and a bed in the Gästhaus
and we cancel what's left

of the tour, to stay
by a lake, with ducks, together.
After each Exit, we agree
is another, and the next.

ROGER McDONALD

1915

Up they go, yawning,
the crack of knuckles dropped
to smooth the heaving
in their legs, while some,
ashamed, split bile
between their teeth,
and hum to drown their stomachs.

Others touch their lips
on splintered wood
to reach for home –
'a bloke's a mug'
thinks one (who sees
a ringbarked hill)
another hisses drily
(leaping burrs).

All dreaming,
when the whistle
splits the pea, as up
they scramble, pockets fat
with Champion Flake
in battered tins,
and letters wadded thick
from Mum (who says
'always keep
some warm clothes on . . .')

Up from slits in dirt
they rise, and here they stop.
A cold long light swings over.

Hard like ice
it cracks their shins –
they feel a drill and mallet
climb their bones, then cold
then warmth as blood spills out from pockets,
chests, and mouths.
No mother comes to help, although
a metal voice is whining
'boys, relax', as one
by one they totter to their knees.

JENNIFER RANKIN

Burning Off

I made my mother walk across dead distances
pacing her at a favourite occupation
while she filled in days between the family meals.

I set her to work at carefully creating hills
and dotting paddocks with a strange calligraphy,
carving upwards into space small pyres.
I watched from underneath the pine.

The midday tree shadows her as she moves
to the lighting of the grass, religious rituals
hang in the air and while I watch
the smoking sculpture creeps towards my pine.

BARRY HILL

A Long Swim

Swimming out there
Musculature in ultramarine,
In weed-green sea
You can think 'mackerel'
Till you're blue in the face
But you go like tow rope –
Heavy, frayed, stretched
From pier to pier
From year to year

Entering at the southern one
Mind finned with intent
Crossing crags and sea-grass
Gutters gouged by ebb tides
Rays much wider than beds
Their glide-aways heavenly
Over sands that cloud the hourglass
In light that breaks the light,
Squid invisible, abalone opalescent,
The flood tide your freedom
Its reverse your test of worth

Emerging at the northern one
Your body out of water
Your flesh, on arrival
The underside of flounder,
Each tooth in your head
A little colder, your sense
Of time like coral

ROBERTA 'BOBBI' SYKES

Cycle

The revolution is conceived
as a babe in the womb;
It is, as a foetus,
An idea – a twinkle only
in men's eyes and a silent knowing
in women;
Yet it lives.

The revolution is alive
while it lives
within us;
Beating, making our hearts warm,
Our minds strong, for we know
that justice is inevitable –
like birth.

Unaware of what they see,
They watch us;
We grow stronger and threaten
to burst our skin;
They do not realise
that the revolution
is near birth

That it threatens to spill
from this succoured womb
To the long-ready world
Which has not prepared
Even in this long time of waiting.

We do not always talk
of our pregnancy
for we are pregnant
with the thrust of freedom;
And our freedom looks to others
As a threat.

Yet we must be free, we know it,
And they know it,
For our freedom is not a gift
To be bestowed,
But torn from those
Who seek to keep us down.

We must stand up, raise our arms
To the sun, breathe deep the free air,
And our children
Cavort as new-born, trouble-free.

The revolution lives. It lives
within us. Birth is imminent.
It cannot be bought off,
pushed back, held off.
The revolution will spring forward
As surely
As the child will leave the womb
– When it is ready;
We must make haste preparing
while biding our time.

JOHN TRANTER

Voodoo

From his rushing-away, from his
ever-receding throne, under a rainy
canopy of trees and scraps of cloud
that topple back, shrink and disappear,
embalmed behind his rear window in a nest of
crushed velvet plush, the flash wog's nodding dog
blinks out his witless approval to the vehicles
that shadow him forever.

His twin the dipping bird sips and sips,
tilts back, cools off, dries out,
dries out utterly, totters weakly
on the lip of philosophy
then dips again.

These two critics teach us how to live,
rehearsing the gap between the no-no
and the drink-again. Their motto? Every day
I will get better at embroidering the lingo
of the tongue-tied doctors of letters; every night,
in the lack of light, I will get better
and better at the negative virtues, telling
girls to piss off, who needs them,
swimming off the edge of the rock
ledge into the plunging broth of deeper waters,
soaring up to the stratosphere, bothering the angels
and yarning with God. My left hand writes it,
my right hand tells me that it's right.

In the pre-dawn rack and bash of winter peak hour
traffic on the Sydney Harbour Bridge you notice them
hefted up over the city like ju-ju dolls
in the trance of a terrible gift. You note
the man with gauntlets and the goggled girl
on motorbikes, the nurses' giggles
in the fogged-up Mini Moke, an ambulance weaving
and howling in the rear-view mirror, the tablets
rattling in the Emergency Bucket, the icy rain
furious and seething on the road, and Noddy
and his loopy brother brooding on it all
for our sake, so that we can see it whole.

Lufthansa

Flying up a valley in the Alps where the rock
rushes past like a broken diorama
I'm struck by an acute feeling of precision –
the way the wing-tips flex, just a little
as the German crew adjust the tilt of the sky and
bank us all into a minor course correction
while the turbo-props gulp at the mist
with their old-fashioned thirsty thunder – or
you notice how the hostess, perfecting a smile
as she offers you a dozen drinks, enacts what is
almost a craft: Technical Drawing, for example,
a subject where desire and function, in the hands
of a Dürer, can force a thousand fine ink lines
to bite into the doubts of an epoch, spelling
Humanism. Those ice reefs repeat the motto
whispered by the snow-drifts on the north side
of the woods and model villages: the sun

has a favorite leaning, and the Nordic gloom
is a glow alcohol can fan into a flame.
And what is this truth that holds the grey
shaking metal whole while we believe in it?
The radar keeps its sweeping intermittent promises
speaking metaphysics on the phosphor screen;
our faith is sad and practical, and leads back
to our bodies, to the smile behind the drink
trolley and her white knuckles as the plane drops
a hundred feet. The sun slanting through a porthole
blitzes the ice-blocks in my glass of lemonade
and splinters light across the cabin ceiling.
No, two drinks – one for me, one for Katharina
sleeping somewhere – suddenly the Captain
lifts us up and over the final wall
explaining roads, a town, a distant lake
as a dictionary of shelter – sleeping
elsewhere, under a night sky growing bright with stars.

Glow-boys

Four a.m. At the reactor an alarm begins
howling. The core's full of shit: get out
the gloves, the phosphorescent rakes.

A burnt-out star hangs low on the horizon.
The Harrisburg glow-boys knuckle down
to work, poking around in the ashes.

They gaze out through glitter: behind the visor
putty imitates a human face, the lips
gritty, frayed, as they reach for speech

across the static field. Now a bell rings
and they wade thigh-deep into the muck,
their eyes the colour of lightning.

Five years of that and they're
too hot to touch; they wake screaming
before dawn, the pillow soaked.

What have they seen: their children's future
flare and crackle, a vast Christmas tree
flashing up from the skyline?

Rake it up, Ratshit! In a month
vacation in the Rockies, drinking rye and
blowing rattlesnakes away with a shotgun.

Now, like any cleaners, they go to work
deft and grumbling, their wives awake
in nylon nighties staring at the ceiling

and the glow of the luminous clock.
The pot of coffee popping on the stove.
The kids asleep, dreaming fitfully.

CAROLINE CADDY

Pelican

Aloof   long nosed conjurer
impeccably out of style   watch him
he will show you the neat trick
of eating.

Dip and glide   another fish pocketed
in the deep box of his bill.

He lifts extendable wings
they are empty.

He points with a cold eye
summons his mate.   They preen
practise sawing each other
in half.

JOANNE BURNS

avon calling

there's dust on the vinyl leather cover of the shakespeare
  sonnets
and summer's humid breath has turned the paper brown
you stare out from the shelf in kodachrome
behind a woolworth's plastic frame
slouched at your desk a blue biro
between your teeth like a thermometer in front
of your clapped out fax machine: a fickle scribe
its messages fading fast;
the brass gods, candlesticks and vases
are tarnished and strewn with dust, there are
no petals in these lines, or darling buds of may –
only the tv knobs intend to gleam naïve
as costume jewels, and listen
is that meals on wheels or the avon lady at the door

ROBERT GRAY

Kangaroo

His hungry face
drifts on the grass, in the way that a final
pencil
will retouch or the artist erase.

Then when he flies, a head that was hieratic
is delicate
and remote, before the powerful tight
basketball attack.

At other times, travels with a retinue; it's done
seated, idle
as someone on a bicycle. (Wheel
and haunch make the same proportion.)

Dogs in pursuit,
he cantilevers on a tail like a tap-root, tears
with stevedore's
hook. While carrying the forepaws of a house pet.

In silhouette, he can almost seem
to make plain
that something unknown
which is able to contain, as one, every extreme.

Garage

In one of the side streets
of a small hot town
on the highway

we saw the garage,
its white boards peeling
among fronds and palings.

The sun had a cut a blaze
off the day. The petrol pump
was from the sixties,

perhaps. Of human scale
and humanoid appearance
it had a presence,

seemed the attendant
of our adventures on the road
the doorman of our chances.

We'd pulled in, for nostalgia,
onto concrete. From where
did this thing's almost

avoidable sense of,
was it sacrifice, remorse,
arise? One felt it

as though it were a line
in the hand, drifted far out
somewhere, unweighted.

Who was this, in faded
cream outfit, with badge,
expressionless small head,

and rubbery arm laid
on the breast, dutifully
or out of diffidence?

Were arms being shown, and in
servitude or willingness?
The stoic discomforts,

implies a rebellion.
Elusively, such feelings
waft through us, but how

interpret them? A person
relied upon, and yet
a danger. Was this

another, or perhaps oneself?
Were we the familiars of something
we cannot know? I looked

down a blank street, of pines,
light poles, old houses
in shadowy yards, which made

a genuflection in approaching
the gentian-coloured hills;
then at the workshop, a dim

barn, or empty corridor
in the galaxy, with somewhere
far along one of its fires

crackling and bursting
hugely; and at the rusted
dog, in its narrow shade.

And on the old bowser –
its sense still proclaimed but
ungraspable, though everything

lay open. Someone shouted
acknowledgement, so we sat
quietly. The daylight

had become an interest
of this place, in its pronounced
contrast with the peculiar

matt blackness of sump-oil
stains, soaked widely
on earth, gravel and cement;

an obscurity as opaque
as the heart, where it kept on
with its tunnelling there.

PETER SKRZYNECKI

Migrant Hostel

Parkes, 1949–51

No one kept count
Of all the comings and goings –
Arrivals of newcomers
In busloads from the station,
Sudden departures from adjoining blocks
That left us wondering
Who would be coming next.

Nationalities sought
Each other out instinctively –
Like a homing pigeon
Circling to get its bearings;
Years and place-names

Recognised by accents,
Partitioned off at night
By memories of hunger and hate.

For over two years
We lived like birds of passage –
Always sensing a change
In the weather:
Unaware of the season
Whose track we would follow.

A barrier at the main gate
Sealed off the highway
From our doorstep –
As it rose and fell like a finger
Pointed in reprimand or shame;
And daily we passed
Underneath or alongside it –
Needing its sanction
To pass in and out of lives
That had only begun
Or were dying.

MARTIN JOHNSTON

Gradus Ad Parnassum

for David Campbell

Over a tabasco sandwich, with black coffee
and a number of cigarettes ('one of my breakfasts')
I've been rereading a poem about *The Shipwreck*
of the Heart, or some such – the title isn't important,
only, of course, the Image – by the well-known

Russian revolutionary poet Vladimir Mayakovsky.
This he wrote immediately before indulging
in the uncharacteristic excess of suicide;
the poem, perhaps because of this, is peculiarly flabby
for this normally vigorous author, is, how shall I put it,
    sentimental.
Of course, he never had a chance to revise it.
So, having nothing better to do at the moment, and in
    accordance
with my (borrowed) idea that we're all one writer
and ought, in any case, to do one another justice,
I thought I might have a go at it
on his behalf. I like to think he wouldn't mind,
though he did once call Dante and Petrarch tongue-tied.

One way of approaching it would be what I'd call the Arnoldian
(cf. *The Scholar-Gypsy*) – the extended thalassic metaphor,
the tang of myth, the vague yearning (perhaps *tristesse*
is more or less the word) after something or other indefinable.
But it would be hard not to be woolly.
Seferis can get away with that sort of thing; but he's a Greek,
in this, as in other lines of business, an advantage.
I don't think it'll do.

Or perhaps something after the manner of Rimbaud,
Le Bateau Ivre, say. It's been done, I grant you
– there's a new Rimbaud every week or so – but it does offer
both astringency and lots of freedom. It's tempting;
and I could invoke Hoffmansthal too, and his incredible boat
'with enormous yellow sails', the ideal dreamscape property
if ever there was one.
Except Rimbaud never had to face

that particular situation; it was always poor Verlaine
who copped it – court cases, absinthe, all very sordid – and *his*
style,
I'm sure of it, would be worse than useless . . .

A good line (ironic distancing) would be the cheerfully morbid
surrealist – black comedy, kitsch, *fantastically* rich
imagery – the sort of thing David Campbell does so well
in his latest book. I mean, you could have these merchants,
whores, and sailors gaping on some picturesque waterfront
as this bloody great red, pulsating thing comes in
beating past the headlands, with Joe the little cabin boy
sticking his head out of the aorta to be sick.
And then Whoompf! the reef, and Squelch! the blood,
and the sun opportunely setting. I mean, it's powerful . . .
but just a little . . . heavy-handed? And critics seem to think
that's all passé. Jim Tulip
wouldn't take it seriously. You can't win.

Or, again, the nebulously cosmic: a giant uvula
suddenly becoming discernible on the skyline –
shades of Fenrir at Ragnarök –
teeth poking through the clouds, a crunching sound,
end, but *end*, of poem. But I've done very similar things
myself, earlier on. I don't want to end up in self-parody,
I know too many critics. And I've been a little unkind
myself, perhaps, on occasion. It would hardly be politic.

And the groovier modern Americans? They seem to be the
context
I'm supposed to work in, though I mostly haven't read them.
But their thing about the quotidian, and the earth,

and the immanence of the tremendous in just about
    everything –
what kind of immanence is left for something tremendous?
Like an extravagantly outsized Russian
about to do himself in, shat with love and the party?
What has that to do with the grass? Tenochtitlan? Cotton
    Mather
or your friend and fellow-poet who happened to drop in?

. . . and one is left, it seems to me, with the techniques and
    words
of Vladimir Mayakovsky, who wrote this poem,
The Shipwreck of the Heart or whatever, just before
shooting himself, if I remember rightly.
I'm not sure that it's much of a poem
but it'll have to do. I'm thirsty to start with
and the pubs have opened, and besides, I think deep down I'm
    hoping
that someone will try to pinch *my* poems, and much good
may it do them: each one the precise, the only possible
delineation of a complex of thinking and feeling;
the explanation of each poem
precisely the poem itself.
Sometimes it's hard to repress a snigger. Still, a beer
and buy the papers and some more tabasco
and maybe another bash at Mayakovsky . . .

RHYLL McMASTER

The Brineshrimp

They have minute faces like walrussed grandpas
and they many-feelered paddle on their backs
with their black dorsal lines and bits of gravel eyes showing up
like bulge-eyed, curled up crowbars.

Nothing like crowbars
but have the strength of obstinacy
to live through a change to fresh water;
to whirr themselves from one cramped fish mouth
to another nearby, inevitable, drawn-in, spat-out death.
All the while on their backs and looking pleasantly ludicrous.

And at the same time to make love to each other –
to cruise around their rectangular chamber of horror
one brineshrimp starting where the other leaves off –
both on their backs.

They flesh-colouredly exist – uncomfortable for the most part –
and desperately love and are lump-throated funny
because they're only very small, water-galumphing
    brineshrimp
and rather untidy –
and they mate and are fruitless.

ALF TAYLOR

Moorditj Yorgah

You are a cruel
Deadly moorditj yorgah
An' um marrdong for you
But um
Just a wintjarren
Nyoongah man
But um gonna try
To get off
Diss gerbah an' gunja
An' be a cruel
Deadly moorditj nyoongah man

You are indeed
A truly deadly solid
Moorditj yorgah
An' um
Jerrepjing something wicked
For you
But um
Just a wintjarren nyoongah man

Um gonna
Get off
Diss gerbah an gunja
An' show you
What a moorditj man
I can be
An gib you
All da lub

Dat I can
But kurndarnj choo
Um shame

PAM BROWN

At the Wall

I'd written myself into a wall
– James Baldwin

our soft little lives
are asleep

sarajevo srebrenica palestine
rwanda kabul kenya

a half-empty bottle
of old formalities
thrown in the mud
'we are all of us in the gutter
but some of us are looking
at the stars'
said o. wilde
not another twenty years
of that, I hope

our feckless little aspirations
require the lowest
common denominator

so show me the book
that shows me

rows of terrariums
growing horrible viral cells

genetic cultures
  dropping enormous
    thick clots

the artists
   are affected
clumsy vision
  stuck with lumps

the artists
    could be
lost   as well

invited
  to a 'private viewing' –
an occasion
  usually called
   an 'opening'

you see
  backward lurchings
& hear vacuous flatteries
  & the S&M pose
  hit hurt ooh ahh
looking like petals
 acting like engines
making minor contributions
 to the 'cutting edge'
(80s talk 90s clothing)

will anyone ever
   agitate
     again ?

when will they occupy
  the privatised academies ?

all talk & theory
  older & older
    less & less wise

statues are toppling
  before they are built

so   at the bar,
  my pal remembers
    a quote
from Mark Twain or someone
  'the means have become
    more expedient
    but the goals are lost'
I write it down
      on the back
  of a blank
        TAB trifecta ticket

here,   in the country
    without guilt,
when will the menacing,
      the history,
            begin ?

MICHAEL DRANSFIELD

Pas de deux for lovers

Morning ought not
to be complex.
The sun is a seed
cast at dawn into the long
furrow of history.

To wake
and go
would be so simple.

Yet

how the
first light
makes gold her hair

upon my arm.
How then
shall I leave,
and where away to go. Day
is so deep already with involvement.

That which we call a rose

Black greyed into white a nightmare of bicycling
over childhood roads harried peaceless
tomorrow came a mirage packed in hypodermic
the city we lived in then was not of your making
it was built by sculptors in the narcotic rooms of Stanley Street
we solved time an error in judgment

it was stolen by the bosses and marketed as the eight hour day

Waking under a bridge in Canberra to chill scrawl
seeing the designs we had painted on its concrete like gnawed
    fresco
Venice with princes feasting while Cimabue sank deeper into
    cobweb
as the huns approached in skin boats
back in the world Rick and George on the morgue-lists of
    morning
one dead of hunger the other of overdose their ideals precluded
    them
from the Great Society they are with the angels now

I dremt of satori a sudden crystal wherein civilisation was seen
more truly than with cameras but it was your world not ours
yours is a glut of martyrs money and carbon monoxide
I dremt of next week perhaps then we would eat again sleep in
    a house again
perhaps we would wake to find humanity where at present
freedom is obsolete and honour a heresy. Innocently
I dremt that madness passes like a dream

Writ out of ashes, out of twenty years of ashes
For George Alexandrov and for Rick

Colonial Poet

today he will write some verses. his schedule
allows for a poem on his travels, or
                roses, or
                a mythological topic.

the day is hot so he selects the past / waterfalls,
dryads, a god or two. from the filing cabinet
of his head, in which legends are filed, alphabetically,
he picks out Hylas and a springside of nymphs. these tiny
    people
come to life for him, obediently; the ingredients mix well –
the beautiful youth / himself / the women / his / who take him
for their own. he makes of this an allegory, displaying his
    knowledge / minimal /
of psychology / referring to another file / and from the news,
a topical allusion. his measured cadences unfold, a page or two
    is covered;
he pauses, reviewing what is written. for him the parentheses
    ripple outward
pleasingly, and he sees in the still pool of his verse
a clear reflection of himself as god.
he rises, leaving the study, it has served its panelled purpose;
    switches off
his music machine. the record, labelled in flawless french
L'Apres-midi etc / returns to yet another file, and his gods and
little people
go home to their woods
as far now from his mind
as the toy soldiers of his childhood

DENNIS HASKELL

At Greenwood, a Meditation

In a humdrum household
occasional cats jackknife over fences,
slink across the path, wide

eyes on guard, whiskers atwitch.
For these dark creatures
my mind wanders
over the other neighbourhood
they sidle silently from
and what water or milk
they hope to lap from
in my head.

Now the hunched and
ricketty figures of houses
slip to one side, in trees
sharply cut blood coloured sap
flows up from each root,
salt scatters from the shaker
over tablecloths lit with stars,
dark, stiff outlines of hills
brood, mysterious, that will
in time become again
suburban, lupin dressed hills . . .

I never can call to them
nor fix how they come
but when I see a mouth
lick up the dabs of sunlight
celebrate / what has then begun,
the twitch of whiskers,
the startling tongue.

JOHN A. SCOTT

My Favourite Things

I'm sorry, but I loved
the ambulance night. How the heat
began to affect people's spelling.
The unusually busy foyer where smoke
handshook its way through the crowds.
I loved the gift-burning. It's how
you come to meet someone tough
like Jane; rising from ammonia
and the mother's club shuffle,
sick to death of sense because it hurts
more than hoses or biography.
I loved the restroom queues, where
the diagnosis gets served through
a shrapnel of make-up: nothing serious
with *you* baby! and the blackmail
of other people's fun pulls out,
muffled, under the specimen moon.
I'm sorry, but I want taxis everywhere.
It's how you talk to someone bright
as Jane: on the switchboard, lost in
an alcoholic drift like Radio India;
unsure of exactly which Post Office
you might be outside. Favourite things:
how you pay for all that applause on
live albums; how Madonna's new clip
has her hosing down the tiles;
how the Pope is here; how the oxygen
masks start to descend. I loved

those shimmering, tumescent days
of casualty; your kind drugged advice.

ALEX SKOVRON

The Steeples

So we continued into the valley of ruined machines
Weaving our trace among the blackened wreckage
The charred distillations of our wizardry and love

We hummed chorales and inhaled the death-smoke
Curling from the steeples in the wavering distance
And we wondered at the implacable grey thunder

The birthquake of the proliferating generations
Who would curse our dim elegance and engineering
The conceits we had nailed upon this landscape

And all the while out machines gazed up at us
Though we had long ceased searching the quiet sky
For a sign of grace or music in the skeleton trees

So what use the rust we scrabbled against rudely
Or the clay-crusted leaves we unearthed to rekindle
The wheels and pulleys that had taunted eternity

We failed of course so we hoisted our memories
Blew the powder of sleep from our bulging histories
Endured a night of tacit copulations and proceeded

VICKI VIIDIKAS

Future

It doesn't really matter if I met him in a bar, picked him up or was picked up; in the morning he pushed me out of bed saying, 'You must go, my wife's due back.' And catching the 7.44 a.m. bus I thought, it doesn't really matter, what did I expect? These are my fingers spread out to touch, the palms turned down, the kisses like nets; these are the lines, when I was a girl the fortune teller said, 'You will travel.'

YAHIA AL-SAMAWY

Variations on My Clay Heartstrings (translation Eva Sallis)

1

Here I am, spreading fresh water, plaintive songs,
Sweet myrtle flowers,
Unsleeping.
I await nightly an apparition from my beloved
Who will hunt for me the bird of drowsiness?

2

Between your eyes and me
There is a forest of exiled trees
Fences of prison cells and a desert of lamentation.
Why do strangers bathe
In my country
In the drizzle of blessed rain
While the grass by the Euphrates bathes in pus and blood?

And why do we own nothing in our homelands
Except elegies?

3
Who will scale the fence of night and distance
And wipe the tears from our eyes
And the disgrace from our foreheads?
Who will return greenness to the grass
And to the river its waters
And peace to Karkh and Rassafa
Without aspiring to the Caliphate?

4
Country of date palms
And teardrops the shape of glittering stars,
If you make the rope into a noose
I will make from it a child's swing,
And from my wound a lily.

5
O winds!
Take the ash of our wounds
And pollinate the flower of revolt or the points of spears
And then perhaps a dawn will break
From the womb of wounds.

6
O time of lamentation
My country
Is as wide as the sky
And as tight as a shroud

KEN BOLTON

Holden Song – or, Homesickness Was His Middle Name

> Here, plastic furniture seems like a good idea,
> more natural on a marble chip
> & concrete terrace, as though
> what we treat as objects,
> they take for granted
>
> (hence 'style'
> and how for us this word belongs in ads
>
> *Roman Poem*, John Forbes

Reading about Marie Henri Beyle
I suddenly wonder if Murray Bail hasn't named
himself
after Stendhal – Marie Beyle. Why shouldn't he
of course, despite . . . Or are the similarities numerous?
Anyway, an act of faith. Cath, Michael, & Di
have gone down to the markets.
I, in an act of enlightened disbelief –
after all I have been before –
remain & quietly read
&, now, inside, write –
another act of faith. As the trams
roll by & traffic noises – horns mostly,
but distant ones – bleat & sigh, complain,
or mechanically & pleasantly
drag the moments by. From where I sit I see,
outside, the white plastic chairs
John was so caustic about, momentarily, in his poem –
& beyond them, six feet further – green shrub

& the pink-&-biscuit-coloured facetted climb
of buildings on the hill opposite: warm, calm, marked by
the grey-white *horizontals* of verandahs –
the *vertical* accents of window frames, aerials,
&, dominant, one dark green pine.
Above, blue sky, & a bit of awning hanging down
                    outside our doorway,
the door I look out to see all this.
John joked severely
that the plastic chairs that, to us,
would look less than ideal
or even cheap, at home in Adelaide
in Rome look sensible, approaching elegance, & closes
with those Australian expatriates
looking fondly on them, turning
their hearts against Australia.

My point? None, as usual.
Two months to go, of our stay here in Rome –
where the chairs look okay, to me,
though, true, I wouldn't like them
at home – where
I can't wait to go
though happy for the time to run out
at its own pace –
where the sight of the first aged Holden
will make me smile – like the thought
'Murray Holden Bail.'

LAURIE DUGGAN

Boredom

(after Ardengo Soffici)

Between 8.45 and 10.10
I have watched the bloodstained world
through a rectangle of red glass
with white lettering:
'Bisleri – sparkling digestive mineral water:
gout cure and uric diet'.

What else should I hope for?
Our fate is death by retail,
our calendar scheduled by economists.

The modernist dream is as dead as Rameses II.
The big cities don't even notice spring
returning each year like an usherette with a tray of cigars,
though the moon's electric crescent promotes itself:
'founded anno one – still going strong';
and the stars always find some muddy pool to wink at
like the smacked-out eyes of streetwalkers.

Trams, yellow housemartins, dip into the streets and are gone;
buses scatter for the suburbs like magnetised filings;
car headlights whirl in primitive blizzards
(the pigeons are mass-produced like pigeons everywhere else).
The sky – full of signwriters –
looks like a lunatic has been loosed with an icing gun,
but the banknotes smell like almond blossoms.

The Town Hall clock is several minutes slow
(what a symbol to live under!).
Everything else repeats itself:
each house, shuttered, as though the apocalypse were
forecast;
each room holds secrets too dull to mention:
bidets, mauve shirts, sweaty skin, suggestive notes, dirty
postcards.
The heart closes its hatches, like a bank teller
on the dot of 3.30 p.m.

Our lives bump together in a gossip-column
assembled by cadet-journalists on the Great Daily.
Imagination belongs only to window-dressers.

The universe, all that tiresome cosmology, disappears with a
stroke.
A new alchemy welds daylight to dusk;
a seasonless glow of artificial fire and mellow acetylene.

'Gentleman wanted:
must have clown-suit, powder and paint,
scarlet quiff, scarlet heart.
Green eyebrows essential.
Should be able to dance,
laugh,
sing;
be a masked god on a highwire
stretched from alpha to omega
over this fleapit, waiting for encores'.

GEOFF GOODFELLOW

The Violence of Work

I work in a factory
Monday to Friday
    punch on   punch off

i work a rotating roster
Monday to Friday
    punch on   punch off

i wear earmuffs & gloves
Monday to Friday
    punch on   punch off

i stamp on a press
Monday to Friday
    punch on   punch off

i still had my fingers last
Monday to Friday
    punch on   punch off

i work on a tally
Monday to Friday
    punch on   punch off

i'm told to work faster
Monday to Friday
    punch on   punch off

i have smoko with Billy
Monday to Friday
    punch on   punch off

i play euchre at lunchtime
Monday to Friday
    punch on   punch off

i just do my best
Monday to Friday
    punch on   punch off

i'm paid the award for
Monday to Friday
    punch on   punch off

i don't complain to the boss
Monday to Friday
    punch on   punch off

but complain to my partner
Monday to Sunday
    want to punch on
        punch on.

ALAN GOULD

Three Icelandic Interiors

Heimaey Eruption, 1973

A Palaeozoic tenure
spits vermilion gobbets
high above these canneries.
This year the spring's no use;
the island eats its cowl.

The wharf's lanterned with nightgowns
as ash invades the kitchens,
bursting like a sea
on heirloom spoons, on clocks
great-grandfathers set ticking.

Offshore the cod shoals poise
remote as stars in space,
and here's a sanctity
of home that is not touched
by yesterday today.

Valleys on the Road to Dalvik

From green to indigo
the valleys intermarry
shoulders, rumps and laps.

All Gisli's kids were poets,
all Egil's sons were dolts.

A woman lugs her bucket
from the talking stream
where once an outlaw gibed,
set upon by many,
out-laughed his grinning wounds.

The rain has won this barn,
the wind throws back the door
and looks you in the eye;
'If you marry me
I'll win the Nobel Prize!'

Akureyri

An Irish Viking built
a shrine upon this site;
a thousand winters gone,
his bones are shingle here,
his blood runs in my veins.

The town boys fish and dream
of Malaga hotels.
Their cod is abbey silver,
their beach digests old nets
and skeletons of boats.

Hoarse the shout at dawn,
a mist takes Eyjafjord,
a trawler's scanner sounds
the wealth of Helgi Magri;
the deeps lap at the shrines.

JENNIFER MAIDEN

Reflected Hearth at Bowen Mountain

This is not a cluster poem.This
is a parallel poem.
Katharine, beautiful as a firelit window
is reflected with her violin, as is
her beautiful violin teacher's fine
kind quirky face. The sky is like
a snow sky, smooth as the crystal hub
in a flame. Breeze tears the treetops.
The primary colours
of someone's neighbouring TV
dance in an upstairs pane, vast glass
where worlds juxtapose unmoved.
If I lean forward
I am in the window, but the fireplace
with its stove and chimney dominates
as if the outside bush were made to frame it,
not just its reflection. The tree boles
lean on the wind fully-charactered
like those by a river, like firewood
in this fire. The sky is not grey but
colourless-cold and vibrant-cold with power.
The fire
in the glass is clearly somehow beyond
the glass. The twin violin bows move
in the glass so there are four, the two
songs, one a jig, become four, yet the black
reflective chamber, the chamber of reflection
in the night glass has silence, even

the woodsmoke smell has a dark
freezing mountain silence in it. Then, too,
even the wind makes no noise, not even in
its real, rough, tuneless thump which is
happening and is one of life's most sudden
noises, like an earthquake's quick door slam.
The bush world, nevertheless, beyond
the stove-starred window is nothing like a door.
It allows no entrance and no exit, reflects
all but is not deflective. Reflects all?
But now the big window pane
is surprisingly selective: reflects
only some objects from the room. The fireplace
like all fire in glass seems ungrounded
and hovers in air. Looking at
the fireplace itself I realise that all
fireplace fires follow laws like mountains
in their natural arrangement. The little
flickering fire mountains have the rhythm
of the mountain winds ouside and, too,
there are redgold landforms, yellow
caves in which one's childhood tried
to see small fire-spirits, the land
in the grate so intricate in flux that
the trees in the window flicker like
the hearth. The light on the violins, however,
is the colour of ironbark honey, not
yellow, not fire. There is no merger.
There is the glass, the room, the woodsmoke
in and out, the falling night, which
doesn't fall because night as always
clambers up from the earth with a

flickering, smoky smell that has a glassy,
glacial clarity, a silent sound.   And I believe no sounds
but two distinct violins, one new and deep,
the other practised, lively.
This poem is a parallel poem.

PHILIP NEILSEN

The Conservative Forest

for Bruce Dawe

This is a family-values forest. The red-checked table cloth
is spread on grass where the canopy has been removed.
The sun shines as required, a hygienic space to celebrate
freedom, strong government, luminous freeways.

The elitists wanted this closed to ordinary people,
and left for soap-fearing ferals, anti-social bushwalkers.
But now it is accessible, with tables made of eucalypt,
trees making a contribution, in full employment.

Long gone is the anarchy of wilderness, the over-excited mind.
Discipline is learned from a neat row of firs, a line of swings
under the Big Axe. The kids, Andrew and Emma, draw houses
with chimney smoke on paper the wood-chips have provided.

But do not relax. Be wary of seductive tunes from the foliage,
of horns and pipes, dangerous nymphs with plausible stories.
They whisper of peace won without cost in blood.
They meddle with gender and leave the young confused.

See them in jester's cloaks, their hair like snakes,
lodged in tree tops or introspective undergrowth,

cursing the honest toil of chainsaw and bulldozer,
the strong orange arms, the friendly giants.

At night you may hear gentle keening, the pioneers whose
prayers and sweat cleansed the scrub, made the ground
sweet for cattle and wheat, braved the savages and gypsies,
carved an asylum under stars for those who followed.

Today is a reunion, mum in her apron, children with toy guns,
dad will polish the four wheel drive. The park awaits our return,
invites us to enjoy the fruits of our labours. Sausages and wine,
the glow of the sacred barbecue. A fire to reflect our hunger.

RICHARD TIPPING

SOFT RIOTS / TV NEWS

6pm july 4

theyre marching on the american consulate

be/cause

theres nowhere else to go

its cold in the city   wind off the water
trains on time

marching
marching for
marching for reasons

in adelaide a man takes off his coat
in melbourne a woman sits down and sighs
in sydney a man changes channels
in brisbane its windy southwest change maximum 25

THE CAMERAMEN ARE READY action
action
the spotlit streets action
spit back cats cars action

a spearhead of radicals bearing red flags urged
on and led by other radicals a drawing of the prime
minister was also burned a petition police wielding
batons kicked and punched 1000 independence day
ball with 99 arrested and constable green hit by
a stone & allowed to leave

i tell ya jude
you cant beat the sheriff

che che che che
che guevara
che che guevara
che che che guevara
che che guevara
che

angelic hip christ holding
bulletholes to his poems :
crucified dead & buried
after three days he didnt
rise / no rock rolled back

who live out your lives
who live out your lives
in darkness
in darkness

a match
three butts
ashes all
on a box
of pins

the police were unable to find a motive for the killing.
they suggested three alternatives :

READY

up against the wall
they pin the target
to your chest & share
your last cigarette

up against the wall
clawing at

AIM

spotlights arclight gutteral swing bark
blinding the wire ripping through your outstretched
fingers tearing at your machinegun gut gut to
shredding clothes a shirt flagged above bones the
wire flashing with the sun wire barbs gaa sssh ing

when i shut my eyes its dark in my brain

zzzooooooooooooomm shot
reversed to full screen
panoramic wall

strung by the hungry prisons of

FIRE

click

goodnight melbourne
lights out adelaide
brisbane shut your eyes
sydney
see you in the morning

JOHN FORBES

Death: An Ode

Death, you're more successful than America,
even if we don't choose to join you, we do.
I've just become aware of this conscription
where no one's marble doesn't come up;
no use carving your name on a tree, exchanging vows
or not treading on the cracks for luck
where there's no statistical anomalies at all
& you know not the day nor the hour, or even if you do
timor mortis conturbat me. No doubt we'd
think this in a plunging jet & the black box recorder
would note each individual, unavailing scream
but what gets me is how compulsory it is –
'he never was a joiner' they wrote on his tomb.
At least bingeing becomes heroic & I can see

why the Victorians
so loved drawn-out death-bed scenes:
huddled before our beautiful century, they knew
what first night nerves were all about.

Ode to Doubt

Luminous substrate
our views are just a veneer on, or like
the slats in a venetian blind
changing with the weather or the mood I'm in –
without you the light drones behind our heads
and we know what the world is like
or better be, if it wants to avoid
the pious grindstone of our self-regard
and tho' certainty has its saints,
to just step outside with you, like drinking
considered as experience,
would make their good deeds nobler
                                        and, if nothing else,
abolish hagiography as a genre
(not to mention theories of reflection
and the clear-eyed luxury of teenage beliefs –
America's tribute to your absence).
We stand to be corrected & sit down unassuaged
because of you. You keep us modest
like the stones I used to shift around as a kid
assuming they needed a change of view. That
was the closest I got to playing God,
as if each brick had a message wrapped around it
or, vice-versa, the world was a fake parcel
                                        with each layer of tissue

gauzy, ornate & gorgeous, keeping us from you.
Blanchot says, 'at the moment of death
we each experience our life as a lie', so
no wonder dying is important to believers.
With you that shade is always there & we become
a happy extension of the rocks & trees,
                                        no longer certain
but a part of what we know.

Love Poem

Spent tracer flecks Baghdad's
bright video game sky

as I curl up with the war
in lieu of you, whose letter

lets me know my poems show
how unhappy I can be. Perhaps.

But what they don't show, until
now, is how at ease I can be

with military technology: e.g.
matching their *feu d'esprit* I classify

the sounds of the Iraqi AA – the
thump of the 85 mil, the throaty

chatter of the quad ZSU 23.
Our precision guided weapons

make the horizon flash & glow
but nothing I can do makes you

want me. Instead I watch the west
do what the west does best

& know, obscurely, as I go to bed
all this is being staged for me.

ANDREW SANT

Mussolini's Umbrella

For now the umbrella
will be banned from the house
as a traitor to rugged
complexions. *Ombrello* –
little shadow; too cute,
mused Il Duce, amid
this century's downpour
of bullets. It rises
abruptly as the national debt
and parades street to street
as a weakness. Let there be
hailstorms, heat, thunder
like jackboots striding
terrible skies; let
them bravely flush out
from cupboard or carboot
this conspicuous wretch
which given speech and
a dig in the ribs might confess
his dandy cheek is the
similitude of a rose
or a peach. Exile
this pansy to wasteland

or the muteness of movies;
seek it if it's stalled
in a cavernous hallway
like a tropical bat –
for it is the downfall
of national weather
and shelters a shadow
where there should be a lout.

PHILIP SALOM

Barbecue of the Primitives

They stand in a roughish circle: a row of backs,
a muddling Stonehenge, half tourist,
half ritual. As the fire is carried out
in boxes, a male and dormant thing, assembled
from clinking cylinders, thin pipes
curling like snakes into the coupling place,
hissing until the match bomps them into flame.
The hot air pouts and silkens,
or crimps like someone beaming down in Star Trek.
The red portable ovens, standing
like UFOs and calling the wilderness
to sit around with its own ether blue as flame.

It pre-empts the liquor, and perhaps the light,
both will fall on the picnickers
like something strong, pre-figuring.
If the city stands fifty dry kilometres
towards the coast, under the radiation
of what it means to be human: this ether of bush
hits them like the weightless falling

of neutrinos, passing through without sensation,
like silent speech. But

only teeth will beam them back
to being primal, and the firejuice of steaks.
It is the only time they give up speech.
They eat, as far above the sky convulses
outward to the tufted body of an eagle
high on ozone and lean entirety of hunger.

Like pets, the cars sit under trees
or curl into their gloss out in the heat.
The insects now seem utterly demented:
each beat a coin in the air's strict metre.
Something is being counted off, by ones.

NICOLETTE STASKO

Dislocation

Each year
my sister sends
a calendar
for Christmas
I use it to keep track
of the days
neat parcels
of time measured
in square inch boxes
I note the names of holidays
we no longer celebrate here
like survivors of a shipwreck
we have forgotten

our visions of home
replaced them
with horizons of ocean
unfamiliar skies
and sun
sorting through
salvaged cargo
for clues

PETER BOYLE

Where the Roads Go After Nightfall

Sometimes a road bends in darkness,
bends from the sheer weight of travelling
across the line into night.
The river hurled under you,
like a great doubt below bridges,
may be there or not.
The stars curve away
and all that life meant –
the naked sweetness of the sky –
disappears with the vanished signposts.
So still, the most distant hills
and the earth just in front of you are one.
You stand on a different path then,
getting used to the empty sky
as it wraps itself about you,
getting used to the worm food,
to the blindness of walking without eyes.
The rush the dead must feel
bleeds suddenly into you

and the unimaginable grows inside you
as a fire can burn for years inside itself
giving out only darkness.

Lonelier worlds stretch endlessly out there:
your feet have taken their first step
into that space:
where the roads go after nightfall.

CHARLES BUCKMASTER

Wilpena Pound

– Where we had stood
at the peak of the mountain
and had first noticed   that we were
inside.

below us, the pass, and about us
a circle of mountains:
red aside orange
the rocks
laced with colour.

and the bushland below
'so dense, in some areas'

– she had said,

'that one can barely pass through it'

The Pound – originally,
a depressed plateau, the centre
having eroded, leaving a natural enclosure

– a plain
circled by mountains.

Where we had stood
by the groupings of boulders, inside the Pound

spread on the rocks, exhausted
by the climb

facing west, toward the sun, the miles
of forest against mountain

the isolation!

winding track, below
through the pass

– the way to the Outside.

Mordor – the mountains –
in the 'other world'.

'This is our home, the place
of our people'

she said
without realizing . . .
'to think that we could
climb down that path, into the forest,
to the centre of the Pound

and never
return again'.

(Taking up your axe – the trees
for your home

. . . at some unmarked spring – bathing your child
in the water of the mountains

. . . Gardens about your cabin

. . . Within the voice of the forest . . .)

This circle of mountains! – a natural
and an un-natural
isolation.

'The tribes of the Ranges
were exterminated'. (Poisoned flour,
'Aborigine Shoots' –
'near here, a massacre, in the 1880s:'
said John.

And for this! –

The Pound stretches twelve miles
– twelve miles of heavily forested plain
thinning on all sides against the mountains.
About and around the centre – the remains of the lost;
where few men have been.
Twelve miles of complete/the final
isolation.

And I had little else to give but love:
now, there is that which we shall take from you,
this land, being
our land:

there is reason for many to be bitter – this land,
your pastures
stained with blood from dark-skinned wounds.

Land of clouds; from the forest and pick up the spear
which fell
from the hand of my brother
as he died
a century past.

Though you refuse our offer; understand, father:
My brothers and I are of the forest
and we are of its nature more fully than you

– the forest
is our home father:
the battle to be fought is our self-preservation.

. . . And I take up that weapon and return
to the hunt.

Sunset. To the west, etched
in a sky of all colour – a lone tree against light:

and to the north, the Pound: a circle of fire.

STEPHEN EDGAR

Ulysses Burning

This room is the darkened theatre. Through the glass
The white veranda frames the stage
Like a proscenium. Garden, street and beach,
River and mountain, layer on layer, reach
Out to the backdrop of the sky
Before which all must pass that has to pass.

The river with its diamond-crusted gloss:

A Petri dish of gel in which
A culture of the sun is flourishing.
On the mountain, which aspires to Monet, cling
Veiled glares, some squeegee smears of cloud.
A creeper on the trellis hangs across

The wall of water, mountain, sky, as though
Its tendrils twined through them, as their
Confection oozes through the lattice squares.
Far out, one lone vermilion sailboard flares,
A soul whose punishment's to flee
The bliss he's riding on, who seems to slow

The vagrant eye to focus, or pulse on
The shuttered eyelid's blindness, less
Impelled to motion by the wind's weak force
Than by some fanciful odylic source;
Or simply, like a solar panel
Prompted with light, pushed by the moving sun.

I look. The people I take in take in
The view they partly constitute.
What here can last the longest? The mountain slopes
Vanish behind the glaze like fading hopes,
Lapsed concentration. The river burns
Away to a vapour. Prickings of a pin,

The glitter points are whiting out my sight.
Two couples amble by, and sun,
Firing the women's dresses, rouses me.
Like spirits out of Dante's *Comedy*
The walking flames sway past, their forms
Wrapped in a fabric of ignited light

Within which step their shadows. As they glide,
They still cling to the view, and I
To them, while brilliant day devours us, body
And sight. And though desire would make them tardy,
They must proceed towards the frame
And disappear as on a pushing tide.

On the river's silver terrace ride remote
Translucent sails of wind-slow yachts,
Combusting in this last declension of
The sun, in motion scarcely seen to move,
Like more of Dante's walking flames,
Ulysses burning, statically afloat.

PETER GOLDSWORTHY

Suicide on Christmas Eve

After the doctor, the steam-cleaners,
more usefully. I drive home to bed
through intersections sequined with glass:
it's Christmas Eve, season of donor organs.

What is the meaning of life? I shake you
gently awake. What answer would satisfy?
you mumble, yawning, from Your Side.
To understand is to be bored, you say,
practising, perhaps, for Speech Night.
Knowledge is a kind of exhaustion, you say.

A child enters our room: is it morning yet?
Not Yet. In another room the lights of the Tree
wink colourfully, and when the telephone rings
again, it is almost, but not quite, in time.

JILL JONES

The 7.17 Silver Machine

Adamstown platform slicks by
rain and night chill, the sparky track.
I'm wired for sound
lucky as heroin boy on the radio
psychedelic, pure and unengaged
apart from electricity skating the rails –
Kotara, Fassifern – and the kids
in pink kicking their cherub runners.
And *hey buddy*, watch that friction
feel the breath of the hawk wind
past Gosford, a floodlit Hyundai lullaby
where each house is an island
yellow out in the dark.
Blonde legs the catwalk of the carriage
I long for her sleepy slide
while our lady of dreams curls up
in green blanket and as her hair hangs down
in the aisle, I'm losing my opinion
the voyeur's defence.
I want to say something like an acoustic guitar
want to slow down, throw away the phone
but we are racing time and track work
as the splayed out, the curved and embryonic lurch
towards dark Sydney – the dome, the nipple
the snow white breasts of midnight
waiting till we step down in the light
and a profusion of shaggy and baggage
our names still manifest.

But now is the hurry
spittle of angels ripples the windows
flecking our ride in a silver machine.

Π.Ο.

Yoori

Yoori is
the greatest painter (in the
World). He lives
in a boarding-House in
Gore St. Fitzroy.
He moved in
about 3 months after
his accident;
And 2 years on
is still a-waiting the Courts;
You can see him
walking into the Albanian joint
across the road;
Or an hour later into ours (or the Turkish
Club next door).
He comes
into the shop
with a large folder (about
once a week);
Sits down by himself
and orders a coffee.
For $5 he'll
draw your portrait
and for 20 he'll paint it.

The others (around the
table) are allowed to look on
and talk; That is,
provided they don't make
too much noise.
His 'style'
can only be described
as being
somehow some-way towards
some mok-Greko-Slav-cum-icon-discipline;
Not too good on foreheads;
Too fat;
Toooo pink;
and somehow two-dimensional;
But REAL
nevertheless (I mean:)
you can tell
who it's suppose to depict.
Anyhow! They like
how he draws;
They roll'em-Up in lackerbands
and take 'em home
to stick-Up on the wall.
Yoori (meanwhile)
is silent; And modest (like an artist
should be);
And when they
give him his money,
he takes it; Like he's earned it!
And never
hangs around too long;

π.ο.

To keep
his talent
sacred.

ANIA WALWICZ

Australia

You big ugly. You too empty. You desert with your nothing nothing nothing. You scorched suntanned. Old too quickly. Acres of suburbs watching the telly. You bore me. Freckle silly children. You nothing much. With your big sea. Beach beach beach. I've seen enough already. You dumb dirty city with bar stools. You're ugly. You silly shoppingtown. You copy. You too far everywhere. You laugh at me. When I came this woman gave me a box of biscuits. You try to be friendly but you're not very friendly. You never ask me to your house. You insult me. You don't know how to be with me. Road road tree tree. I came from crowded and many. I came from rich. You have nothing to offer. You're poor and spread thin. You big. So what. I'm small. It's what's in. You silent on Sunday. Nobody on your streets. You dead at night. You go to sleep too early. You don't excite me. You scare me with your hopeless. Asleep when you walk. Too hot to think. You big awful. You don't match me. You burnt out. You too big sky. You make me a dot in the nowhere. You laugh with your big healthy. You want everyone to be the same. You're dumb. You do like anybody else. You engaged Doreen. You big cow. You average average. Cold day at school playing around at lunchtime. Running around for nothing. You never accept me. For your own. You always ask me where I'm from. You always ask me. You tell me I look strange. Different. You don't adopt me. You laugh at the way I speak. You think you're better than me. You don't like me. You don't have any interest in another country. Idiot centre of your own self. You think the rest of the world walks around without shoes or electric light. You don't go anywhere. You stay at home. You like one another. You go crazy on Saturday night. You get drunk. You don't like me and you don't like women. You put your arm around men in bars. You're rough. I can't speak to you. You burly burly. You're just silly to me. You big man. Poor with all your money. You ugly furniture. You ugly house. Relaxed in your summer stupor. All year. Never fully awake. Dull at school. Wait for other people to tell you what to do. Follow the leader. Can't imagine. Work horse. Thick legs. You go to work in the morning. You shiver on a tram.

Little Red Riding Hood

I always had such a good time, good time, good time girl. Each and every day from morning to night. Each and every twenty-four hours I wanted to wake up, wake up. I was so lively, so livewire tense, such a highly pitched little. I was red, so red so red. I was a tomato. I was on the lookout for the wolf. Want some sweeties, mister? I bought a red dress myself. I bought the wolf. Want some sweeties, mister? I bought a red dress for myself. I bought a hood for myself. Get me a hood. I bought a knife.

DAVID BROOKS

The Cold Front

It was coming

the cold front
and the complex weather

we returned
and the difficult loves were waiting

the long conversations
with pain in the final sentences

winter
gathering her parcel for the victory

stones, feathers, bottles
brimming with light

the troops
breaking in through the syllables

the empty cups
sitting before us in the snow

this
like all the others

a lullaby

a few grains of salt at the centre

CHRIS MANSELL

Definition Poem: Pissed as a Parrot

For those of you who are etomylogically inclined
I would like to take this opportunity
to explain to you the derivation of the expression
pissed as a parrot.

Sidney Baker in *The Australian Language* indexes
    Paroo Dog
    Parrot
    Parson's pox
There is no entry under *pissed.*
He also gives
    Proverbial, come the
    Piss, panther's
and Pseudoxy.

Parrot on page 55 is a sheep
which has lost some of its wool
If the sheep's fly-blown it's a rosella.

Wilkes in his *Australian Dictionary of Colloquialisms*
lists only to piss in someone's pocket
(refer Kylie Tennant, Bray, Hardy & Herbert)
Pissant around (Dymphna Cusack)
and Pissant, game as a.
There is no mention of any parrot in any condition at all.

In *Collins English Dictionary* (Australian Edition)
you will find definitions for
    piss
    piss about

Pissaro
piss artist
and piss off.

Parrots appear in their psittaciformes capacity
which I found meant having a short hooked bill,
compact body, bright plumage, and an ability to mimic.
It was not entirely clear whether this referred to birds.

Parrot-fashion had nothing to do with anything.

Roget's *Thesaurus*
Nuttal's *Dictionary of Synonyms and Antonyms*
Stillman's *Poets Manual and Rhyming Dictionary*
Webster's *Treasury of Synonyms, Antonyms and Homonyms*
and the *Shorter Oxford English Dictionary*
were no help at all.

I thought *Usage & Abusage*
being by Partridge
could be illuminating, but it appears
that neither piss nor parrots are abused.

I refused to consult Strunk's *Elements of Style*
on the grounds that on the backcover blurb
has quotes from the *Greensboro Daily News*
and *The Telephone Engineers and Management Journal*.

But I went to afternoon tea
in the School of Chemistry at the University of Sydney
at 4 pm on Thursday 6 November
and there, Dr A.R. Lacey, physical chemist, MSc Phd,
informed me, in his capacity as a true blue,
down to earth, dinky-di, grass roots Aussie that

when working on his horse study in the Wingecarribee Shire
he had observed that Gang Gang cockatoos
fall with paralytic suddenness
from the branches of Hawthorn bushes
after ingesting the berries.

Incredibly, *The Reader's Digest Complete Book of Australian*
Birds
makes no mention of this.

KEVIN HART

Gypsophila

Another day with nothing to say for itself –
Gypsophila on the table, a child's breath
When breath is all it has to name the world

And therefore has no world. It must be made:
Her shadow sleeping on the wall, the rain
That pins fat clouds to earth all afternoon,

A river playing down the piano's scales.
This is the strangest of all possible worlds
With foam upon the beach, the sea's dead skin,

And lighting quietly resting in each eye.
Like gypsy camps or love, it must be made,
Undone, then made again, like the chill rain

That falls without hope of climbing back,
Content to leave its mark, for what it is,
Upon the window or in the child's mind.

Gypsophila on the table, rain outside,
The child will tune the world to her desire
And make another world to keep in mind:

These breaths of air in which we softly wrap
The rain's glass stems to let them fall again
In sunlight, or flower for ever in the mind.

A world of things with nothing at all to say,
A margin that absorbs our silences:
The child must take the lighting from her eye

And place it in the sky, her shadow must
Be told to fall asleep. This strangest world
In which we say *Gypsophila, Baby's breath* –

Father

Some nights fat Death heaves up to me
And wheezes, 'Now your Father's here,'
And, if I can, I squint to see
All those he has in tow back there

And then some nights I can't resist
And chat about the dead this year
And, if I can, stretch out a fist
And filch a little mouse all fear

And then mad Death lays down the law
And drags out Dad for me to see
And I reach out a bony claw
And watch him pull him back from me

DOROTHY PORTER

Bluebottles

In living there is always
the terror
of being stung

of something
coming for you
on the unavoidable wave.

In living there is always
the terror
of the alien boneless
thing

of something
blue
coming for you
from the blue and salty sea
spat
on your bare and shrinking
skin.

In living there is always
the terror
of the poison finding
your heart

of something
whose stingers
will stretch over you

like stars
with an ancient burning
patience.

PMT

The moon is out this morning.
Full,
        and the yellow
             of old dentures.
Nothing like a moon
        in a fastidious T'ang poem
it stares through
        the mist, the traffic, my windscreen,
like a mesmerising chilblain.

The radio is a box of 'Fantales';
        gossip, rubbish
              and caramel.
I chew on it
thinking about
              my long weekend
              my lover's delectable mouth.
But the moonlight
        splashes on my driving hands
              like freezing water
and I count my jerky heart-beats
             backwards.

JAVANT BIARUJIA

Georges Braque

a curmurring deadened by cotton wool escapes
it renounces clouds as useless pretension
it has never left a lucumo in a cramp
mawbound in its wool
it has never had numbles

moist cow putty breezes past the sea lion
thewy whaups and whimbrels say aye
belles laides only know how to say i
to tequilla to tragopans
and cool rosé auks on pedestals

a grotesque humming yelt crits a krummhorn luff
it shrewdly embowels emblic fruits
like emboxed fewtrils
embailed like the merry wives of Cremorne
and solemn lubbards in love

JENNIFER HARRISON

Funambulist

Coins fill the busker's hat;
it's true, a thief will steal from the blind.
Satellites spin delicate journeys
in the woods above. Space

the guestroom we never had.
Malleable, down below,
in the mute neon between streets,
we've touched only the details of maps.

Believing ourselves beamed upon,
we script new mercy themes
and here are the things I carry:
a silver bell, a desk, a lock of hair,

some laurel flowers, a lantern,
a *bonbonnière*, three scarves,
a black cat, a peacock, a box of rain,
a streak of lightning,

a ladder, a pipe, a coffin, a fan,
a pumpkin, a skull, a book of law.
Believing myself beamed upon,
I carry one clap of thunder, some shrimps

and a globe, a bag of nails, a carton of *crème*,
a roly-poly of doves.
I carry the city, the cleft mirror,
the faked fight of the fist on the drum.

PETER ROSE

Rattus Rattus

Even at midnight
the pontiff's window is open,
framing the next blessing or admonition.

Combing the colonnade
late tourists shop for symbols.

In the square
a thousand chairs
pray to a vacant altar.

Chesty bells convulse a dozen times.
'Electric', you mutter.

Amputees put away
their disabilities and dream.

Handsome carabinieri
erect barriers to Bernini's scheme.

Beside each column
a metal detector
radiates our nothingness.

Following the Tiber home,
footsore and fascinated,
we watch a stupendous rat,
bigger than a monstrance,
mapping the slimy historic bank.

OUYANG YU

Moon Over Melbourne

in a night without time
when I mourn over the loss of
an ancient Chinese poem
a thousand years ago about now

but moon over melbourne
that knows nothing of *that*
a young one just 200 seconds old
with a man-made light that is not only cold

you mooch over melbourne
in an air-conditioned mood

how is it you look so bloody australian
so i-wouldn't-care-less tonight?

you have driven so many poets crazy in China
over the centuries
Li Bai with your nostalgic light at his bedstead
Li Yu with emotions so entangled he could hardly cut them loose
because of you
Du Fu with you surging in the mid-stream of the yangtze
Wen Tingyun with you in a frosty cock-crowing morning
Wang Wei with you shining through the pine trees
Zhang Ji with you down at midnight full of frost and the
    arriving of a passenger boat
ouyang yu with you wandering lonely across a heavenly desert

moon over melbourne you bloody australian moon
you hang on you all right you no worries mate
you make me sick home sick

you put every body to a multicultural sleep
who know not what it means by
one dancing with oneself and one's shadow under you

so contented with sharing the feeling
of planting proudly the rag of a flag
among your rocks

never mind their colonising instinct
for they lose you as soon as they touch you
tonight you belong to me

the Chinese are so poetically cheap
remember they say thousands of years ago in a poem:

for all the breeze and moon I get I don't need to spend a penny

the happiest are not the expensive

you are long colonised by us, by me
caught with lyrical lines
tamed with sleeplessness
Sinicized in a single character: 月

moon over melbourne
you can't stop drunken engines
the weekend rage on a.b.c
the nameless night bird screeching grotesquely

moon over melbourne
mourn over melbourne
for the irretrievable poems lost to you
for the sleepy souls who wouldn't care less
for the nights that are so displaced here
for the dogs that bark so loyally

for me
for me
who refuse to go out again
dreading the sight of you
dreading the slightest suggestion of a memory
dreading so bloody dreading to see
the bloody bastard moon

over melbourne

JUDITH BEVERIDGE

The Domesticity of Giraffes

She languorously swings her tongue
like a black leather strap as she chews
and endlessly licks the wire for salt
blown in from the harbour.
Bruised-apple eyed she ruminates
towards the tall buildings
she mistakes for a herd:
her gaze has the loneliness of smoke.

I think of her graceful on her plain –
one long-legged mile after another.
I see her head framed in a leafy bonnet
of balloon-bobbing in trees.
Her hide's a paved garden of orange
against wild bush. In the distance, running
she could be a big slim bird just before flight.

Here, a wire-cripple –
legs stark as telegraph poles
miles from anywhere.
She circles the pen, licks the wire,
mimics a gum-chewing audience
in the stained underwear of her hide.
This shy Miss Marigold rolls out her tongue

like the neck of a dying bird.
I offer her the fresh salt of my hand
and her tongue rolls over it
in sensual agony, as it must

over the wire, hour after bitter hour.
Now, the bull indolently
lets down his penis like a pink gladiolus
drenching the concrete.

She thrusts her tongue under his rich stream
to get moisture for her thousandth chew.

The Shark

We heard the creaking clutch of the crank
as they drew it up by cable and wheel
and hung it sleek as a hull from the roof.

Grennan jammed open the great jaws
and we saw how the upper jaw hung from
the skull. We flinched at the stench of blood

that dripped on the fishhouse floor, and
even Davey – when Grennan reached in
past the scowl and the steel prop for the

stump – just about passed out. The limb's
skin had already blanched, a sight none
of us could stomach, and we retched –

though Grennan, cool, began cutting off
the flesh in knots, slashing off the flesh
in strips; and then Davey, flensing and

flanching, opened up the stomach and
the steaming bowels. Gulls circled like
ghouls. Still they taunt us with their cries

and our hearts still burn inside us when
we remember, how Grennan, with a tool,
took out what was left of the child.

S. K. KELEN

Atomic Ballet

Like integers that deal with themselves
and each other   market forces

make smarmy bastards rich for no real reason
wipe whole families off the slate

who head for mean streets
as the old man's made redundant

bank managers shake their heads
at all the fibro they've inherited

and fate wrapped messily in newsprint . . .
Ah, living under the triffid's whip

wonder where the strange disease came from?
Released from a satellite launched by our taxes.

The mass media entertain with the latest
movements of the atomic ballet.

GIG RYAN

Swoons

She tells of her swoons
many and varied, smitten and occult
and then the wholesome novelist's parents appear, endearingly
and play their squeamish assessment
Green necklace, the sad viola focuses
Drums accompany the shot of the window

You look the future in the artery
You look love in the foot
enjoying the emptiness
as the no-story play's women skeet and blip
The meaning of her song, frayed and timely,
slats through the personality's dull work
in a sorority of fame

How should I capture the blue newspapers
the hanging cords

Travel

Birds waver and spear through the hotel window
Trees majestic and brushed
in the streets of Morocco
or the plains of Troy
If you gave me a mountain
His faded hands throw the poems away
The great trees flick in the courtyard
and shallow tram tracks mossed
Snowing fir tree, laced with dust

Broken flowers
in the airport's smoked limbo
You stick with those you hurt
His fuchsia dress, empanelled and cohesive
inert as a stump
Dollar-obsessed pragmatist
baking in your landscaped garden
You kiss the cigarette's fund
Greetings in Dutch

SARAH DAY

Antarctic Ships

A tawdry brass band extracts too much emotional mileage.
The usual streamers span the gap –
slack, then tightening to a tug on the heart
at either end – the intrepid and those farewelling them
at the freight docks of Hobart's port.

Rust-repellent orange or vermilion
these ships have to be noticed
in southern seas
where waves rise mythically
and icesheets creep insidiously towards June.

The names, *Aurora Australis, L'Astrolabe,*
called on curiously from the skies, are irresistible.
And so is the destination. You want to be up there too
waving goodbye to the known from the decks,
heading off to landscapes of perpetual whiteness.

That titled vision has some allure – the thirty-degree list,
The bloodstopping notion of deep green fathoms

above which these tubs valiantly ferry
like little emblems of life itself.
Who knows mortality like a sailor?

Unable to see near distance
the seekers return from sea, ice and frozen sky
and you are envious of the point
on which their sights are set,
the diminished gravity of the close-up.

And you want to go where those forklifters
sitting dormant up there on the decks
have been. You want to vault over the rail,
seize some of the clay that's stuck to the grill
in the palm of your hand.

LIONEL FOGARTY

Jukambe Spirit – For the Lost

Jukambe
Don't we all have your spirit
Bleed sores between teeth
Feeding lighting rocks
My Jukambe will devote, come giant shelter.
My distant Jukambe host a tribe
I'm with your journey standing tall striped away
felt intervals for coastal Murris
are relation to Yoogum Yoogum.
How several mountains came
one loving brainy social wantness
Yea Jukambe fruit a result
But most us live city private

our knowing each cone is lumped
killing important
My tribe were among white mans ownership
grouped they claimed on Jukambe tear
and distant areas
Roasted raw the bunya nut
unripened ceremonies
initiation coming over elaborated wide territories
now massed by houses and sales
my people nutritious a seed
and brings boils over their bodies
if they wanta get unsick
Nature, Jukambe might tell or lend.
Collectively my people now
I don't see at grassland or hill creek track
where Jukambe worked and played.
Yea my some communication, still many tribespeople
dialect young and old, not sold.
Yea, bunya pines brighten old Jukambe members Yoogum.
individual; to keep children Yoogum
The stories, bodies and mind, exact
cause hard telling all youse
Jukambe is my people, cause white mans name taken place
Relived, I am. In your spirit, Jukambe.
29/11/82

I am Not Santa

Black santa is sad cos he found he's sacked
The Christmas has come again
messing up the family's saving

The kids at school sing praises
of a silent holy night and a
tree to be cut down for presents
And they wait for the big red
bearded white santa man to
come down the chimney
And they think this is true
but the jingle media suck dem
in to buy everything at high price.
And what the black parent
say to their childrens is, who
the bloody hell is christ coming
here and stealing our culture
with deer and sledges?
Then you all turn and sing
merry christmas, well this
is a profit making business
for the rich, don't you know childs?
Christmas destroy the poor
and it's a fake unto happiness
Christmas is against the Murri
belief cos it celebrate one man
birth and not all men.
Sure you'll get me to a black santa
but remember I'm just cringe
inside cos you're too young
to explain the political cultural
sad oppressed nature this so-called
xmas caused to our people before.
And even right here, the image of
santa forgets neglects the poor dark
childrens even white kids, why?

cos santa is the capitalist who's there to
fool you and drain your dad and mum of
every money they have.
Now how can you be merry when your
cuz relative got nothing or people starving or
people live in bad homes.
How can you merry on
a day when the world is at war for peace.
Well if in your heart you want to be merry then do it every
moon, full star shine and dawn morning
And catch the sun up before SANTA comes and
takes your PRESENTS!

PAUL HETHERINGTON

Skin

What I happen at, I do. It's like a skin
I've gradually put on, testing the fit,
tucking here and there until it seems
the only one I have, or could have grown;
that any clone would step out from its culture
with just these mixed and known proclivities,
standing, walking, speaking in my way.
Impatience, love or quixotic doubt
could each be argued an essential feature
and yet a secret twin would always be
caught up in divergent circumstance –
much like a mirror dissenting from my glance –
and would shift towards increasing distance
slantwise, in his own trajectory.

MERLINDA BOBIS

going ethnic

When I met you,
you even wished to learn
how to laugh in my dialect.

Between the treble of bees
and the deep bass of water buffalos
on TV's 'World Around Us'.
Between the husk and grain of rice
from an Asian shop.
Between my palms
joined earnestly
in prayer,

you searched for a timbre
so quaint,
you'd have to train your ears
forever, you said.

And when I told you how we village girls
once burst the moon with giggles,
you piped, 'That must have been
a thrilling sound,
peculiar, ancient
and really cool –

can't you do that again?'

PHILIP HODGINS

Shooting the Dogs

There wasn't much else we could do
that final day on the farm.
We couldn't take them with us into town,
no-one round the district needed them
and the new people had their own.
It was one of those things.

You sometimes hear of dogs
who know they're about to be put down
and who look up along the barrel of the rifle
into responsible eyes that never forget
that look and so on,
but our dogs didn't seem to have a clue.

They only stopped for a short while
to look at the Bedford stacked with furniture
not hay
and then cleared off towards the swamp,
plunging through the thick paspalum
noses up, like speedboats.

They weren't without their faults.
The young ones liked to terrorize the chooks
and eat the eggs.
Whenever he started doing this
we'd let him have an egg full of chilli paste
and then the chooks would get some peace.

The old one's weakness was rolling in dead sheep.
Sometimes after this he'd sit outside

the kitchen window at dinner time.
The stink would hit us all at once
and we'd grimace like the young dog
discovering what was in the egg.

But basically they were pretty good.
They worked well and added life to the place.
I called them back enthusiastically
and got the old one as he bounded up
and then the young one as he shot off
for his life.

I buried them behind the tool shed.
It was one of the last things I did before
we left.
Each time the gravel slid off the shovel
it sounded like something
trying to hang on by its nails.

MIKE LADD

Junior Football

I like to watch the primary colours clash
and hear the caws beside the boundary line,
the *round the necks!* and *in the backs!*
I like the hawks and bulls and lions
on homemade banners flapping in the wind –
the team 'runners' with arthritic hips,
the car horns from the hill that greet a goal,
collective groans that echo round a miss.
Sweet oranges that grin from plastic buckets,
clouds of liniment in tatty changing rooms,

the smell of mud and grass between the sprigs
that clatter onto concrete like sudden hail.
Half-time: aunts and uncles tong the barbie.
I like the hiss and then sometimes the taste
of sausages spitting their social grease.
Coaches: circled by the teams, philosophic,
or ranting bitter losers who swear at kids.
Umpires: just older than the under fourteens,
or pushing fifty, a kick or two behind the game,
inventing which way to give the frees.
The beer-holding, fag-smoking parents
overweight in Saturday's tracky daks
cheer their progeny surging down the wings.
The rumble of the boots like horses' hooves,
the thump and tumble of the ball –
this high ritual, that lifts suburban roofs.

ADAM AITKEN

Saigon the Movie

James Bond flies into Phuket, which he pronounces
Fukit and this announces the demise
of the colonial era.
My mother sits on the Left Bank, harvesting rice.
The Baron announces his arrival
with a slice of lemon between his teeth and
Panama with razors embedded in its rim, to wear
to restaurants with a view of crossfire.

The iron butterfly folds back her wings, and rests awhile
on the pillows of this city.
But they are soaked

with the formalin of diplomacy
and the perfumes of an irresistible corruption.

Finally the old merchants
dig up their gold and re-invest in a
coat of arms they wire to a security gate.
Guard dogs with degrees, and lap-dog breeds
that do not bark.
Here a childhood made sensitive to bombs,
a kindergarten closed down with prayer,
American linguists in a helicopter, dropping
ration packs of Chicklets and brand new grammar.

KATE LILLEY

My Bad

In the doghouse my date barks back
bite-size annihilation

Behind the door the facts
the jokes of one awaiting trial

Am I under-administration
or beginning to free associate?

Enter the poltergeist girls
with the hands of stenographers

Burning glances at smoko
moaning after lights out

JORDIE ALBISTON

Inventory
(or What to Bring When Setting Up a Colony)

2 Barrels of Tar   700 Grubbing-Hoes
6 Hogsheads of Vinegar   12 Ox-Bows
Augers   Adzes   20 Pit-Saws   Forges
Fish-Hooks   Thousands of Drawers

100 Plains Measures   30 Box-Rules
60 Padlocks   5 Sets of Smiths' Tools
1 Bible   40 Barrows   700 Bowls
700 Clasp-Knives   Chaldrons of Coal

40 Camp-Kettles   700 Felling Axes
A Dozen Tin Saucepans   700 Hatches
6 Pounds of Spices   50 Hay-Forks
14 Fishing-Nets   Loads of Salt-Pork

6 Harpoons   50 Puncheons of Bread
1 Loom for Canvas   200 Canvas Beds
Shoe Leather   Iron Shovels   10,000
Bricks   3 Dozen Flat Iron Candlesticks

Scissors   Stockings   Spindles   Caps
1 New Machine for the Dressing of Flax
Handkerchiefs   Harnesses   Hinges and
Hooks   Pins   Pincers   1 Prayer-Book

Ploughs   Petticoats   Pounds of Sewing-
Twine   Canteens   Combs   Coils of
Whale-Line   Hackles   Hats   Handfuls
of Nails   The surplus of England's gaols

LISA BELLEAR

Women's Liberation

Talk to me about the feminist movement,
the gubba middle class
hetero sexual revolution
way back in the seventies
when men wore tweed jackets with
leather elbows, and the women, well
I don't remember or maybe I just don't care
or can't relate.
Now what were those white women on about?
What type of neurosis was fashionable back then?
So maybe I was only a school kid; and kids, like women,
have got one thing that joins that schemata,
like we're not worth listening to,
and who wants to liberate women and children
what will happen in an egalitarian society
if the women and the kids start becoming complacent
in that they believe they should have rights
and economic independence,
and what would these middle class kids and white women do
with liberation, with freedom, with choices of
do I stay with my man, do I fall in love with other
white middle class women, and it wouldn't matter if
my new woman had kids or maybe even kids and dogs
Yes I'm for the women's movement
I want to be free and wear dunlop tennis shoes.
And indigenous women, well surely, the liberation
of white women includes all women regardless . . .
It doesn't, well that's not for me to deal with

I mean how could I, a white middle class woman,
who is deciding how can I budget when my man won't
pay the school fees and the diner's card club simply
won't extend credit.
I don't even know if I'm capable
of understanding
Aborigines, in Victoria?
Aboriginal women, here, I've never seen one,
and if I did, what would I say,
damned if I'm going to feel guilty, for wanting something
better for me, for women in general, not just white
middle class Volvo driving, part time women's studies
students
Maybe I didn't think, maybe I thought women in general
meant, Aboriginal women, the Koori women in Victoria
Should I apologise
should I feel guilty
Maybe the solution is to sponsor
a child through world vision.
Yes that's probably best,
I feel like I could cope with that,
Look, I'd like to do something for our Aborigines
but I haven't even met one,
and if I did I would say
all this business about land rights, maybe I'm a bit
scared, what's it mean, that some day I'll wake up
and there will be this flag, what is it, you know
red, black and that yellow circle, staked out front
and then what, Okay I'm sorry, I feel guilt
is that what I should be shouting
from the top of the rialto building
The women's movement saved me

maybe the 90s will be different.
I'm not sure what I mean, but I know that although
it's not just a women's liberation that will free us
it's a beginning

ALISON CROGGON

The Elwood Organic Fruit and Vegetable Shop

I will go walking in Elwood with my mind as smooth as a
marrow
winking at the unruffled sky throwing its light down for free
letting the gardens exude their well-groomed scents and
thinking everything good
to the Elwood Organic Fruit and Vegetable Shop:
for the counter is democratically in the centre and everyone
smiles
for people go on with the civil business of buying and selling
under the handwritten notices
for bawling children are solaced with grapes and handled to
leave no bruises
for the mangoes are soft yellow thighs and the strawberries are
klaxons of sweetness
for the mignonette purses its frilly lips and snowpeas pout
their discreet bellies and the melons hug their quirky shapes
under their marvellous rinds
for onions ringing their coppery globes and o the silver shallots
and the hairy trumpets of leeks
for the cabbages folding crisp linens and the broccolis
blooming in purple tulles and the dense green skirts of
lettuces,
for peaches like breasts of angels and passionfruits hard and

dark and bursting with seed in your palm
for the dull gold flesh of pontiacs and knotty umbers of yams
and new potatoes like the heels of babies
for the tubs of sweet william and heart-lifting freesias and
orchids damp and beautiful as clitoral kisses
for poignant basil and maiden-haired fennel and prim blue-
lipped rosemary and o! irrepressible mint!
how they nestle up the vegetables, promising them the
fragrance of their ardour!
the marriages which await them! the lips that moisten to meet
them! glorious speech of the earth!

Ode

We were woken too early, before the moths had died in the
streets,
when buds had barely hardened in the frost, when stars are
hurtful
and famished. They took us through gardens and past the halls
where once we had lingered, past the houses and doused
markets.
Our footsteps echoed back like iron. Of course we were
frightened,
that was a given, of course we remembered photographs we
had studied
that then had nothing to do with us. The empty light of
morning
made anything seem possible, even freedom, even God. We
stumbled
on familiar roads, and everything turned away from us,
lamp-posts, windows, signs. They weren't ours any longer.

Even the air
greeted us differently, pinching our skin to wake us from its dreams.

*

Words of course were beyond us. They were what killed us
to begin with. They were taken away from the mouths that loved them
and given to men who worked their sorceries in distant cities,
who said that difficult things were simple now and that simple things
no longer existed. It was hard to find our way, we understood
the tender magic of hands, we knew the magic of things not spoken,
but this was a trick we couldn't grasp. It lifted the world in a clump of glass
and when everything came back down the streets had vanished.
In their places were shoes and clotting puddles and sparking wires
and holes and bricks and other things that words have no words for
and that silence swelling the noise until you can't hear anything at all.

*

It's said that the dead don't dream, but I dream of flowers.
I could dream so many flowers – lilies like golden snow on water,
hyacinths the colours of summer evenings or those amaranths they call

love-lies-bleeding. I dream of none of those. I dream instead
of wind-blown roses that grew in our shabby yard, of daisies
glimpsed through the kitchen window, of marigolds that
glowed
through nets of weed. But most of all, I dream of red anemones
that never grew in my garden. They rise on slender stalks,
their seven-petalled heads bobbing and weaving in the wind.
Wind-flowers, Pliny called them, because they open only in the
wind,
and the wind scatters their petals over every waste in the
world.

LUKE DAVIES

North Coast Bushfires

Reverence. How the afternoon
comes down on you like that.
In a microsleep you can travel
hundreds of metres – into trees
and cars. I thought I would
just close my eyes. After that
it is all pretty random.
The universal joint, the bearing pins.

So I tried to focus on clouds.
They billowed just like anvils.
I smelled smoke long before the cops
closed off the highway.
On backroads the sunlight slanted
through dust and I pictured the roll
of the earth. The sky turned orange.
But everyone had the same idea.

At dusk a black soot filled
the valley where a lone tree stood.
It was like driving through fog, only
it burnt the throat. Then lightning
lit that tree which said, 'I have
grown into a god.' And stray thoughts
were telling me how badly I needed
a motel. Because life is long.

EMMA LEW

The Clover Seed Hex

Once my foot was like a cube of sugar.
I ran deep in the village, playing on a drum,
happy even with the stones on the road.
I swept the air like this with my hand.
Like a dove, but my father was behind me.

The one I took was a poor man, the one
who limped, and it turned out badly.
It is said that a married man and woman
must be like a tomb. There was a stranger
who followed me home also. He put
his eye to the keyhole and looked at me.
He was a man already. I didn't see him.
I turned the water jug over on its mouth.

Men are never afraid. They know everything,
not like women, and in other ways
we have taken their hardness. A woman
has to be fine and weak. He loves her tears.
One man came close to me after a time,

and during the small feast I answered, 'Yes.'
Childlessness can come of dishonour.
In other words, mine was a black deed.

The mothers of the boys are passing
on the opposite side of the street,
the Nile side. They say, 'So-and-so
was ruined because of her.' Let them
talk and pass. I walk in fields
I am unfamiliar with, and it may be that
when I fall down I am under some spell.
In any case, half of beauty is darkness.
Are these things in our hands?

CHARMAINE PAPERTALK-GREEN

Culture Way

Homeswest give ole man
Ebiction notice yesterday
He bin sick long time
Diabetes, kidneys
Homeswest reckon he
Got too many 'lations
Visiting, making big noise
And trouble late at night
He can't tell countryman
'Shoo, shoo,
Go away'
That not his culture
That not his tradition
Where that homeswest ALO now?
That the one should help him

Where the Aboriginal housing mob
To explain cultural ways?

Ole man being shoved back
Anderson street way
That not solve anything
Homeswest must be too lazy
To accept that culture way.

Wanna Be White

My man took off yesterday
With a waagin*
He left me and the kids
To be something in this world
Said he was sick of being
Black, poor and laughed at
Said he wanted to be white
Have better clothes, a flash car
He said me and the kids
Would give him a bad name
Because we are black too
So he left with a waagin

East coast Australian term for 'white woman', derived from 'white gin'.

CRAIG SHERBORNE

Strapper

Cow sucked-up marshy cud,
had chewing gum jaws;
wore a head, a kettle
that steamed in the cold;
made a nest of her legs
and sat on it –
the elephant of birds.

Horse lived in a straw hotel,
had me to pour the oats
for tea, a silver service of tin.
He was something that should
have been horned.
He licked the bottom of his cup
and only made snorts
nor let me take his winter coat.
I'd go to brush away
his dusty sticks, the mud
of journeys, but he shook
and stamped the fist of his hoof.
When I dared, with my muck-sack open,
I carried the bags he dropped at his feet.

M.T.C. CRONIN

The Flower, The Thing

for Greg McLaren

Urgently, now, before us, the flower, the thing,
entered before any window would allow it,
always living, always posthumous, breached
by the world and unabstracted. Give luck
to your eye if you see it, miracle to your nose
if you smell it, and completion to your skin
rubbing the sunset into the flower's hydris sea.
Don't be afraid of looking for the word which
will describe this perfectly for with the help
of the body the world will rise up, catch the wind,
and float to the clear surface of the waiting water.
Do you recall the world? Place your hand
on the place where it was cut from you and you
will know what pushes us to leave meaning.
Do we think, adrift, we will forget or be forgotten?
The flower answers that the mood has decided
its method of flying, its rest. The flower says
I have believed enormously, have you? And so,
the vulture, the hat, the hand, the cobra, the dog,
the sand, the arm, the trail, the reed, the two reeds,
the foot, the bone, the leaving, the basket, the back,
the folded cloth, the jar, the stand, the gold, the rope,
the tether, the sound, the viper with horns and the
sound of these like pins in the throat which are eased
by water . . . and always now, before us, *the thing* . . .

JOHN KINSELLA

Drowning in Wheat

They'd been warned
on every farm
that playing
in the silos
would lead to death.
You sink in wheat.
Slowly. And the more
you struggle the worse it gets.
'You'll see a rat sail past
your face, nimble on its turf,
and then you'll disappear.'
In there, hard work
has no reward.
So it became a kind of test
to see how far they could sink
without needing a rope
to help them out.
But in the midst of play
rituals miss a beat – like both
leaping in to resolve
an argument
as to who'd go first
and forgetting
to attach the rope.
Up to the waist
and afraid to move.
That even a call for help
would see the wheat

trickle down.
The painful consolidation
of time. The grains
in the hourglass
grotesquely swollen.
And that acrid
chemical smell
of treated wheat
coaxing them into
a near-dead sleep.

TRACY RYAN

Hair

The length
of my body is an odd
nudity, what is it
doing there, how
did the hair
get pared down
to just
these patches
we cultivate
like fetishes
meant to excite
when we want
to play animal
or we control
to stress and make
the difference
between sexes

as if otherwise
we couldn't find
ourselves.
I can't force
what once was
to grow now
in a strange season.
I'm caught
between
the dream of befores
that paralyses
and the need
of my own nakedness
which is there,
which is there.

MICHAEL FARRELL

nude descending a liftshaft

she gets up removes her gender which
the mission wont require the nudes initials
arent tattooed as far as past observers
could tell were not privy its happening the
emptiness which freaks out conservatives
with their lift manuals & repertoires of
degas etcetera oh no does the operation
involve violence are the former touts
at bottom sing out nude of descending
vibrations i glanced at such a nude one
night while reading the well moonlite
the twyborn affair i descended into

the underworld of australian fiction
there are many emptinesses give me
the rough teeth the subliminal gums
the open mouth of the pub sloth
i & the visiting execs take the stairs
which afford a view of the empty city
theres nothing significant in this
conversationwise we think the nude
we hear wild animals in footsteps
some things are too heavy to carry
the invisible nude assumes a new
eroticism are there attendants first
aid givers insurance covers calmly
we await the crash with paperbacks
scoffing at the critical remarks
heard from radio news ambulance
workers secretaries so much wasted
ability a thought we read in each
others minds mentally slapping into
fictions our falls & little fetishes

CORAL HULL

Sharpies

we decide to have a picnic/ on the way home from
school/ we settle down/ beneath a council gum/ in
front of someone's frontyard/ diane spreads out a
brown & yellow chequered tea towel/ over december
thistles & hidden bindis/ it is very hot/ the tea
towel is soft against our legs/ our uniforms short/
we have saved half our lunch/ diane's homemade cup

cakes/ with sour mock cream/ half a plastic bottle
of iced red cordial/ a vegemite sandwich on thick
white bread/ two chocolate wheatens wrapped in wax
paper & a soapy orange/ diane has saved her salt 'n'
vinegar chip crumbs/ i liked them the best/ because
that's where the flavour was strongest/ i always
said: save me the crumbs diane/ save me the crumbs/
& she always did/ we picked a quiet street/ off gill
avenue/ in case our parents came looking for us/
more than likely/ it would be diane's parents/ who
were over protective/ & we ate/ & we gossiped/ &
no one bothered us/ & then it was 5.30 p.m./ we packed
up real quick/ & diane went home & got into trouble/
& when i got home/ mum was cleaning the kitchen
blinds/ & she didn't even look at me/ as she asked:
where have you been?/

our primary school relief
teacher/ mrs hay/ tells us/ that she keeps a lot of
cats/ she is fifty years old/ she sits in front of
the class/ her legs wide apart/ & tells us stories/
& we could all see her undies/ big white ones/ with
thick elastic/ & there was blood/ on the front of
them/ none of us knew what had happened to her/ she
was so big & old/ & so boisterous/ none of us talked
whilst she was talking/ mrs hay tells us/ about
girls 'n' boys being kidnapped/ & put into glad bags/
into car boots/ & about their underpants/ & what
had been done to them/ & about the mother crying
on the news who said/ that her little girl/ always had
a clean frock on/ & her father who said: i washed her
socks every night/ children dumped/ in ditches/ off
the road/ down by shady creeks/ where no one went/

in their singlets/ & underpants/ mrs hay says: never
talk to strangers/ & warren lewington asks: is the
easter bunny okay?/ & was santa okay/ to talk to at
christmas?/ & she never answered straight off/ &
suddenly/ none of us really knew how safe the easter
bunny was/

friday afternoon/ after school/ diane's
mother gets tiddly/ & cooks us raspberry jam tarts/
she tells us about strangers/ & what they do to
children/ on school holidays/ my grandmother/ makes
me pray for lost children/ last seen together/ a
brother & sister & friend/ on a beach/ in south
australia/ their parents looking for them/ & me
praying/ that jesus/ friend of all children/ would
bring them back/ diane's mother tells us/ how they
find the skulls of children/ buried in the bush/ &
sometimes little pairs of grey school shorts/ &
another time a boy's tooth/ he must have been very
frightened/ he must have run through the bush/ to
get away/ children run a lot/ & mostly are very fast/
at school/ we practise our running in the playground/
& we climb the monkey bars/ we pretend that a
sharpie is after us/ & some of the older kids/ show
me a sharpie's footprint/ embedded in the stone roof/
of the girls' toilets/ i could just about make it out/
but then a big huntsman/ scampered out of a corner/
& we all screamed & ran out into the playground to
play hopscotch/

at playlunch/ we stand along the
wire fence/ on the very edge/ of the school
playground/ on sharpie patrol/ the teachers had
told us/ to keep an eye out for sharpies/ & to

report any sightings/ to the local head mistress/
no one could be trusted/ gnarled old women/ with
their shopping trolleys/ waved at us/ from across
the street/ passing truck drivers/ honked their
horns/ on their way through/ to the blue mountains/
& we all jumped up & down & squealed in the wind/
then we got bored with looking for sharpies & played
skipping/ at home time/ the german bus driver/ who
makes us sit three to a seat/ who sometimes squashes
us four to a seat/ even though half the bus is empty/
so that the corners of our square brown school bags/
scratch our legs/ well/ we call him 'sharpie'/ because
that is exactly what a sharpie would do/ if he was
a busdriver/ & when he is not working/ for neville's
private bus company/ we know he is a sharpie

PETER MINTER

Life™

In another complicated manoeuvre
    we watch bats feeding in the figs, fat drops of bat shit
    something to really think about as I look up &
imagine David Attenborough hanging close by, his camera
right where my head is. A bat looks straight into my eyes
    mammal to mammal

& I keep filming, sheet lightning and the odd bolt
    post-gothic behind lush fig branches, night storms
    cracking east toward Bondi and the headspace docos over
        that way.
All this at the bus stop on Hay street, waiting with you
for a ride home. The Year of the Monkey

is just beginning, city a little crazy on cordite,

red lanterns & the endless bats. Overhead
people watch ads as they glide by in a monorail,
look out at fluorescent high-rise &
down at us and the *big leather bees*
or so you say they're called, making me laugh
with that fake English accent, my eyes' aperture

widening to take in the distance
between image, language and object. Which is just
as it should be – commentary on bat-world
made up on the spot in a 'naturalistic' way,
all wet and exciting – then our machine home
in the mid-summer-night air, so *down-town* and *stuffed.*

GABRIELLE EVERALL

Queen of Suburbia

My mother said
the queen is an Aries
and so am I
I sell steak knives
door to door
teaching French feminism
on the sly
my knives make
a stainless diadem.

I drop booklets:
steak knives for the cause
on people's doormats
walk on private property

flirt with the
man of the house
finally starting to feel
apart of the community.

ANITA HEISS

I'm Not Racist But . . .

I'm not racist but . . .
Why can't I climb Ayers Rock?
Why don't they get jobs like everyone else?
Did you hear the one about?
Why are Aborigines so angry?
Why don't they just get over it – the past is the past?
Why do I have to say sorry for something I didn't do?

I'm not racist but . . .
They're all drunks!
They don't wash!
The kids roam the streets at night!
They look dangerous!!!

I'm not racist but . . .
I wouldn't pick one up in my cab
I wouldn't want my daughter to marry one
I wouldn't rent my flat to one
I wouldn't employ one

I'm not racist because . . .
I played football with one once
I worked with one once
I use the word Koori
I let them sit next to me on the bus

I walked over the Harbour Bridge
I signed a hand
I gave money to one begging on the street

I'm not racist . . .
I'm simply privileged by being white.
I'm just speaking from a position of power.
I'm just *observing* the *obvious.*

I'm not racist . . .
I'm just following the lead of my prime minister!

Canada, 2002

BRONWYN LEA

These Gifts

Days like these – cool afternoons
in late summer, a rain so delicate
you can sit in the backyard and let the mist
drizzle your face. There's no grass,
of course. A late heat wave has bleached
the lawn, burnt off the last of the tree ferns.
Just last week, children and the elderly
were suffering from heatstroke. Yet
these gifts that arrive late season –
an apology you hadn't dared hope for,
a rush of poems, an impromptu patience
with the world. You rest your head
against a silky oak, and by your cheek
two butterflies coupled in flight
sex it up. And the day has charmed you
with ephemera before you can object.

MILES MERRILL

Night's Knows

If Night had a nose
of course it would be running
from the bridge on down.
Night's thick calves would cha-cha-cha
holes in your dance floor.
It's hair? Black fire; under control
but still dangerous.
Night's face: Venus in the open sky,
a mask over back alleys wet with trash.
But its eyes are green flashing lights saying 'Go-go-go-go . . . '.
Night's body of course would be heavenly
with little needle holes to let the stars shine through.
If night were me I'd kill the sun and never let you go.
Beats like a big bass drum.
Moans like scotch pouring through a saxophone.
Night's lips would always be pouting and puckered on some
    poor, cheap, sick movie star.
It's voice a ka'billion cars
RevRevRevvvving with alarm.
I tell you It breathes
sweet magnolia breeze.
When morning comes creeping in that back door
and all sane people are asleep,
there's just me and you
playing in the abandoned puddles of dawn.
And that's night. Isn't it?

JOHN MATEER

Cemitério Da Ajuda

We would expect families to be living in the vaults,
so many are small stone houses with painted doors and
curtained windows,
the coffins mirror-smooth and on bunks along two walls,
and there are fewer than have been abandoned
on any street in an actual city. Through one grimy window
I see a shelf like a mantelpiece with framed photos
of a woman as a child and as a teenager and then of her as a
bridesmaid.
On the clean floor there's a line of yellow teddy-bears
and in a darkened corner, encircled by fallen petals, a vase of
roses.
Why am I looking in on this sadness? In another vault,
across from the grey dusty coffins, broken shelves;
and in another, a monochrome studio-portrait of the entire
family
as would be hung with pride above a matriarch's bed.
Why am I weeping again as I never do in my adopted country?
Why, as I am wandering the streets of memorial homes and
cenotaphs,
hiding in the shade of Cyprus trees charred by the noon sun?
When I cross paths with the three old women bundled in their
black,
they don't murmur *Bom dia*. To them I am less than the dead,
not even a curator of remains, not even a ghost-writer – *a*
tourist.
I'm sick of this. I can't stop weeping.

LOUIS ARMAND

Biodegradable

arriving elsewhere, there are fundamental questions
of locality, modularised space –
the dividing line
of separate hypotheses, & the river
charting a passage
of illicit traffic, carnal (the bare 'that it is'
in the 'nothing of the world') –
a bridge flares into view & recedes again into urban
renewal, like time
suddenly focused on some inevitable
statistical average –
a cognitive sculpture arching out of bipolarity,
disorder in the barely initiated
idea, a mere ornament of
style – above the skyline remote etymologies wink
conspiratorially, faux blond
in a fugitive
midnight hustle: then
just as soon it's over again, the agitation
passing to usedness,
wastage – a damaged landform stag-
gering upright & dissolving in brief nocturnal laughter

JUDITH BISHOP

Rabbit

Life shivers between yourself and us: help us to stretch
toward the kingdom of our burrows in the earth: we'll never occupy
again the silk-soft that was a womb, but we wander the night grass
with you,
searching for a tenderness, an innocence at birth: until the quiet
winds cut
the quiet breath from your mouth and your hindquarters stamp,
Quickly, I must go –

Rabbit, winding up your stride, in your alignment, recalling full
stretch,
a god's arrow-head, shaft, lengthening from nose to tail, aching
to occupy
the whole damn bubble of the moment of each movement: if you
made it, what would snap, whose shining fingers, what scene
would cut
abruptly to another, what deity float gently in to bid us her
good night?

Rabbit, laid ragged at the fold of day's field, where the sparrow-
hawk
stretched
the stars' scarf across her wing: with your velvet heart, you
occupied
the blood's old theatre: with your hushed ballet of spring, you
performed the coiled rites you have taught us tonight: showed
our ropes of matter cut
by the one puppet-master, hanging in his own winds.

MICHAEL BRENNAN

Flowers

My father reached
down tried to take
a flower from
my brother.

My brother was a box
covered in flowers.
I was terrified.
He might fall in too

trying to reach
that flower,
that flower that
should never bloom.

I was terrified
he would fall in,
that they would all
fall in, my family.

I would reach down
and find only
flowers dried and
crushed into scent.

I was falling or
I was a box now
covered in flowers.
I could smell

their rich scent
drying the breeze,
mixing with earth,
I could feel

his hand reaching,
it was my hand,
my father's hand,
my brother's hand.

KATE FAGAN

Concrete Poem

The beginning of duration
The infinity of cells
The form of unknowing
The hopelessness of dropped articles
The foot following the hand
The enticement of proclamations
The factual storm breaking between cables
The loss of a single throat
The particularities
The restaurant the satellite the city
The ambivalence of hours
The finity of care
The naming of difference
The reappearance of history
The violence in repetition in repeating
The repetition of ritual
The stealing light
The floor as we cross it
The unanswerable question of occurrence

The leaves the rivers the glass the dust
The absolute relevance
The petal as it falls
The book as it falls
The capital returning
The centralisation of numbers
The faces on ships and under fences
The domestic ear of infinite justice
The continuous event
The evening of a globe
The end of solid impossibility

MIRIAM WEI WEI LO

Searching for Words

Our bedsheets never really needed washing before. Could have had them on for months and they wouldn't get as dirty as they do after one day with David. Sand. Biscuit crumbs. Bits of banana. When he has a cold, smears of snot. As if our bed were a giant handkerchief. A catch-all. Like the Chinese term for bib: 围都都 [wei dou dou], which means, literally, to cover or protect everything, to enclose or surround. Except it's colloquial.

The term. Can't find it in the dictionary. It's what the Taiwanese lady at the local fruit and veg calls a bib, in her language alive and kicking like the baby in her belly. She smiles as she stands on a crate, reaching up for the cucumbers, stopping to shift the tomatoes, the hands that lovingly lift soft fruit sometimes coming to rest on the bulge beneath her shirt, as if she were patting it into place, like some strangely quivering melon. There is an art to arrangement. Ripe peaches on top. Grapes sit next to bananas, and beside the bananas an embankment of navel oranges.

I think about this as I survey our garden. To the right, the neat order of the semi-circular bed, clipped hedges of box, everything trained into symmetry. To the left, the madcap riot of the vegetable patch, feral watermelon threading its way through the mesclun lettuce.

Perhaps it's colloquial. Most of the vegetable seedlings brought in from the shops get chewed up by slaters or snails. What survives comes up from the compost. There must be a word for this. Something specific to a time, a place. Something idiomatic. Like the precise shape of a pregnant woman's belly. Like the state of our bedsheets after David's been in them one Thursday afternoon, sand, biscuit, banana, and snot in cunning arrangement – an unforseen gift, given with the grace of reckless abandon.

ALI ALIZADEH

Rumi

I escaped from the city
barefooted. I escaped from the fires

naked, except for the bag
of ancient books

slung over my back.
I ran into the desert. The horsemen

chased. Their torches
had coloured the tenements.

I ran for months. Finally
on a glorious night

I stopped. The raiders had given up
on me. I was alone

with the moon and the sand-dunes.
I looked down at my feet.

They were skinned.
I looked at my trace: red footprints

dark on the glowing plain.
I thought about my tribe

butchered as sacrificial beasts.
I remembered their smiles

before the flames. On the holy night
I knelt before the moon

and wept. In the desert
tears are elixir. From their pool

a fountain bubbled. I cleaned my scars
in the water. The books

weighed on my body. I took them out
and one by one

dipped them into the spring.
All knowledge, all art, and all history

drowned before my eyes. Freed
from the clutch of paper

words' ink dissolved in the lake.
I then drank. I was saved.

JAYA SAVIGE

The Master of Small Violences

He wakes at ten, opens up a can of tinned peaches
and hacks at the succulent halves with a fork taken
from the dish-rack, the only clean utensil left
after a week of neglecting the washing up.
Pushing past split fly-screens in tatters after
making the mistake of feeding next-door's cat,
he flicks some of the syrup at a largish ant crawling
along a frond and four varieties of flies swarm
in like a squadron heeding the sticky reveille.
Some of the syrup hits a spun leaf so that
a spider worries for its sack, stumbles forth,
forelegs raised to attack the assailant, mimicker
of the elements, which it is unable to locate, aimless
in defence. He finds himself inspired each time
a Christmas beetle's wings close incorrectly.
The cat bears gifts: chewed cockroaches beckon
from its jaws. After lunch, ants scamper over crumbs,
march toward a crack, drown, fall off the stainless
splashback. Now the sun's warm paws reach in
through the kitchen window, toying with each web
as at a fraying hem. The sink fills with this predatory
warmth: it is the day drowns them, he is blameless.

Biographical notes

ADAM AITKEN (b.1960) was born in London. He spent some of his childhood with relatives in Thailand before moving to Sydney. He has earned his living as an English teacher, a poetry editor and reviewer, and as a lecturer in cultural studies and creative writing. His collections include *Letter to Marco Polo*, *In One House*, and *Romeo and Juliet in Subtitles*. A fourth book, *Eighth Habitation*, is forthcoming in 2008.

JORDIE ALBISTON (b.1961) was born in Melbourne. She holds a PhD in literature and two of her works, including *The Hanging of Jean Lee*, have been adapted by Andrée Greenwell for music-theatre. Her other books of poetry include *Nervous Arcs* and *Vertigo: a cantata*.

ALI ALIZADEH (b.1976) was born in Iran and migrated to Australia at age fifteen. His books include *Eyes in Times of War*, *Fifty Poems of Attar* (with Ken Avery), *eliXir: a story in poetry*, and the novel *The New Angel*. His writing interests include dissent, history and spirituality.

YAHIA AL-SAMAWY (b.1949) has published many volumes of poetry in Arabic. He was born and educated in Iraq. Imprisoned and tortured under Saddam Hussein's regime, he fled and spent years in exile before migrating with his family to Australia. He now lives in Adelaide. His translator, Eva Sallis, is an Australian novelist who has studied Arabic for many years. She lives in Adelaide.

LOUIS ARMAND (b.1972) is a Sydney-born writer and visual artist living in Prague. His collections of poetry include *Land Partition* (2001), *Inexorable Weather* (2001), *Strange Attractors* (2003), *Malice in*

Underland (2003) and *Picture Primitive* (2006). He is also the author of several volumes of prose fiction, criticism and theory, including *The Garden* (2003), *Menudo* (2006), and *Solicitations: Essays on Criticism and Culture* (2005). He is the editor of *Contemporary Poetics* (2007).

E. J. Rupert ATKINSON (1881–1961) was born in Bendigo, Victoria. Atkinson spent considerable periods of his life in England, Europe, and the US. Atkinson's volumes of poetry include *The Shrine of Desire* (1906) and *A Flagon of Song* (1921). He also wrote for the theatre. Atkinson eventually lived in Melbourne, on the inheritance left by his father.

ARTHUR BAYLDON (1865–1958) was born in England. Before his arrival in Australia in 1889, he had already published two volumes of poetry, and they might be the underpinning of his 'voice', though the second edition of *The Oxford Companion to Australian Literature* says of Bayldon: 'A typical *Bulletin* poet, reflected the ambivalent attitude of the day towards the outback and bush life.'

'WILLIAM BAYLEBRIDGE' (William Blocksidge) (1883–1942) was born in Brisbane as Charles William Blocksidge. Baylebridge left for England in 1908, and returned to Brisbane in 1919. After further travel, he eventually settled in Sydney. Often privately printing his works, he later rejected his first two publications, and constantly revised older work before republishing. Baylebridge was a controversial, and now basically forgotten poetic figure. There is much that is conceptually and politically repugnant in his work, and in many ways he expresses a proto-typical fascism.

BRUCE BEAVER (1928–2004) was born in the Sydney seaside suburb of Manly. He was the author of more than a dozen books of poetry and several novels. Beaver's many honours include a Poetry Society Award, the Patrick White Award, the Bicentenary Award for Poetry, the Christopher Brennan Award, and an Honorary Doctorate from the University of Sydney awarded posthumously in 2004. His poetry volumes include *Odes & Days* (1975) and *Anima and Other Poems* (1994).

LISA BELLEAR (1961–2006) was from Stradbroke Island (Minjerriba). She was Goenpul of the Noonuccal people. An activist for her people and indigenous rights in Australia, she was a noted performer. In 1999 she wrote: 'This is Aboriginal land. Our country was invaded some two hundred and ten years ago. As a writer, artist, activist, my work will always address these issues.' Her volume of poetry *Dreaming in Urban Areas* was published in 1996.

JUDITH BEVERIDGE (b.1956) has published three books of poetry all of which have won major prizes, most recently *Wolf Notes* (2003). In 2005 she was awarded the Philip Hodgins Memorial Medal for excellence in literature. A fourth book is due out in 2009. She is currently the poetry editor for *Meanjin*.

JAVANT BIARUJIA (b.1955) is an Australian poet and playwright of mixed Celtic and Mediterranean descent. His most recent publication is *Pointcounterpoint: New & Selected Poems* (2007).

JUDITH BISHOP (b.1972) lives in Sydney. Her first book of poetry, *Event*, was published by Salt Publishing in 2007. Her poems have appeared in numerous journals in Australia, the US and UK, and in anthologies including *The Best Australian Poems* series, *The Best Australian Poetry* series, *The Oxford Book of Modern Australian Verse*, the *Singapore-Australia Anthology of Poems* (2007), and *Contemporary Australian Poetry* (2007) (in Chinese translation). She is currently working on a second book of poems.

JOHN BLIGHT (1913–95) was born in South Australia, but raised in southeast Queensland. Blight was part-owner of a number of timber mills. He also did stints as an accountant and later a professional writer. His first collection of poetry was *The Old Pianist* (1945), and his *Selected Poems* 1939–1990 were published in 1992. His reputation largely rests on his numerous sonnets on sea themes, of which he wrote multiple books, though the themes of his poetry, taken across his oeuvre, are wide-ranging, as he noted himself.

BARCROFT BOAKE (1866–92), born in New South Wales, was committed to a vision of the bush, though this was conditioned by his 'melancholia'. Assistant to a surveyor, drover, boundary-rider, he lived the bush life from 1886 to 1891, after which time he returned to Sydney. In 1892 his body was found in scrub, hanged by his own stockwhip; he was twenty-six. Only one volume of his poetry appeared: *Where the Dead Men Lie, and Other Poems*, with notes and a memoir by A. G. Stephens, was published posthumously in 1897.

MERLINDA BOBIS (b.1959) is a Filipino-Australian who writes in English, Pilipino and Bikol. She is the author of a book of short stories, a novel, four plays and a number of poetry collections, including *Summer Was A Fast Train Without Terminals* (1998).

KEN BOLTON (b.1949) was born in Sydney. He lives in Adelaide and manages the Dark Horsey Bookshop at the Experimental Art Foundation. He edited *Otis Rush* magazine and runs Little Esther Books. His poetry volumes include *Untimely Meditations & other poems* (1997) and *At The Flash & At The Baci* (2006). Bolton is also an art critic.

'THE BOULDER BARD' ('WILLY-WILLY') (n.d.), as noted by William Grono, the editor of an anthology of Western Australian poetry, *Margins: A West Coast Selection of Poetry* 1829–1988, '"The Boulder Bard" published several poems, sometimes as "Willy-Willy", in 1899: identity unknown. According to the *W. A. Post Office Directory* a William Williams lived in Hopkins Street, Boulder in 1899.'

PETER BOYLE (b.1951) lives in Sydney. His collections of poetry include *The Blue Cloud of Crying* (1997), *Museum of Space* (2004), and *Reading Borges* (2007). Forthcoming works include a collection of collaborative poems with M.T.C. Cronin and a long work, *The Apocrypha of William O'Shaunessy*, fictive translations of imagined classical texts.

J. BRENCHLEY (n.d.). His volume of poetry, *May, Blossom and Wattle* was published in 1876 in Melbourne.

CHRISTOPHER BRENNAN (1870–1932) was born and educated in Sydney. Brennan became Associate Professor in German and Comparative Literature at Sydney University, but was dismissed in 1925 for 'scandalous behaviour', by which was meant his alcoholism and his affair with Violet Singer, whose death in tragic circumstances shortly afterward left Brennan a shattered man. Brennan's literary criticism, as well as his poetry, introduced an enthusiastic knowledge of French Symbolist poetry into Australia, although Brennan did not necessarily see himself as a symbolist. He refused to compromise his ideas and intellectualism for the sake of the reader's comfort, and almost revelled in his 'difficulty'.

MICHAEL BRENNAN (b.1973) was born in Sydney and is currently a lecturer in the Faculty of Policy Studies, Chuo University, Tokyo. His first collection, *The Imageless World* (2003) was short-listed for the Victorian Premier's Award for Poetry and won the Mary Gilmore Award. His books include *Absence and Negativity in Australian Literature* (editor, 2000), *The Imageless World* (2003), *Language habits* (2006), 空は空 *Sky was sky* (with Akiko Muto, 2007), *Atopia* (with Kay Orchison, 2008), and *Unanimous Night* (2008). He is the Australian editor of www.poetryinternational.org and director of Vagabond Press.

JOHN LE GAY BRERETON (1871–1933) was born in Sydney. A friend to C. J. Brennan, Brereton went on to be Professor of English Literature at Sydney University. A supporter of Henry Lawson and other writers, Brereton was a generous literary figure of the time. He co-wrote *Mask* with Brennan in 1913 to celebrate the twenty-first anniversary of the Women's College of Sydney University.

ELIZABETH DEBORAH BROCKMAN (1833–1914) is a major 'undiscovered' poet of the nineteenth century. Born in Edinburgh, she arrived in Western Australia in 1840. Living in and around the Avon and Swan rivers, she contributed poems and a column on the condition of the colonial woman to the Western Australian Church of

England magazine. Her single volume of poetry, *Poems*, was published by family members a year after her death.

DAVID BROOKS (b.1953), a novelist, short-fiction writer and essayist, as well as poet, divides his working time between the Blue Mountains and Sydney, where he teaches Australian literature at the University of Sydney, and is co-editor of the journal *Southerly*. His work has been translated into several languages.

PAM BROWN (b.1948) has published many books. The most recent is a collection of collaborative poems written with the Seattle-based Egyptian poet Maged Zaher, called *farout_library_software* (2007). Her book *Dear Deliria* (2003) was awarded the NSW Premier's Prize for Poetry in 2004. A new collection, *True Thoughts*, is due from Salt in 2008.

VINCENT BUCKLEY (1925–88) was born in Romsey, Victoria, educated in a Jesuit College in Melbourne and eventually held a Personal Chair in Poetry at Melbourne University. His Irish Catholic background strongly informed his personal, academic and poetic identity. He published a number of critical works and edited others, including *The Faber Book of Australian Verse* (1991). An influential figure in academic poetic circles in Melbourne, Buckley's volumes of poetry include *The World's Flesh* (1954) and *Golden Builders* (1976).

CHARLES BUCKMASTER (1951–72) was born in Gruyere, Victoria. He edited the magazine *The Great Auk* and published two volumes of poetry, *Deep Blue and Green* (1970) and *The Lost Forest* (1971) in his short lifetime. *Collected Poems*, edited by Simon MacDonald, was posthumously published in 1989.

FREDERICK SPENCER BURNELL (1880–1958) was born in Sydney. Burnell's two volumes of poetry were *Before Dawn and Other Poems* (1912) and *A Sallet of Songs* (1920). He published *How Australia took German New Guinea* (1915), after accompanying the New Guinea expedition as special correspondent for the *Sydney Morning Herald*.

JOANNE BURNS (b.1945) lives in Sydney. She has had over a dozen collections of her poems published. Her latest collection *an illustrated history of dairies* was published by Giramondo Publishing in 2007.

CAROLINE CADDY (b.1944) was born in Western Australia and spent part of her childhood in both the US and Japan. She has published eight volumes of poetry, and has won a number of major awards. Her most recent volume is *Esperance: New and Selected Poems* (2007).

ADA CAMBRIDGE (1844–1926) was born in Norfolk, England, and arrived in Victoria in 1870 with her Anglican curate husband. Cambridge had lost three of her children by the time she left for England again in 1912, only returning to Australia after the death of her husband in 1917. A prolific novelist, Cambridge also wrote three volumes of poetry.

DAVID CAMPBELL (1915–79) was born at Ellerslie Station, Adelong, in the southern highlands of New South Wales. He attended Jesus College, Cambridge, where he played Rugby Union and received a BA. During World War Two, he served as a reconnaissance and bomber pilot; he was awarded the DFC. After the war, he became a farmer in the Canberra district. His first book of verse was *Speak with the Sun* (1949), and he went on to publish over fifteen volumes of poetry and prose. He was poetry editor of *The Australian* newspaper in 1964 and '65. Campbell started out as poet of the local landscape but unexpectedly changed to a looser form of versification and more contemporary themes with an occasional slightly surreal tone.

CAROLINE CARLETON (1820–74), a true poet of South Australia, published the first book by a woman there, *South Australian Lyrics* (*c.* 1860). Carleton arrived in Australia from England in 1839. After the death of her doctor-husband, she ran a school in Adelaide.

MARCUS CLARKE (1846–81), born in London, left for Australia in 1863. He edited and wrote for a number of influential Australian journals, and was the author of one of the greatest Australian novels,

His Natural Life, which originally appeared in the popular serialised fashion of the time from 1870–72 in the *Australian Journal*. He was a founding member of Melbourne's literary Yorick Club.

SARAH COLLINS (n.d.) was published in the *Colonial Times* in 1839.

ALISON CROGGON (b.1962) is a writer who lives in Melbourne, Australia. She has published six collections of poetry and *The Books of Pellinor*, a popular series of fantasy novels. She is also the Melbourne theatre critic for the *Australian* newspaper. Her next book of poetry, *Theatre*, is forthcoming from Salt Publishing.

M. T. C. CRONIN (b.1963) has published numerous collections of poetry, including several in translation, and a number of volumes collaboratively written with the Australian poet Peter Boyle. She currently lives with her partner and three young daughters on an organic farm (specialising in fresh Spanish produce) situated in Maleny, Queensland.

ZORA BERNICE MAY CROSS (1890–1964) was born in Brisbane, and went on to become a journalist and freelance writer in Sydney. Cross was one of the most original and dynamic Australian poets, but barely recognised as such. Cross's work includes the volumes *Songs of Love and Life* (1917) and *The Lilt of Life* (1918). Her best-known poem is 'Elegy on an Australian Schoolboy', written for her younger brother killed during the First World War, but Cross also wrote intense love poems, as well as deeply felt and investigative poems of motherhood.

VICTOR J. DALEY (1858–1905) was born in Ireland in 1858. Daley arrived in Australia in 1878. After a somewhat wandering life that included clerical work in Adelaide, prospecting on the Queanbeyan goldfields, and literary journalism in Sydney and Melbourne, his first book of poetry, *At Dawn and Dusk* (1898) appeared the year he settled permanently in Sydney.

LUKE DAVIES (b.1962) is the author of three novels and five books of poetry. *Totem* won the *Age* Book of the Year, the John Bray and the Grace Leven prizes, and the Philip Hodgins Memorial Medal for poetry. *Running With Light* won the Judith Wright prize. His novels are the cult bestseller *Candy, Isabelle the Navigator,* and the recent *God of Speed. Candy,* for which Davies co-wrote the screenplay, was released as a film in 2006, starring the late Heath Ledger.

JACK DAVIS (1917–2000) was born in Perth and raised in Yarloop, Western Australia. A Nyungar man, he was a spokesman and activist for his people. His many public roles included director of the Aboriginal Centre in Perth and the Chairman of the Aboriginal Lands Trust in WA. Among his volumes of poetry were *The First-Born and Other Poems* (1970) and *John Pat and Other Poems* (1988). Davis also wrote short stories and an autobiography, and was an editor and a major playwright, whose plays include *The Dreamers* (1982) and *No Sugar* (1985).

BRUCE DAWE (b.1930) was born in Fitzroy, Victoria. After leaving school at sixteen, he worked in various occupations (labourer, farm-hand, clerk, sawmill-hand, gardener and postman) before joining the RAAF. He left the RAAF in 1968 and began a teaching career. Bruce Dawe has published twelve books of poetry. Dubbed 'the poet of suburbia', Bruce Dawe has received numerous awards for his poetry including: the Grace Leven Poetry Prize (1978), the Patrick White Literary Award (1980), and the Christopher Brennan Award (1984). In 1984, Dawe's collected edition, *Sometimes Gladness,* was named by the National Book Council as one of the ten best books published in Australia in the previous decade and is presently in its 5th edition. In 1992 Dawe was awarded the Order of Australia (AO) for his contribution to Australian literature.

SARAH DAY (b.1958) was born in England and lives in Hobart with her partner and their two daughters. Her fifth and most recent book, *The Ship* (2004) won the Judith Wright Calanthe Queensland Premier's Award, the University of Melbourne Wesley Michel Wright Prize, and was joint winner of the Judith Wright ACT Award for poetry.

C. J. DENNIS (1876–1938) was born in Adelaide, but eventually found his way to Victoria. His books of verse became a publishing sensation, with remarkable sales figures. Intensely nationalistic, spoken in a verse approximating the vernacular, witty with their linguistic and social humour, these works touched on how many Australians saw themselves. In 1919 *The Sentimental Bloke* appeared as a silent movie. Dennis was never to repeat the success of these works, despite a list of other publications. Then-Prime Minister Joseph Lyons referred to Dennis as the "Robbie Burns of Australia" after the poet's death, but the success of Dennis's poetry is now more seen as a phenomenon of his times.

ROSEMARY DOBSON (b.1920) was born in Sydney and lives in Canberra. She was an editor for Angus & Robertson, as well as an art teacher. Her books of poetry include *In a Convex Mirror* (1944), *Cock Crow* (1965), and *Untold Lives and Later Poems* (2002). She is widely acknowledged as one of the most significant Australian poets of the last six decades.

MICHAEL DRANSFIELD (1948–73) was born in Sydney. Though he died at the age of twenty-four, he left a significant body of poetry both in print and unpublished. Associated with drug subcultures, and having, in fact, published a volume entitled *Drug Poems* (1972), Dransfield's legacy is strongly literary, ranging from politically radical to culturally conservative. The same could be said of the poems themselves: conceptually and formally ranging from the innovative and challenging to the formally and textually 'traditional'. His volumes of poetry include *Streets of the Long Voyage* (1970) and the posthumous *Memoirs of a Velvet Urinal* (1975). His poetry helped define a certain poetics within Australia, during the Vietnam era.

LAURIE DUGGAN (b.1949) was born in Melbourne and currently lives in England. His most recent books are *The Passenger* (2006), *Let's Get Lost* (with Pam Brown and Ken Bolton, 2005), *Compared to What: Selected Poems 1971–2003* (2005), and *Mangroves* (2003). Shearsman have also republished his 1987 documentary poem *The Ash Range* (2005). A selection of earlier work, together with journals and critical articles, may be found online at the auslit site.

JAS H. DUKE (1939–92). Anarchist. Dadaist poet. Concrete and visual poet. Sound poet. Lived in England and Germany as well as Australia. In the late 1960s he starred in a number of movies directed by Jeff Keen. He was a founding member of the Poets Union. A posthumous collection, *Poems of Life & Death*, was published in 2003.

ELIZA HAMILTON DUNLOP (1796–1880) was born in County Armagh, Ireland. She and her family arrived in Port Jackson in 1838. Her husband was a magistrate and Protector of Aborigines; she transcribed the poetry of Wullati into English. She collated vocabularies and held a lifelong interest in the indigenous people whose lands encompassed Wollombi, where she died and was buried.

GEOFFREY DUTTON (1922–98) was born at Anlaby, the oldest stud sheep station in South Australia. At Magdalen College, Oxford, he read English under C. S. Lewis. Dutton became founding editor of Penguin Books Australia in 1962 and then co-founder of Sun Books, *Australian Letters* and the *Australian Book Review*. He was also founding editor of the *Bulletin Literary Supplement* and, later, of the *Australian Literary Magazine*. He published over fifty books, including works of poetry, biography, art and literary criticism, fiction and children's writing. Among his books of poetry were *Findings and Keepings* (1970) and *Selective Affinities* (1985).

'E' (MARY FULLERTON) (1868–1946) was born in North Gippsland, Victoria, and journeyed to England in 1921, where she died a quarter of a century later. Her first volume of poetry was *Moods and Melodies: Sonnets and Lyrics* (1908). Among her other works is *The Australian Comic Dictionary of Words* (1916). Her later use of the pseudonym 'E' was out of respect for Emily Brontë and Emily Dickinson. She was a feminist and friend of Miles Franklin.

STEPHEN EDGAR (b.1951) lives in Sydney. He has published six collections of poetry, the most recent being *Other Summers* (2006). His previous book, *Lost in the Foreground*, won the Grace Leven prize in 2004. In 2006 he was awarded the Philip Hodgins Memorial Medal for literature.

GABRIELLE EVERALL (b.1968) published her first book of poetry, *Dona Juanita and the Love of Boys*, in 2007. She has performed at the Big Day Out; Putting On An Act, National Young Writers' Festival, Overload, Emerging Writers' Festival, etc., and has been published in *The Salt Reader*, *Short Fuse*, *The Sleeper's Almanac*, *Cordite* and *The Broadkill Review*.

KATE FAGAN (b. 1973) is a former editor of the US-based journal of innovative poetry *How2*, and is from one of Australia's pre-eminent folk music families, The Fagans. Her books of poetry include *The Long Moment* (2002), *Thought's Kilometre*, and *return to a new physics* (2000). Her album *Diamond Wheel* (2007) won the National Film & Sound Archive Award for Best Folk Album. www.katefagan.com.

W. S. FAIRBRIDGE (1918–50) was born in Perth, Western Australia. After a short life during which he worked as a research officer for the CSIRO, his poetry was published posthumously as *Poems* (1950).

MICHAEL FARRELL (b.1965) is currently working on a PhD thesis. His books are *ode ode*, *a raiders guide*, and *BREAK ME OUCH*, the last being graphic poetry. Future projects include a fictional homage to Barbara Pym, a lesbian and gay anthology, and a book on the billycan in Australian poetry.

BARRON FIELD (1786–1846) arrived in Australia from England in 1817 as judge of the Supreme Court of NSW, and left Australia in 1824. He produced a two-poem book *First Fruits of Australian Poetry*, which was published by the Government Printer in 1819 (a second edition contained four new poems). As well as authoring *Geographical Memoirs of New South Wales* (1825), he was an editor of Shakespearean works, was a friend of Charles Lamb, and wrote for Leigh Hunt's *Reflector*.

ROBERT DAVID FITZGERALD (1902–1987) was born at Hunter's Hill in Sydney. FitzGerald was a surveyor whose work took him to Fiji to survey traditional tribal boundaries, and eventually to the Department of the Interior in Australia. FitzGerald's poetry is philosophical, often rhetorical and even didactic, more than the meditative to which it aspires, but it ranges widely in time and space, and is genuinely intellectual and conceptual. His poetry volumes include *The Greater Apollo: Seven Metaphysical Songs* (1927) and *Moonlight Acre* (1938). FitzGerald was also a prominent critic.

LIONEL FOGARTY (b.1958) was born at Cherbourg Aboriginal Reserve in southeast Queensland. His involvement in the struggle has been through various organisations, including Aboriginal Legal Service, Aboriginal Housing Service, Black Resource Centre, Black Community School and Murri Coo-ee. In 1980 his first book of poetry, *Kargun*, was published, and distributed widely in the community. Since then he has published eight volumes of writing.

MARY HANNAY FOOTT (1846–1918) was born in Glasgow, and arrived in Australia in 1853. Though educated in Melbourne and a student at the National Gallery Art School, she moved to Queensland after her marriage and lived on a station with her husband until his death in 1884. She then became literary editor of the *Queenslander*. Her poetry volumes are *Where the Pelican Builds and Other Poems* (1885) and *Morna Lee and Other Poems* (1890).

JOHN FORBES (1950–98) was born in Melbourne, and studied at the University of Sydney. He worked as a furniture removalist and creative writing teacher, and was founding editor of the occasional journal *Surfers Paradise*. One of the most influential poets of his generation, his relatively small oeuvre is much admired and imitated. His books include *Stalin's Holidays* (1991) and the posthumous *Damaged Glamour* (1998). For some of us, he and his work remain one of the reasons poetry should be written.

LEON GELLERT (1892–1977) was born in Walkerville, South Australia. He had been a school teacher before the war. Gellert was wounded at Gallipoli. With the publication of his book *Songs of a Campaign* (1917), he was considered the pre-eminent Australian poet of the Great War. Later, he worked as editor and journalist for a range of publications, including *Art in Australia* and the *Sydney Morning Herald*.

KEVIN GILBERT (1933–93) was born in Condobolin, New South Wales, of the Wiradjuri and Kamilaroi peoples. He served fourteen years in jail after the death of his wife during a domestic dispute. He went on to become a renowned lino printmaker, playwright, activist and political commentator. He was instrumental in establishing the Aboriginal Tent Embassy, and in 1973 he wrote *Because a White Man 'ill Never Do It*, the first major political work by an Aboriginal author. In 1979 Kevin's oral history *Living Black* won the National Book Council award.

MARY GILMORE (1865–1962) was born near Goulburn, New South Wales. Gilmore's little formal education did not stop her becoming a teacher. She was a supporter of the shearers' strike of the 1890s, and was dedicated to the working class and labour movement. Her poetry was featured in the Red Page of the *Bulletin* in 1903. Her first volume of poetry, *Marri'd and Other Verses*, was published in 1910. In the later stages of her eminent and public life, Gilmore lived in King's Cross, Sydney. She is one of the great figures of Australian social history and literature.

PETER GOLDSWORTHY (b.1951) divides his time equally between writing and medicine. He has won major literary awards across many genres – for poetry, the short story, the novel, for an opera libretto, and most recently for theatre. His novels have been translated into many languages; five are currently in development as movies. A new novel, *Everything I Knew*, is due out in late 2008.

GEOFF GOODFELLOW (b.1949) knows about the violence of work. He has lived it . . . along with many of his family members. Geoff has written about the struggle of 'ordinary' Australians for twenty-five years, and has published a number of collections of poetry. His *Poems for a Dead Father* (2002) was short-listed for the *Age* Book of the Year Award.

W. T. GOODGE (1862–1909) was London-born, and arrived in Sydney in 1882. William Thomas Goodge has a reputation as a fine comic journalist and writer of 'light verse'. The second edition of Goodge's *Hits! Skits! and Jingles!* (1899/1904) was illustrated by Norman Lindsay.

ADAM LINDSAY GORDON (1833–70), horse-breaker, steeplechaser, parliamentarian, cavalryman and poet, is an important figure in Australian balladry. Gordon suffered from 'melancholia'. Having lost money on earlier works, including *Sea Spray and Smoke Drift*, he self-published *Bush Ballads and Galloping Rhymes* in 1870. Shortly after, despite positive responses from Henry Kendall and Marcus Clarke, he shot himself in the head at Brighton. Most published versions of 'The Sick Stockrider' omit the last stanza. Gordon removed it from the manuscript at the suggestion of the *Colonial Monthly*.

ALAN GOULD (b.1949) is a poet, novelist and essayist who lives in Canberra. His *The Past Completes Me – Selected Poems* 1973–2003 won the Grace Leven Prize for 2006, while his novel, *The Schoonermaster's Dance* was co-winner of the *Courier-Mail* Book Of The Year in 2001. He has a volume of poems, *Folk Tunes* and a novel, *The Lakewoman*, forthcoming.

JOHN GRANT (1776–n.d.) was born in Buckinghamshire, England. Grant was transported to New South Wales in 1803 (for wounding an opponent in a duel). His opposition to the conditions of punishment led to his being sent to Norfolk Island where he was treated severely. Grant returned to England after Macquarie issued a pardon in 1811.

ROBERT GRAY (b.1945) will publish his *Collected Poems* and a memoir with Giramondo in 2008.

MARY LEMAN GRIMSTONE (*c*.1796–1869) was born in Hamburg, and arrived in Van Diemen's Land in 1826. Her *Woman's Love*, published in 1832, is said to be among the first novels written in Australia. Richard

D. Jordan and Peter Pierce, in *The Poet's Discovery*, claim that Grimstone might be regarded as a 'proto-feminist'.

RODNEY HALL (b.1935) was born in England and arrived in Australia after World War Two. A renowned novelist, he has twice won the Miles Franklin Award (for *Just Relations* in 1982 and *The Grisly Wife* in 1994) and has been three times nominated for the Booker Prize. His volumes of poetry include *The Autobiography of a Gorgon* (1968) and *The Most Beautiful World* (1981).

PHILIP HAMMIAL (b.1937) has had twenty collections of poetry published, two of which were short-listed for the Kenneth Slessor Prize. *Bread* was published in 2001, and *In the Year of Our Lord Slaughter's Children* in 2004. He is also a sculptor (thirty-three solo exhibitions) and the director of The Australian Collection of Outsider Art.

LESBIA HARFORD (1891–1927) was born in Melbourne, and attended the University of Melbourne, where she graduated in law and philosophy. She held a wide variety of jobs, including work as a machinist in a clothing factory. Socially and ethically radical, Harford was concerned for the wellbeing of the working class, particularly women; she also wrote of gender and sexual freedom, equality, and the beauty of the immediate. Harford's work was collected after her death by Nettie Palmer.

CHARLES HARPUR (1813–68), arguably the greatest Australian poet of the nineteenth century, was born in Windsor, New South Wales. He worked as a post-office clerk, farmer and gold commissioner. Harpur is seen as the first non-indigenous 'native-born' Australian poet to make the Australian environment his primary subject matter. Harpur was also concerned with the rights of Aborigines and social equality in the colonies, and justice at large.

JENNIFER HARRISON (b.1955) is a Melbourne poet and child psychiatrist. Her fourth collection, *Folly & Grief*, was published in 2006. A volume of new and selected poetry is forthcoming from Black

Pepper. She is currently co-editing an anthology of Australian women's poetry on the subject of motherhood and parenting.

J. S. HARRY (b.1939) lives in Sydney and has published eight poetry collections. The most recent, *Not Finding Wittgenstein* (2007), was short-listed for the Adelaide Festival Poetry Award. She received the Christopher Brennan Award for poetry in 2000 and won the *Age* Poetry Book of the Year Award (2008). Her poems have been translated into Italian, Spanish, Polish, Arabic and German.

KEVIN HART (b.1954) teaches at the University of Virginia in Charlottesville. His most recent collection of poems is *Young Rain* (2006), and the latest selection of his poems is *Flame Tree: Selected Poems* (2002). He has also translated Giuseppe Ungaretti's poems, and edited *The Oxford Book of Australian Religious Verse.*

W. HART-SMITH (1911–90) was born in England, spent his childhood in New Zealand, and arrived in Australia in 1936. A true trans-Tasman poet, Hart-Smith moved between New Zealand and Australia frequently. While in Australia he associated himself with Jindyworobakism. Hart-Smith was deeply interested in Australian Aboriginal myths and legends, as well as those of New Zealand – Aotearoa – Maori people. His works include *Columbus Goes West* (1943), *The Unceasing Ground* (1946), and *Christopher Columbus: A Sequence of Poems* (1948). Much of his poetry is characterised by a pared-back lyricism and sharpness of imagery.

GWEN HARWOOD (1920–95) began writing poetry in her late thirties, and many of her early poems were printed under pseudonyms such as Walter Lehmann and Miriam Stone. Her volumes include *Poems* (1963), *The Lion's Bride* (1981) and the award-winning *Bone Scan* (1989). Harwood was awarded Honorary Doctorates of Letters from the Universities of Tasmania, Queensland and La Trobe. Her last volume, *The Present Tense,* was published just prior to her death.

DENNIS HASKELL (b.1948) is the author of five volumes of poetry, the most recent, *All the Time in the World* (2006), won the WA Premier's

Prize for Poetry. His *New and Selected Poems* will be published by Salt in 2009.

ANITA HEISS (b.1968) (Wiradjuri nation) is an author, poet, satirist and social commentator. Anita's published works include the novel *Not Meeting Mr Right*, the kids' novel *Yirra and her Deadly Dog, Demon*, and the poetry collection *I'm Not Racist, But . . .* In 2004 she was listed in the Bulletin/Microsoft Smart 100.

PAUL HETHERINGTON (b.1958) is the author of eight volumes of poetry, most recently *It Feels Like Disbelief*. His poetry awards include a 2002 Chief Minister's ACT Creative Arts Fellowship. He was founding editor of the journal, *Voices* (1991–97), and edited and introduced the final three volumes of the four-volume edition of the diaries of the artist Donald Friend.

DOROTHY HEWETT (1923–2002), the poet, novelist and playwright, was born in Wickepin, Western Australia, and lived for many years in the Blue Mountains in New South Wales. Her poetry received many awards and was published internationally and her plays received critical acclaim.

CHARLES HIGHAM (b.1931) was born in London. He was a book reviewer for the *Sydney Morning Herald* and literary editor of the *Bulletin* (1964–67). His poetry volumes include *The Earthbound and Other Poems* (1959). He moved to the US and has published a number of biographies there.

BARRY HILL (b.1943) has received national awards in several genres: poetry, nonfiction, the essay. His short stories have been widely anthologised, and translated into Japanese and Chinese. His recent work includes the multi-award winning *Broken Song* (2002), a monumental study of frontier history and translation poetics. He has published six books of poetry and is at present Poetry Editor of *The Australian*. He lives in Queenscliff, Victoria, where he has been writing full-time since 1975.

FIDELIA HILL (1794–1854) wrote *Poems and Recollections of the Past* (1840), the first bound book published in Australia by a woman, and the first poetry whose subject-matter was the colony of South Australia. Hill spent only a few years in South Australia and eventually died in Launceston.

PHILIP HODGINS (1959–95) was widely published in Australia and appeared in journals in Europe, the UK, Asia and North America. His awards included the Wesley Michel Wright Prize for Poetry, the Bicentennial Poetry Book Award, the New South Wales Premier's Award for Poetry, the Grace Leven Prize, and the National Book Council Poetry Prize. He died in 1995 of leukaemia.

HARRY HOOTON (1908–61) was born in England, and in 1924 moved to Australia, and lived mainly in Sydney. Inspired by Lawson among others, he was a poet of the people, a Utopian anarchist. His collections of poetry include *These Poets* (1941) and *It Is Great To Be Alive* (1961).

A.D. HOPE (1907–2000) was born in Cooma, New South Wales. Alec Derwent Hope's first collection, *The Wandering Islands* (1955), received immediate international acclaim and established him as one of the world's masters at once of the iambic pentameter and of heterosexual eroticism, though in fact his subject range is far wider and more challenging than the latter would suggest and incorporates some extraordinary investigations into the nature and limitations of human thought. Through the 1950s Hope was Head of English at Canberra University College, where he introduced the first tertiary courses in Australian Literature. In 1960 he became the foundation professor of English at the Australian National University. Almost half of his remarkable oeuvre was produced in the two decades after his retirement in 1968.

PETER HOPEGOOD (1891–1967) was born in England, where he had worked as a freelance journalist and illustrator. Cedric 'Peter' Hopegood moved to Western Australia in 1924 for health reasons. During World War Two, he lived in Melbourne and worked for the ABC. A self-styled mystical visionary, Hopegood could make statements that were, unsurprisingly, vastly insensitive to indigenous peoples, in his quest for a world myth-orientated vision. His first volume of poetry is *Australia Pan and Other Verses* (1932); his best-known work is *Circus at World's End: An Assembly of Verse* (1947).

RICHARD HOWITT (1799–1870) produced *Impressions of Australia Felix . . . Australian Poems* (1845), the first book of verse to come out of Victoria. He was only in Australia for a few years, arriving at Port Phillip in 1840 and departing for England in 1844. He later published *Gipsy Kings and Other Poems* (1845) and *Wasp's Honey, or Poetic Gold* (1867).

W. FLEXMORE HUDSON (1913–88) was born in Charters Towers, Queensland, but moved to South Australia as a boy. His working life ranged from teacher to sailor. Another Jindyworobak, though one with an individualised way of seeing the Australian landscape, Wilfred Frank Flexmore Hudson edited the 1943 *Jindyworobak Anthology*. His poetry deeply and sensitively connects with Australian landscapes, conceptually and sensually. His books of poetry include *As Iron Hills* (1944).

CORAL HULL (b.1965) is a writer, poet, artist, photographer and theorist living in Darwin. She has authored over fifty books. She is an ethical vegan and an animal rights advocate. She is the Director of The Thylazine Foundation.

REX INGAMELLS (1913–55) was born in Orraroo, South Australia. Ingamells is possibly more significant for his role in one of Australia's few cohesive literary movements than for his poetry. Ingamells founded the Jindyworobak Club in 1938. The influence of Jindyworobakism on Australian poetry is extensive, if much debated. Ingamells's poetry volumes included *Gumtops* (F. W. Preece, Adelaide, 1935) and *Come Walkabout* (Jindyworobak, Melbourne, 1948). He worked in Adelaide and Melbourne.

MARTIN JOHNSTON (1947–90) was born in Sydney. He spent fourteen years of his childhood in England and Greece. His parents, the writers George Johnston and Charmian Clift, returned with Martin to Australia in 1964. Apart from an innovative novel, *Cicada Gambit*, he published a number of volumes of poetry, including *The Typewriter Considered as a Bee Trap* (1985). John Tranter edited a posthumous edition of his work, *Martin Johnston: Selected Poems and Prose* (1993).

JILL JONES (b.1951) won the 1993 Mary Gilmore Award for *The Mask and the Jagged Star* and the 2003 Kenneth Slessor Poetry Prize for *Screens, Jets, Heaven: New and Selected Poems*. Her most recent books are *Broken/Open* and *Speak Which*. She has been translated into Chinese, Dutch, French, Italian and Spanish.

NIKOS KALLINIKOS (1884–1976) was born in Ithaka, Greece and died in Adelaide. His work has been featured in *Greek Voices in Australia* (1987), edited by George Kanarakis.

NANCY KEESING (1923–93) was born in Sydney. After studying at the University of Sydney, she worked as a social worker and later a freelance writer. An editor and well-known literary figure, she wrote criticism, biography, memoir, children's novels, and volumes of poetry, including *Imminent Summers* (1951) and *Hails and Farewells* (1977).

ANTIGONE KEFALA (b.1935) was born to Greek parents and grew up in Romania. She now lives in Sydney and has worked as a teacher, in libraries, and as an arts administrator. Her latest book is *Sydney Journals: reflections 1970–2000* (Giramondo Publishing).

S. K. KELEN (b.1956) was born, grew up and educated in Sydney, but has lived and worked in Canberra since 1990. His poems have been published widely in Australia and abroad since the early 1970s. He has travelled with intensity and written many poems in and about East Asia and the Pacific. His most recent books are *Goddess of Mercy* (2002) and *Earthly Delights* (2006).

HENRY KENDALL (1839–82) is placed alongside Harpur as one of the finest Australian poets of the nineteenth century. Born in New South Wales, Kendall's life was almost destroyed by alcoholism and attendant poverty. Kendall moved between Sydney and Melbourne (where he was part of the Yorick Club) to escape his problems. Legend has him emerging to clarity in the early 1870s, having spent time in Gladesville asylum. In 1881 he was made inspector of the forests by Henry Parkes. *Leaves from the Australian Forest* (1869) and *Songs from the Mountains* (1880) are both essential volumes of Australian poetry.

JOHN KINSELLA (b.1963) is the author of more than thirty books published in Australia and internationally. Prizes and awards for his work include the Grace Leven Poetry Prize, the South Australia Festival of Arts John Bray Award for Poetry, *The Age* Poetry Book of the Year Award, The Western Australian Premier's Book Award for Poetry (three times) and the Arts Queensland Judith Wright Calanthe Award.

MIKE LADD (b.1959) is currently producer and presenter of ABC Radio National's *Poetica* program. He lives in Adelaide and has published six collections of poetry, the most recent being *Transit*. In 2006 he was awarded the Barbara Hanrahan Fellowship and was a guest of Venezuela's World Poetry Festival.

PADDY LANDO-NADDI (n.d.–1934) lived for a long time at De Grey Station. According to Auslit, he was a butcher.

JOHN DUNMORE LANG (1799–1878) was born in Scotland, and arrived in Sydney in 1823. He was the first Presbyterian minister in Sydney, and eventually became Moderator of New South Wales. He was an editor of various publications, including the *Colonial Observer*. His poetry was collected in *Sacred and Secular: Written Chiefly at Sea Within the last Half-century* (1872). Lang is a key figure in the development of Australian poetry, and was committed to the cessation of convict transportation. The full version of 'Colonial Nomenclature' appears here, showing its imperialist undercurrents.

HENRY LAWSON (1867–1922) occupies an immense space in the Australian literary and national psyche. Lawson wrote of the bush from the perspective of its people. He had no great sympathy for the place he came out of. He grew up on the Grenfell goldfields, and this rough-and-tumble world implanted itself deep in his psyche, along with the tensions between his Norwegian sailor father and Australian-born mother, Louisa Lawson. Lawson's personal life was dominated by alcoholism, disappointment and depression.

LOUISA LAWSON (1848–1920), often only cited as Henry Lawson's mother and publisher of his first book, was a considerable literary and political figure in her own right. From 1888 to 1905 she founded and edited *Dawn*, a significant journal for women. Her volume of poetry *The Lonely Crossing and Other Poems* appeared in 1905.

BRONWYN LEA (b.1969) is the author of *Flight Animals* (2001) and series editor, with Martin Duwell, of *The Best Australian Poetry* series. Her latest book, *The Other Way Out*, is forthcoming from Giramondo.

CAROLINE LEAKEY (1827–81), poet and fiction writer, published *Lyra Australia, or Attempts to Sing in a Strange Land* (1854). Born in Exeter, England, she sailed for Van Diemen's Land in 1847, lived in Hobart, and returned to England after a number of years. Charitable, religious, and author of the convict novel *Broad Arrow*.

GEOFFREY LEHMANN (b.1940) has published eight volumes of poetry. His best known is *Spring Forest* (1994). He has co-edited, with Robert Gray, two anthologies of Australian poetry, and is the author of two children's books and *Australian Primitive Painters*. He is Chairman of the Australian Tax Research Foundation.

EMMA LEW (b.1962) has published two collections of poems: *The Wild Reply* (1997) and *Anything the Landlord Touches* (2002).

KATE LILLEY (b.1960) grew up in Perth and Sydney. After completing her PhD on Masculine Elegy at the University of

London, she spent four years as a Junior Research Fellow at Oxford University. Since 1990 she has taught feminist literary history and theory at the University of Sydney and has published widely on early modern women's writing and contemporary poetry. She is the editor of *Margaret Cavendish, The Blazing World and other writings* (Penguin Classics). Her one poetry volume, *Versary*, was published by Salt Publishing.

KATE LLEWELLYN (b.1940) is the author of nineteen books, including *The Floral Mother & Other Essays* and *Playing with Water: A Story of a Garden*. She is the co-editor of *The Penguin Book of Australian Women Poets*. Her memoir, *The Waterlily: a Blue Mountains Journal*, sold over 30 000 copies. She is currently the recipient of a Senior Writers Fellowship from the Literature Board. Her autobiography, *The Dressmaker's Daughter*, was published in 2007.

MIRIAM WEI WEI LO (b.1973) is thirty-five and still looking for the music of words as she stands at the kitchen sink. Her first collection, *Against Certain Capture*, won the Western Australian Premier's Prize (for poetry) in 2005. She lives with her husband and three small children in Margaret River.

JAMES McAULEY (1917–76) was born in Lakemba, New South Wales, in 1917. He served in the Australian Army Directorate of Research and Civil Affairs, and lectured at the Australian School of Administration. In 1956 he became editor of *Quadrant*. In 1961 he accepted an invitation to become Reader in Poetry at the University of Tasmania, and subsequently was appointed Professor of English.

GEORGE GORDON McCRAE (1833–1927) was born in Scotland. McCrae arrived in Port Phillip in 1841. Along with Clark, Gordon and Kendall, McCrae was part of the Melbourne literary gatherings known as the Yorick Club, which was vital to the development of Melbourne's literary sensibilities in the 1860s and '70s. He is known as the 'Father of Victorian Poetry'.

HUGH McCRAE (1876–1958) was born in Melbourne, and was the son of poet George Gordon McCrae. As a young writer and illustrator, he was influenced by those orbiting around Norman Lindsay. He moved to Sydney in 1904, and went to America in 1914 to face extreme financial difficulty pursuing the life of actor-artist. Kenneth Slessor believed that McCrae's first volume of poetry, *Satyrs and Sunlight: Silvarum Libri*, decorations by Norman Lindsay (1909), brought modernism to Australian poetry.

RONALD McCUAIG (1908–93) was born in Newcastle. McCuaig became a journalist, working for radio, *Smith's Weekly*, and the *Bulletin* (writing topical verse under the pseudonym 'Swilliam'). His first volume of poetry was *Vaudeville* (1938). McCuaig was a satirist who brought smart twists to his 'light verse'. Peter Kirkpatrick has noted what a 'severe self-critic' McCuaig was, that his slim oeuvre has a touch of 'perfectionism'.

NAN McDONALD (1921–74) was born in Sydney. After World War Two, she was publishing editor at Angus & Robertson. Her volumes of poetry include *Pacific Sea* (1947) and *Selected Poems* (1969).

ROGER McDONALD (b.1941) was born in Young, New South Wales, and attended the University of Sydney. The author of six novels, including *1915* and *The Ballad of Desmond Kale*, which won the Miles Franklin Award in 2006, he was poetry editor at the University of Queensland Press from 1969–76. His poetry volumes include *Airship* (1975).

DOROTHEA MACKELLAR (1885–1968) was born into privilege in Sydney. 'My Country', originally published in London as 'Core of My Heart', is one of the best-known Australian poems. Her books of poetry included *The Closed Door and Other Verses* (1911) and *Dreamharbour and Other Verses* (1923). She travelled widely and had an interest in European languages.

KENNETH MACKENZIE (1913–55) was born in Perth, Western Australia. He moved to Sydney in 1934, working as a journalist, and publishing various novels under the name of Seaforth Mackenzie, including *The Young Desire It* and *The Refuge*.

RHYLL McMASTER (b.1947) has written six poetry books and won four awards, including the Victorian Premier's and Grace Leven Prizes. *On My Empty Feet* was adapted as an ABC radio play. The limited edition *Evolutionary History of Edward Kelly in Primary Colours* was published in 1999.

FRANCIS MacNAMARA ('FRANK THE POET') (*c.* 1810–61+) was transported to New South Wales in 1832. Born in Ireland, he served regular time on a chain gang. He eventually wrote the immortal 'The Convict's Tour to Hell'. A thief and something of a radical, he has become a somewhat legendary satirist and an 'anti-authoritarian', almost resistance figure. Other sources claim that he was born in 1811 and died in 1868.

JENNIFER MAIDEN (b.1949) has had sixteen books published: fourteen poetry collections (some including short prose) and two novels. She has won the NSW Premier's Prize twice, the Victorian Premier's Prize and the Christopher Brennan Award for lifetime achievement. Her most recent collection, *Friendly Fire* (2005), from which 'Reflected Hearth' is taken, won both the *Age* Poetry Book of the Year and the *Age* Book of the Year.

'ERN MALLEY (1918–43)' is a hoax poet whose life and work were created in October 1943 by James McAuley and Harold Stewart. Malley was supposedly born in Liverpool (UK) in 1918, dying in Sydney, after a period of working and living in Melbourne as an insurance salesman and watch repairer, at the age of twenty-five. McAuley and Harris's purpose was to trick Max Harris, editor of the Adelaide-Melbourne literary and art magazine *Angry Penguins* into publishing the work of their dead, pseudo-avant-garde, working-class poet, which he did, in a special 'Commemorative' issue in 1944. McAuley and Stewart's counterfeit poet and his inauthentic compositions have attracted interest within the experimental traditions.

DAVID MALOUF (b.1934) was born in Brisbane and writes novels, short stories and poetry. He has published seven collections of poetry including *Bicycle and Other Poems* (1970), and most recently *Revolving Days: Selected Poems* (UQP).

JOHN MANIFOLD (1915–85) was born in Melbourne, and was of a wealthy background. Attended Cambridge University, and became a member of the Communist Party. Returned to Australia in 1949; moved to Brisbane. Established the Realist Writers Group. His *Collected Verse* was published in 1978. He collected and edited bush songs and ballads, including *The Penguin Australian Song Book* (1964).

LEONARD MANN (1895–1981) was born in Melbourne, and served with the AIF in World War One, before studying law. He eventually became a public servant and retired to a life of farming. Novelist and poet, Mann published volumes of poetry, including *The Plumed Voice* (1938) and *The Delectable Mountains and Other Poems* (1944).

FREDERIC MANNING (1882–1935) was born in Sydney, where his father was four times Lord Mayor. Manning left for England at the age of sixteen for eighteen months, returning to Australia for a further three years, then returning again to England. During World War One he served with the British army in France. He wrote the significant war novel *The Middle Parts of Fortune: Somme and Ancre* (1929).

CHRIS MANSELL (b.1953) was born in Sydney. Her *Mortifications & Lies* (2005) was described as '. . . an important book, both stylistically and thematically a ground-breaking book.' Earlier work includes: *Head, Heart & Stone, Redshift/Blueshift, Day Easy Sunlight Fine, The Fickle Brat,* and *Stalking the Rainbow*. Chris Mansell's latest collection is *Love Poems* (2006).

JOHN MATEER (b.1971) has published chapbooks in Australia, South Africa, Indonesia and Japan, and several books of poems in Australia, as well as a prose travelogue, *Semar's Cave: An Indonesian Journal*. His collections include *The Ancient Capital of Images* (2005), *Elsewhere*

(2007), and *Ex-White*, a gathering of all of his South African poems, which will be published in Europe in 2009.

'FURNLEY MAURICE' (FRANK WILMOT) (1881–1942) was born in Collingwood, and Wilmot's pseudonym combines Ferntree Gully and Beaumaris, two of his favourite places in Melbourne. His working life was dedicated at first to Cole's Book Arcade, and then to Melbourne University Press, where he worked until his death. Of his volumes of poetry, *Melbourne Odes* (1934) remains strongly influential. He was one of the generators of modernism in Australian poetry.

MILES MERRILL (b.1970) tours his monologues and poems internationally. His shows 'Lamp Post Incantations' (Sydney Opera House, 2006) and 'Slamming' (Sydney Festival, 2005) won him critical acclaim. Publications include *What Night Knows* (audio, 1998), *Dirty Curly* (audio, 2008), *Miles Merrill – The Reel* (DVD, 2006), *The Asia Literary Review* (2007), and *Terra: Anthology* (2007).

PETER MINTER (b.1967) is a leading author and editor of numerous books of poetry, including blue grass, and the *Macquarie PEN Anthologies of Aboriginal and Australian Literature*. He is a recipient of several prestigious literary prizes, awards and grants, and lectures in Indigenous Studies and Poetics at the University of Sydney.

E. G. MOLL (1900–97) was born in Murtoa, Victoria. Ernest George Moll spent much of his life in the US, leaving Australia in 1920. After his studies, Moll became Professor of English at the University of Oregon from 1928–66. Thompson, Slessor, and Howarth, in a biographical introduction to Moll in their edition of *The Penguin Book of Australian Verse* (1958), are keen to assert the Australian credentials of this expatriate poet: '. . . poems, although they bear traces of American influence, are typically Australian in their outlook and subject-matter.'

IAN MUDIE (1911–76) was President of the Fellowship of Australian Writers, a history writer, anthologist, poet, lecturer, conservationist, and Jindyworobak. Mudie believed in the values of the bush, Aboriginal tradition, and a patriotic devotion to Australia. He was born in Hawthorn, South Australia. His own volumes of poetry include *Corroboree to the Sun* (1940) and *Look, the Kingfisher* (1970). He also compiled *Poets at War: An Anthology of Verse by Australian Servicemen* (1944) and the 1946 *Jindyworobak Anthology*.

MUDROOROO (b.1938) was born in Narrogin, Western Australia. He was known as Colin Johnson and published the black bodgie novel *Wild Cat Falling* in 1965. He spent seven years in India, returning to Australia in 1975, and publishing several novels, a play, and works on Aboriginal mythology and literature. He has been living in Nepal for several years completing a biographical cycle.

LES MURRAY (b.1938) is one of Australia's leading poets and one of the greatest contemporary poets writing in English. His work has been published in ten languages. He has won many literary awards, including the Grace Leven Prize (1980 and 1990), the Petrarch Prize (1995), and the prestigious TS Eliot Award (1996). In 1999 he was awarded the Queens Gold Medal for Poetry on the recommendation of Ted Hughes.

PHILIP NEILSEN (b. 1949) published his fifth collection of poetry, *Without an Alibi*, in 2008. He is also a widely published and translated fiction writer, the editor of two collections of Australian satirical poetry (with Penguin and UQP) and professor of creative writing at QUT.

JOHN SHAW NEILSON (1872–1942) was born at Penola, South Australia. Receiving little formal education and doing itinerant rural labouring jobs, Neilson spent much of his life struggling with failing eyesight – reciting (according to popular anecdote) his verses for transcription by fellow workers. His *Collected Poems* was published in 1934, eighteen years after his first volume appeared. Sometimes described as deceptively simple, his work combines an intense lyrical acuity with lightness of touch and an apparent naivety, melded with an unusual, off-beat way of seeing.

OODGEROO NOONUCCAL (Kath WALKER) (1920–93) was born Kathleen Jean Mary Ruska on Stradbroke Island (Minjerribah), in Moreton Bay. She became a prominent poet, recognised as one of Australia's first published Aboriginal women authors. She played a pivotal role in bringing about the 1967 referendum. In 1970, Oodgeroo was appointed a Member of the Order of the British Empire for services to the community. She returned it in 1987 in protest against the Australian bicentenary celebrations. Oodgeroo's work has been recognised by numerous awards, including the Mary Gilmore Medal (1970), the Jessie Litchfield Award (1975), and the Fellowship of Australian Writers' Award.

Π.O. (b.1951). Born Katerini/Greece, 1951 * Came to Australia 1954 * Raised: Fitzroy [inner suburb of Melbourne]. Occupation: draughtsman. Has published numerous magazines *FITZROT*, 925, etc. Has represented Australia in the US, Thailand, Germany, Colombia. Is the editor of ~~UNUSUAL WORK.~~

BERNARD O'DOWD (1866–1953), born at Beaufort, Victoria, was a poet with a mission, which was encapsulated in his presidential address to the Literature Society of Melbourne, published in 1909, 'Poetry Militant: An Australian Plea for the Poetry of Purpose'. O'Dowd claimed that 'the real poet must be an Answerer, as Whitman calls him, of the real questions of his age'. A radical socialist, he left his first wife in 1820 to live with Marie Pitt, herself a socialist poet.

OUYANG YU (b.1955) has published forty-three books in the field of fiction, nonfiction, poetry, literary criticism and literary translation. His latest publication of nonfiction is *On the Smell of an Oily Rag: Speaking English, Thinking Chinese and Living Australian*.

JAN OWEN (b.1940) is a South Australian poet whose sixth book, *Poems* 1980–2008, was published by John Leonard Press in early 2008. She has been a writer in residence in Italy, Malaysia and France and has received various grants and prizes, most recently the 2007 Max Harris Award.

GEOFF PAGE (b.1940) is a Canberra-based poet who has published eighteen collections, as well as four verse novels and other works. His most recent books are *Seriatim* (2007), *Agnostic Skies* (2006), 80 *Great Poems from Chaucer to Now* (2006), and *Lawrie & Shirley* (2007).

EDWARD VANCE PALMER (1885–1959) was born in Bundaberg, Queensland. Palmer travelled to Russia and Asia, South and North America. He served in the AIF. An influential 'man of letters', he wrote biographical criticism, essays, drama, fiction, and poetry. His first volume of poetry was *The Forerunners* (1915). An overt nationalist, he perceived Australian literature as part of the entire national experience.

CHARMAINE PAPERTALK-GREEN (b.1962) was born near Mullewa, Western Australia. Her surname is in recognition of her mother's maiden name. She is from the Wajarri/Amangu people on the maternal side and the Bardimia people of the Murchison on the paternal side. Her collection of poetry is *Just Like That* (2007). She has published in various anthologies over a long period of time.

A. B. PATERSON (1864–1941) was born near Orange, New South Wales. Andrew Barton Paterson's was an intense and 'adventurous' life, from Sydney solicitor to war correspondent during the Boer War, to ambulance driver in France during World War One, to being made a major with the AIF in Egypt. Renowned as Australia's foremost 'bush balladist', he also wrote novels, worked as an editor, and pastoralist. The publication of *The Man from Snowy River, and Other Verses* brought him extensive fame throughout Australia.

GRACE PERRY (1927–87) was born in Melbourne, and graduated in medicine from the University of Sydney in 1951. Perry was founder-editor of *Poetry Australia*, which began in 1964. Prior to that, she had edited *Poetry Magazine* from 1961. Her volumes of poetry include *Red Scarf* (1963) and *Berrima Winter* (1974). She led an intense life of editing, farming, publishing (she founded South Head Press in 1964), and working as a paediatrician.

GLEN PHILLIPS (b.1936) has published five collections of poetry, the most recent being *Spring Burning* (1999). Glen's poems have been published in journals and newspapers in Australia, Asia, America and Italy. He has been invited to read poetry at Cambridge University (UK) and Kenyon College, Ohio, and at universities in Australia, Italy, China, India, Thailand and Singapore. His poems have been broadcast on SBS television, ABC TV and Radio, and on commercial and regional radio stations.

JAMES PICOT (1906–44) died in the service of the AIF as a POW on the Burma–Thailand Railway. Born in England, he arrived in Australia in 1923 and studied at the University of Queensland, from which he graduated. His poems appeared posthumously as *With a Hawk's Quill* (1953).

DOROTHY PORTER (b.1954) has published six collections of poetry and five verse novels. Her verse novel, *The Monkey's Mask*, has been adapted for radio, stage and film. Two of her verse novels, *What a Piece of Work* and *Wild Surmise*, were short-listed for the Miles Franklin Award. Porter also writes libretti and song lyrics.

HAL PORTER (1911–84) was known primarily as a novelist, short-fiction writer, and autobiographer, but Porter also wrote three collections of poetry, the first of which was *The Hexagon* (1956). Born in Melbourne in 1911, Porter eventually became a teacher. In 1939 he was in a severe road accident that kept him hospitalised for a year. A variety of jobs followed until he joined the Occupation Forces in Japan from 1949–50. Back in Australia, he was a librarian from 1953–61 before taking up writing full time.

PETER PORTER (b.1929) was born in Brisbane; he has lived in London since 1951. He has published over thirty books, of which twenty are devoted to poetry. He is also a reviewer, broadcaster and working journalist. He returns frequently (as possible) to Australia. Latest publications include *Collected Poems*, 1961–99, 2 vols. (1999); *Max is Missing* (2001); *Afterburner* (2004); *Eighteen Poems* (2006). A forthcoming collection, *Better Than God*, is due out in 2009.

JENNIFER RANKIN (1941–79) was born in Sydney, and studied at the University of Sydney. She worked for a time in England. Her poetry volumes include *Ritual Shift* (1976) and *The Mud Hut* (1979). A posthumous *Collected Poems* (1990) was edited by Judith Rodriguez.

ELIZABETH RIDDELL (1910–98) was born in Napier, New Zealand, and moved to Australia in 1928. A Walkley Award-winning journalist, she lived in England from 1935 to 1939, then ran the *Daily Mirror*'s office in New York until 1944, when she returned to London, and came back to Australia in 1946. Her *Selected Poems* was published in 1992.

MICHAEL MASSEY ROBINSON (1744–1826) was Australia's first 'poet laureate'. Blackmailer, forger, and thorn in the side of officialdom, Robinson published twenty of his odes in the Sydney *Gazette*, writing in honour of the birthdays of George III and Queen Charlotte from 1810 to 1820.

ROLAND ROBINSON (1912–92) was a dedicated follower of Rex Ingamells and the Jindyworobaks. Born in County Clare, Ireland, he arrived in Australia in 1921. With little formal schooling, he did numerous jobs in outback western New South Wales. He published his first volume of poetry *Beyond the Grass-tree Spears* in 1944. Robinson felt deeply and spiritually connected to the Australian landscape. Not only did Robinson collect such stories, and translate Aboriginal poetry, but he wrote his own poetry in the context of Aboriginal narratives, issues and beliefs.

JUDITH RODRIGUEZ (b.1936) has been awarded the South Australian Premier's Prize for Literature and the FAW Christopher Brennan Award. She wrote the play *Poor Johanna* with Robyn Archer, and the libretto for Moya Henderson's opera *Lindy*. Her latest publication, *Manatee*, contains recent and older poems.

ERIC ROLLS (1923–2007) was born at Grenfell, New South Wales, and was a farmer, a poet, and historian. His books of poetry include *Sheaf Tosser* (1967) and *The Green Mosaic* (1977). His historical book *A Million Wild Acres* (1981) is considered a classic work.

PETER ROSE (b.1955) is the author of five poetry collections, including *Rattus Rattus: New and Selected Poems* (2005). His family memoir, *Rose Boys*, won the National Biography Award in 2003. He edited *The Best Australian Poems* 2007. A former OUP publisher, he is the editor of *Australian Book Review*.

DAVID ROWBOTHAM (b.1924) is eighty-four and nearly blind. Nevertheless he goes on writing. He published his first poem in the Toowoomba Grammar magazine at the age of fourteen, and has never stopped since. It was this lifelong commitment to Australian literature that gained him the Patrick White Award 2007. He also holds other honours. He has contributed to more than 100 anthologies.

GIG RYAN (b.1956) is poetry editor for *The Age*. A freelance reviewer, poet and song writer, she is also a musician with the band Driving Past. Her books include *The Division of Anger* (1980) and *Heroic Money* (2001). She lives in Melbourne.

TRACY RYAN (b.1964) was born in Western Australia, and has spent some years living in Britain and the US. She has published five collections of poetry and two novels, with a third novel due out in late 2008. She has worked in libraries, bookselling and community journalism, as well as teaching at various universities. She has two children.

PHILIP SALOM (b.1950) has won two Commonwealth Poetry Prizes in London, three WA Premier's Prizes and two Newcastle Poetry Prizes. *The Well Mouth* was an *SMH* Book of the Year. More recently he has won the Christopher Brennan Award – a lifetime award for poetry – and the Australia Council's Major Writers Fellowship for 2006/2007. His books include *The Well Mouth, A Cretive Life, Toccata and Rain, Sky Poems,* and *New and Selected Poems*.

ANDREW SANT (b.1950) lives alternately in Australia and the UK. His collection *Tremors – New & Selected Poems* was published in 2004. His most recent book is *Speed & Other Liberties* (2008). He is currently living in London while being Writing Fellow at the University of Chichester.

JAYA SAVIGE (b.1978) was born in Sydney, and grew up on Bribie Island, Queensland. His first collection, *Latecomers* (2005) was awarded the 2006 NSW Premier's Kenneth Slessor Prize for Poetry.

JOHN A. SCOTT (b.1948) was born in England. A renowned innovative novelist, Scott is also a significant innovative poet. His poetry volumes include *The Barbarous Side Show* (1975), and *St Clair* (1996).

TOM SHAPCOTT (b.1935) lived in Queensland for forty-seven years. Public accountant and poet (yes!). Moved to Melbourne in 1982. Director, Literature Board 1983–90. First novel published in 1980. Inaugural Professor of Creative Writing at Adelaide University, 1997–2005. Over fifty books published, mainly poetry. Most recent volume: *The City of Empty Rooms* (2006).

CRAIG SHERBORNE (b.1962) published his first poetry collection, *Bullion*, in 1995, and his verse play, *Look at Everything Twice for Me*, in 1999. *Necessary Evil* was published in 2006. His memoir *Hoi Polloi* (2005) was short-listed for the Victorian and Queensland Premiers' prizes. Its acclaimed sequel, *Muck*, was published in 2006.

R. A. SIMPSON (1929–2002) was born in Melbourne. Ron Simpson figured heavily in Melbourne's poetry scene throughout his life, and is often associated with other Melbourne poets like Chris Wallace-Crabbe and Vincent Buckley. He was poetry editor of *The Bulletin* 1963–65 and of *The Age* 1969–98. Simpson published four volumes of poetry during his lifetime, and a posthumous collection of poems and drawings, *The Sky's Beach*, was published in 2003.

ALEX SKOVRON (b.1948) is the author of four collections of poetry, most recently *The Man and the Map* (2003), and a prose novella, *The Poet* (2005). A volume of prose-poems, *Autographs*, is due in 2008. He was born in Poland, arrived in Australia in his tenth year, and lives in Melbourne, where he works as a freelance editor.

PETER SKRZYNECKI (b.1945) was born in Germany, and came to Australia in 1949. He has published sixteen books of poetry and prose. Poetry books include *Immigrant Chronicle* (1975) and *Old/New World: New & Selected Poems* (2007). He is an adjunct associate professor in the School of Humanities and Languages at the University of Western Sydney.

DOUGLAS B.W. SLADEN (1856–1947) only spent a brief period in Australia: he arrived in Australia from England in 1879 and returned in 1884. In that time, however, he studied law in Melbourne, and was the first appointee to the Chair of History at Sydney University. A poet in his own right, his major contribution to Australian literature was its promotion back in Britain and his anthologising of its poets, including the anthology *A Century of Australian Song* (1888).

KENNETH SLESSOR (1901–1971) was born at Orange, New South Wales. Slessor is the core of post-World War One Australian modernism. A life in journalism, which eventually saw him made an official war correspondent from 1940–44, anchored his writing. He largely stopped writing poetry in 1944. His later activities included editing Sydney's literary journal *Southerly*. His reputation primarily rests on *One Hundred Poems:* 1919–1939 (1944), where we find a poetry of great diversity in subject and style, that ranges from the overtly lush to the ironically restrained, but with a steady and recognisable poetic diction. Primarily conservative and critical of modernity, Slessor's poetry also marvels at the force and impact of language, of words themselves. It is a unique poetry that can barely be imitated.

VIVIAN SMITH (b.1933) has published eight collections of poetry, most recently, *Along The Line* (2006). His early poems of Tasmanian landscape and history appeared in the first *Penguin Book of Australian Verse*. He speaks French and German and has translated numerous poets from these languages and edited anthologies of Australian poetry. His later work has become more surrealistic and experimental.

NICOLETTE STASKO (b.1950) was born in the US of Polish and Hungarian ancestry, and emigrated to Australia in 1979. She has published five volumes of poetry and a bestselling nonfiction work, *Oyster*. She is also a reviewer, editor, essayist and teacher. Her volumes of poetry include *Glass Cathedrals: New and Selected Poems* (2006).

DOUGLAS STEWART (1913–85), narrative poet, bush balladist and nature lyricist, published many books of poetry, verse plays, criticism and short stories and edited several anthologies. He was literary advisor to Angus & Robertson Publishers from 1961 to 1973. He died in 1985.

HAROLD STEWART (1916–95) was born in Sydney. Apart from his co-authorship of the 'Ern Malley' poems with James McAuley, he published poetry volumes that include *Phoenix Wings: Poems 1940–46* and *Orpheus and Other Poems* (1956). He moved to Japan in 1966 and eventually joined the Shinshu Buddhist sect.

RANDOLPH STOW (b.1935) is acknowledged as one of Australia's finest writers. He graduated from the University of Western Australia and has lectured in English at the Universities of Adelaide, Western Australia and Leeds. He has also worked as an anthropologist in New Guinea. Stow has published many novels as well as poetry and opera libretti. His many literary awards include the Miles Franklin Award (for *To the Islands*) in 1958 and the Patrick White Award in 1979. He lives in England.

JENNIFER STRAUSS (b.1933), born at Heywood, Victoria, is a poet and academic, who has published four collections of poetry – most recently, *Tierra del Fuego: New and Selected Poems* – edited two anthologies of Australian poetry and *The Collected Verse of Mary Gilmore*, and co-edited *The Oxford Literary History of Australia*.

ROBERTA 'BOBBI' SYKES (b.1943) was born in Townsville, Queensland. An activist for black causes, she was first executive secretary to the Aboriginal Tent Embassy to Canberra in 1972, and founded the Black Women's Action group. Sykes received a PhD from Harvard. Her oeuvre includes the three-volume autobiography, *Snake Dreaming*

(1997–2000), as well as the poetry volumes *Love Poems and Other Revolutionary Actions* (1979) and *Eclipse* (1996).

NORMAN TALBOT (1936–2004) was born in Suffolk, England, and migrated to Australia after having completed a PhD in American Literature at Leeds University. He took up a lectureship at the University of Newcastle and, in time, became intimately connected with the publication and promotion of Hunter Valley writers. His collections of poetry include *Poems for a Female Universe* (1968), and *Four Zoas of Australia* (1992), which carried an introduction by Gwen Harwood.

ALF TAYLOR (b.1947) was born in Perth. He spent his younger years with his family in Perth, then joined his brother at New Norcia Mission. Alf spent the rest of his childhood there. As a young man he worked around Perth and Geraldton as a seasonal farm worker. He then joined the armed forces and was based at various locations around Australia. Alf then left the armed forces and went home. After a marriage, seven children (only two of whom survived), and a divorce, Alf Taylor found his voice as a writer and poet . . . although it is a gift he believes he was born with.

ANDREW TAYLOR (b.1940) is the author of more than fourteen books of poetry, the libretti of two operas, and the critical study *Reading Australian Poetry* (1987). His most recent major publication is *Collected Poems* (2004). A new collection, *The Unhaunting*, will appear late in 2008.

COLIN THIELE (1920–2006) was born in Eudunda, South Australia. Strongly associated with the South Australian literary community, he was also an Australian nationalist. A high school teacher, Thiele went on to be director of Wattle Park Teachers' College. Thiele wrote in many genres; two of his most famous works were novels for children, *The Sun on the Stubble* (1961) and *Storm Boy* (1963). His poetry volumes include *The Golden Lightning* (1951) and *Selected Verse* (1970).

RICHARD TIPPING (b.1949) grew up in Adelaide, South Australia, and studied in humanities at Flinders University. He has been active in poetry, sculpture, printmaking, photography, music, film and video, with a common interest expressed in the title of his doctorate as 'Word Art Works: visual poetry and textual objects'.

CHARLES TOMPSON (1807–83) produced *Wild Notes from the Lyre of a Native Minstrel* (1826), a landmark volume for the reason that it is the first volume of poetry published by a 'currency lad' – a 'native-born' non-indigenous Australian. Tompson was a public servant. He has been termed an 'early conservationist'.

JOHN TRANTER (b.1943) has published more than twenty collections of verse. His collection of new and selected poems, *Urban Myths: 210 Poems* won the Victorian Premier's Prize in 2006 and the New South Wales Premier's Prize in 2007. In 1992 he edited (with Philip Mead) the *Penguin Book of Modern Australian Poetry*. He has lived at various times in Melbourne, Singapore, Brisbane and London, and now lives in Sydney, where he is a company director. He is the editor of the free Internet magazine *Jacket* (jacketmagazine.com), and in 2004 he initiated the Australian Poetry Resources Internet Library (april.edu.au).

DIMITRIS TSALOUMAS (b.1921) was born on the island of Leros, educated in the Italian language, and writes in Greek and English. He arrived in Australia in 1952 and studied to become a secondary school language teacher in Melbourne, retiring in 1982. His first poetry volume in English, *The Observatory*, was translated by Phillip Grundy. Collections such as *Falcon Drinking* (1988) and *The Barge* (1993) were written in English. He has published six collections of poetry in Greece.

DAVID UNAIPON (1872–1967) is said to be the first Australian writer of Aboriginal descent to have published a book in Australia. Unaipon was Ngarrindjeri, born at Raukkan in South Australia. His book *Native Legends* appeared in 1929. Unaipon was also a preacher and an inventor, and wrote his autobiography, *My Life Story*, in 1954. A strong influence on the welfare of indigenous people in South Australia, tireless and driven in his beliefs, Unaipon has become an icon. His portrait is on the Australian fifty-dollar note.

VAL VALLIS (b.1916) was born in Gladstone, Queensland and published the poetry collections *Songs of the East Coast* (1947) and *Dark Wind Blowing* (1961). Receiving a PhD from London University, he taught at the University of Queensland. He also lectured at the Queensland Conservatorium of Music.

'VIATOR' (CHARLES W. ANDREE HAYWARD) (1866–1950) was born in England. The Rugby and Oxford-educated Hayward arrived in Western Australia in 1894 to work as a journalist and editor. In 1922 he travelled to Sydney and joined the *Bulletin*, where he remained until his death, writing under a collection of pseudonyms. His volume of poetry, *Along the Road to Cue and Other Verses*, appeared in Geraldton, Western Australia, in 1897.

VICKI VIIDIKAS (1948–98), poet, short-story writer and free-spirit from the Balmain group of modern poets and 'Generation of 68', was born in Sydney of Estonian and Australian parentage. *Condition Red*, *Wrappings*, *Knabel*, and *India Ink* reflect the inner rawness of her emotional experiences, the transient relationships and her love of India.

BRIAN VREPONT (1882–1955), violinist and poet, whose real name was Benjamin Arthur Trubridge, was born in Melbourne, and studied and taught at the Melbourne University Conservatorium. He spent some time in Queensland and Western Australia, and his first volume of poetry was *Plays and Flower Verses for Youth* (1934).

CHRIS WALLACE-CRABBE (b.1934) is a Melbourne poet and art critic. His new collection is *Telling a Hawk from a Handsaw* (2008) while his recent essays are gathered in *Read It Again* (2005). An ardent conservationist, he chairs the newly established Australian Poetry Centre.

ANIA WALWICZ (b.1951) has published *Writing, Boat, Red Roses*, and has a collection, *Palace of Culture*, forthcoming in 2008. She also writes material for theatre and opera, and records her work performed – see her latest *Voiceprints* CD.

FRANCIS WEBB (1925–73) was born in Adelaide, but grew up in Sydney. He lived abroad in the 1940s, coming back from Canada to Sydney where his first work, *A Drum for Ben Boyd* (1948), was illustrated by Norman Lindsay. He spent most of the remainder of his life in mental institutions, suffering from schizophrenia, but was consistently supported through publication.

RICHARD WHATELY (1787–1863) never travelled to Australia. A deeply committed opponent of transportation, he was also a professor at Oxford, and later Anglican archbishop of Dublin.

JUDITH WRIGHT (1915–2000) was born on her family property near Armidale, New South Wales. She came to prominence through publication of *The Moving Image* (1946) and *Woman To Man* (1949). Her long partnership with scientist Jack McKinney and their life at Mount Tamborine in Queensland, engendered a strong political edge to her later writings on conservation, the value of Australian wildlife and Aboriginal rights. In 1972 she moved to Braidwood, where she both worked and lobbied for these concerns.

WULLATI (n.d.). L.E. Threlkeld wrote: 'There is a god of Poesy, Wallati [sic], who composes music, and who [. . .] is inspired with the supernatural gift. This very individual, Wullati, or as the white folks used to call him, Woolaje, lived near to our establishment, he was esteemed highly by the tribes [. . .] enliven[ing] the midnight hour with his song and dance, assisted with his own voice and musical accompaniment of two sticks, beating time to the divine inspiration of the sacred muse. The song composed by Wullati, translated and published, some years ago by Mrs E.H. Dunlop, is an excellent specimen of the Poetry of the Aborigines, and ought not to be lost though the Poet and his tribe is now no more.'

FAY ZWICKY (b.1933) was born Melbourne. She was formerly a musician and a teacher of literature. She has won the Patrick White Award (2005) and the Christopher Brennan Prize for Poetry (2006).

Acknowledgements

First, I'd like to thank Clive Newman, who has put so much time into the organisational processes behind this anthology: my heartfelt thanks. Thanks, too, to editor Bridget Maidment for the dedicated work. Also thanks to my partner, Tracy Ryan, for her support. Special thanks to Peter Pierce and Philip Mead, who have read and commented on the introduction and section commentaries, and have also given feedback for various biographical notes and other issues. Philip also provided the biographical notes for David Campbell and Ern Malley; I thank him too for helping me prune my introductory texts down to size. For help with a variety of biographical notes, tracking of permissions, and fixing dates of texts, special thanks to David Brooks (specifically for A. D. Hope's biographical note, and also for his comments and input on others), Vivian Smith, Pam Brown, Dennis Haskell, Peter Kirkpatrick, Philip Butterss and John Tranter. My thanks to Tom Thompson for his support. I'm also grateful to Steve Kinnane for his help. Thanks to James Quinton for library work and photocopying, and to the many poets with whom I have discussed issues relating to this volume. Finally, thanks to Bob Sessions at Penguin for his enthusiasm and support.

Most contemporary biographical notes were provided by the poets themselves, some by their agents and representatives – thanks to Tom Thompson in a variety of these capacities. The biographical notes I compiled drew on a variety of sources, including the online *Australian Dictionary of Biography*, the AustLit database, *The Oxford Companion to Australian Literature* (2nd ed. William H. Wilde, Joy Hooton, and Barry Andrews (eds), OUP, Melbourne, 1994), *Australian Literature: A Bibliography to 1938 by E. Morris Miller, Extended to 1950, edited with a Historical Outline and Descriptive Commentaries* by Frederick T. Macartney (Angus & Robertson, Melbourne, 1956), *The Poets' Discovery: Nineteenth-Century Australia in Verse* (Richard D. Jordan and Peter Pierce (eds), MUP, Melbourne, 1990), and a variety of one-off sources. I take responsibility for subjective comments embedded in various biographical notes.

JOHN KINSELLA

The inclusion of the early material by indigenous Australians is considered essential to provide a comprehensive overview of poetry in this country. Although every effort has been made to seek formal permissions from the custodians of these works, it has not proved possible in some cases. The editor and publisher respect the originators of the material and the custodians of the work and would be pleased to hear from persons who may enable them to make contact with the custodians.

The use of the term 'Anonymous' throughout the anthology to indicate unknown authorship is not to intended to diminish the agency of individuals or communities connected with the creation of songs or texts.

For permission to reprint the poems in this anthology, acknowledgement is made to the following:

Adam Aitken: 'Saigon the Movie' from *In One House* (2006), Angus&Robertson/ HarperCollins in association with Paper Bark Press to the author. **Jordie Albiston:** 'Inventory' from *Botany Bay Document* (1996), Black Pepper to the author. **Ali Alizadeh:** *'Rumi' from Eyes in Times of War* (2006), Salt Publishing to the author. **Yahia Al-Samawy:** 'Variations on my Clay Heartstrings' from *Two Banks with No Bridge* (2005), Picaro to Eva Sallis. **Anon.:** 'To the Editor, Sydney Gazette' from Threlkeld, L.E. *The Muses – Poetry*. (1974) Australian Institute of Aboriginal Studies. **Anon.:** 'Two Aboriginal Songs' from Paterson, A. B. (ed) *The Old Bush Songs*, (1905) Angus and Robertson. **Louis Armand:** 'Biodegradable' from *Land Partition* (2001), Textbase to the author. **Bruce Beaver:** 'Ode XIII' from Odes & Days (1967), Angus & Robertson to Brenda Beaver. **Lisa Bellear:** 'Women's Liberation' from *Dreaming in Urban Areas* (1996) to University of Queensland Press. **Judith Beveridge:** 'The Domesticity of Giraffes' from *The Domesticity of Giraffes* (1987) Black Lightning Press; and 'The Shark' from

HEAT, vol. 8 (2004) to the author. **Javant Biarujia:** 'Georges Braque' from *Australia: Redoubt, 1989 – collected in Calques* (2002), Monogene to the author. **Judith Bishop:** 'Rabbit' from *Event* (2007) to Salt Publishing. **John Blight:** 'Flatworms' from *Selected Poems* (1976), Thomas Nelson to Arts Queensland. **Merlinda Bobis:** 'going ethnic' from *Summer Was a Fast Train without Terminals* (1998), Spinifex Press to the author. **Ken Bolton:** 'Holden Song' from *At the Flash & at the Baci* (2006), Wakefield Press to the author. **Peter Boyle:** 'Where the Roads Go After Nightfall' from *Museum of Space* (2004) to University of Queensland Press. **Michael Brennan:** 'Flowers' from *Unanimous Flight* (2008), Salt Publishing to the author. **David Brooks:** 'The Cold Front' from *The Cold Front* (1983), Hale & Iremonger to the author c/o Tim Curnow. **Pam Brown:** 'At The Wall' from *This World. This Place* (2004), University of Queensland Press to the author. **Vincent Buckley:** 'Secret Policeman' from *Arcady and Other Places* (1966), Melbourne University Press. **Charles Buckmaster:** 'Wilpena Pound' from MacDonald, S. (ed.), *Collected Poems* (1989), University of Queensland Press. **Frederick Spencer Burnell:** 'A Mangrove Swamp' from Mackaness, G. (ed.), *Poets of Australia* (1946), Angus & Robertson. **joanne burns:** 'avon calling' from *penelope's knees* (1996), University of Queensland Press to the author. **Caroline Caddy:** 'Pelican' from *Letters from the North* (1985), Fremantle Arts Centre Press to the author. **David Campbell:** 'Harry Pearce', 'Hawk and Hill' and 'Windy Gap' from *Collected Poems* (1989), Angus & Robertson to HarperCollins Publishers. **Alison Croggon:** 'The Elwood Organic Fruit and Vegetable Shop' from The Blue Gate (1997), Black Pepper Publishing; and 'Ode' from *Salt* magazine to the author. **M. T. C. Cronin:** 'The Flower, The Thing' from *The Flower, The Thing* (2006), University of Queensland Press to the author. **Zora Bernice May Cross:** 'Sonnets of Motherhood' from *The Lilt of Life* (1918), Angus & Robertson; and 'Love Sonnets' from *Songs of Love & Life* (1917), Angus & Robertson to April Hersey. **Luke Davies:** 'North Coast Bushfires' from *The Best Australian Poems 2003* (2003), Black Inc. to the author. **Jack Davis:** 'Rottnest' from *Black Life: Poems* (1992), University of Queensland Press; and 'Death of a Tree' and 'Mining Company Hymn' from *Jagardoo: Poems from Aboriginal Australia* (1977), Methuen of Australia to Curtis Brown. **Bruce Dawe:** 'Elegy for Drowned Children', 'A Public Hangman Tells His Love' and 'Homecoming' from *Sometimes Gladness* (2006) to Pearson Education Australia. **Sarah Day:** 'Antarctic Ships' from *Antarctic Ships* (2002), Arc Publications to the author. **C. J. Dennis:** 'The Mooch of Life' from *The Sentimental Bloke* (1996) to ETT Imprint. **Rosemary Dobson:** 'In the End is My Beginning', 'The Mirror' and 'Folding the Sheets' from *Collected Poems* (1991), Angus & Robertson to the author. **Michael Dransfield:** 'Pas de Deux for Lovers', That Which We Call a Rose' and 'Colonial

Poet' from *Michael Dransfield: A Retrospective* (2002) to University of Queensland Press. **Laurie Duggan:** 'Boredom' from *Mangroves* (2003), University of Queensland; and 'Compared to What' from *Compared to What* (2005), Shearsman to the author. **Jas H. Duke:** 'Positive Poem' from *Poems of War and Peace* (1987), Collective Effort Press to Π.O. **Geoffrey Dutton:** 'Burning Off' from *Selected Poems (*1993), Angus & Robertson to Curtis Brown. **Stephen Edgar:** 'Ulysses Burning' from *Corrupted Treasures* (1995), William Heinemann Australia to the author. **Gabrielle Everall:** 'Queen of Suburbia' from *Dona Juanita and the Love of Boys* (2007) to the author. **Kate Fagan:** 'The Concrete Poem' from *Meanjin*, 61(3) (2002) to the author. **Michael Farrell:** 'Nude Descending in a Liftshaft' from *ode ode* (2002), Salt Publishing to the author. **Robert David Fitzgerald:** 'The Wind at Your Door' from *Forty Years' Poems* (1965), Angus & Robertson. **Lionel Fogarty:** 'Jukambe Spirit – For the Lost' and 'I am not Santa' from *Collected Poems* (2008), Salt Publishing to the author. **John Forbes:** 'Death: an Ode', 'Ode to Doubt' and 'Love Poem' from *Collected Poems* (1999) to Brandl & Schlesinger. **Kevin Gilbert:** 'Shame' from *The Blackside – People Are Legends and Other Poems* (1990), to Hyland House Publishing. **Mary Gilmore:** 'Fourteen Poor Men', 'Nurse No Long Grief', 'Remembrance' and 'The Myall in Prison' from *A Passionate Heart* (1980), Angus & Robertson to ETT Imprint. **Peter Goldsworthy:** 'Suicide on Christmas Eve' from *New Selected Poems* (2000), Duffy and Snellgrove to the author. **Geoff Goodfellow:** 'The Violence of Work' from *Punch On Punch Off* (2004), The Vulgar Press to the author. **Alan Gould:** 'Three Icelandic Interiors' from *The Past Completes Me: Selected Poems* (2005), University of Queensland Press to the author. **Robert Gray:** 'Garage' and 'Kangaroo' from *New Selected Poems* (1998), Duffy and Snellgrove to the author. Revised versions appear in the anthology. **Rodney Hall:** 'Mrs Macintosh' from *Heaven, in a Way* (1970), University of Queensland Press to the author. **Philip Hammial:** 'Exile' from *Black Market in the Wild Life* (1996), Penguin Books Australia to the author. **Jennifer Harrison:** 'Funambulist' from *Folly & Grief* (2006) to Black Pepper. **J. S. Harry:** 'A Quality of Loss' from *Hold, for a Little While, and Turn Gently* (1979), Island Press to the author. **Kevin Hart:** 'Gypsophila' from *Flame Tree: Selected Poems* (2001) to Bloodaxe. **W. Hart-Smith:** 'Space' from *Poems of Discovery* (1959), Angus & Robertson; and 'Limpets' from Dibble, B. (ed.) *William Hart-Smith: Selected Poems, 1936–1984* (1985) Angus & Robertson to Brian Dibble. **Dennis Haskell:** 'At Greenwood' from *Abracadabra* (1993) to Fremantle Arts Centre Press. **Anita Heiss:** 'I'm not racist, but' from *I'm Not Racist, But* (2007) to Salt Publishing. **Paul Hetherington:** 'Skin' from *Conversations: Occasional Writing from the Research School of Pacific and Asian Studies* and *It Feels Like Disbelief* (2007), Salt Publishing to the author.

Dorothy Hewett: 'Country Idyll', 'Psyche's Husband' and 'Yealering in the Mind' from *Collected Poems* (1995) to Fremantle Arts Centre Press. **Charles Higham**: 'The War Museum at Nagasaki' from *The Voyage to Brindisi and other Poems* (1970), Angus & Robertson to the author. **Barry Hill**: 'A Long Swim' from *The Best Australian Poems 2004* (2004), Black Inc. to the author. **Philip Hodgins**: 'Shooting the Dogs' from *Selected Poems* (1997), Angus & Robertson to HarperCollins Publishers. **A. D. Hope**: 'The Death of the Bird', 'Australia' and 'Hay Fever' from *Collected Poems 1930–70* (1972), Angus & Robertson to Geoffrey Hope. **Harry Hooton**: 'Words' from *Poet of the Twenty-First Century* (1990), Angus & Robertson to Margaret Fink. **W. Flexmore Hudson**: 'Drought' and 'Bashō' from Eliot, B. (ed.) *The Jindyworobaks*, (1979) University of Queensland Press to Melbourne University Press. **Rex Ingamells**: 'The Golden Bird' from *Selected Poems* (1944), Georgian House to ETT Imprint. **Coral Hull**: 'Sharpies' from *William's Mongrels* (1996), Penguin Books Australia to the author. **Martin Johnston**: 'Gradus Ad Parnassum' from *The Sea Cucumber* (1978) to University of Queensland Press. **Jill Jones**: 'The 7.17 Silver Machine' from *Broken/Open* (2005), Salt Publishing to the author. **John Kinsella**: 'Drowning in Wheat' from *The Hunt* (1998), Fremantle Arts Centre Press to the author. **Nancy Keesing**: 'Revelation' from *The Woman I am* (1995) State Library of NSW Press to the State Library of NSW. **Antigone Kefala**: 'The Alien' and 'The Wanderer' from *The Alien* (1973), University of Queensland Press to the author. **S. K. Kelen**: 'Atomic Ballet' from *Atomic Ballet* (1991), Hale & Iremonger to the author. **Mike Ladd**: 'Junior Football' from *Transit* (2007), Five Islands Press to the author. **Paddy Lando-Naddi**: 'White Engine Against Black Magic' from Brandenstein, C. G. and Thomas, A. P. (eds), *Taruru: Aboriginal Song Poetry from the Pilbara* (1974), Rigby. **Bronwyn Lea**: 'These Gifts' from *The Other Way Out* (2008), Giramondo to the author. **Geoffrey Lehmann**: 'Pear Days in Queensland' from *Collected Poems* (1997), Heinemann to the author. **Emma Lew**: 'The Clover Seed Hex' from *Anything the Landlord Touches* (2002), Giramondo Publishing to the author. **Kate Lilley**: 'My Bad' from *Jacket* magazine, vol. 27 (2005) to the author. **Kate Llewellyn**: 'Breasts' from *Honey* (1988), Hudson Publishing to the author. **James McAuley**: 'Holiday', Self-portrait Newcastle, 1942', 'Pietà' and 'Terra Australis' from *Collected Poems 1936–1970* (1971), Angus & Robertson to HarperCollins Publishers. **Miriam Wei Wei Lo**: 'Searching for Words' from *Meanjin* 63(2) (2004) to the author. **Hugh McCrae**: 'Camden Magpie' from *Selected Poems* (1965), Angus & Robertson to ETT Imprint. **Ronald McCuaig**: 'Love Me and Never Leave Me' from *Collected Poems* (1992), Angus & Robertson to ETT Imprint. **Nan McDonald**: 'The Hawk' from *Selected Poems* (1969), Angus & Robertson to HarperCollins Publishers. **Roger McDonald**: '1915' from *Airship*

(1974) to University of Queensland Press. **Kenneth Mackenzie:** 'Caesura' and 'The Snake' from *Selected Poems* (1976), Angus & Robertson to ETT Imprint. **Rhyll McMaster:** 'The Brineshrimp' from *The Brineshrimp* (1972), University of Queensland Press to the author. **Jennifer Maiden:** 'Reflected Hearth at Bowen Mountain' from *Friendly Fire* (2005), Giramondo Publishing to the author. **Ern Malley:** 'Dürer: Innsbruck 1495' and 'Petit Testament' from *Collected Poems* (1993), Angus & Robertson to ETT Imprint. **David Malouf:** 'At a School Athletics Day' from *David Malouf: Poems 1959–89* (1992) to University of Queensland Press. **John Manifold:** 'The Tomb of Lt John Learmonth, AIF' from *Selected Verse* (1948) from Dennis Dobson to University of Queensland Press. **Chris Mansell:** 'Definition Poem: Pissed as a Parrot' from *Head, Heart & Stone* (1982), Fling Poetry to the author. **John Mateer:** 'Cemétario da Ajuda' from *Best Australian Poems 2007* (2007), Black Inc. to the author. **Miles Merrill:** 'Night's Knows' from *What Night Knows* (CD) (2005), Hunters and Gatherers to the author. **Peter Minter:** 'Life™' from *Blue Grass* (2006), Salt Publishing to the author. **Ian Mudie:** 'Underground' from *The Blue Crane* (1959), Angus & Robertson to ETT Imprint. **Mudrooroo:** 'Blotched Country Boy' from *Pacific Highway Boo-Blooz* (1996), University of Queensland Press to ETT Imprint. **Jimmy Murray:** 'Thunder' from Duwell, M. and Dickson, R. (eds), *The Honey-ant Men's Love Song* (1994), University of Queensland Press. **Les Murray:** 'Widower in the Country', 'The Grassfire Stanzas', Bats' Ultrasound' and 'The Quality of Sprawl' from *Collected Poems* (2006), Black Inc. to the author. **Π.O:** 'Yoori' from *The Fitzroy Poems* (1989), Collective Effort Press to the author. **Oodgeroo Noonuccal:** 'Municipal Gum' from *The Dawn is At Hand* (1966), Jacaranda Press; and 'Namatjira' and 'Gooboora, the Silent Pool' from *My People* (1970), Jacaranda Press to Denis Walker. **Jan Owen:** 'Blue Bowl' from *Eating Durian and Other Poems* (2002), Picaro Press to the author. **Ouyang Yu:** 'Moon Over Melbourne' from *Moon Over Melbourne* (1995), Papyrus Publishing to the author. **Geoff Page:** 'Smalltown Memorials' from *Smalltown Memorials* (1975), University of Queensland Press; and 'Inscription at Villers-Bretonneux' from *Collecting the Weather* (1978), Makar Press to the author. **Charmaine Papertalk-Green:** 'Culture Way' and 'Wanna be White' from *Just Like That* (2007), Fremantle Arts Centre Press to the author. **Grace Perry:** 'Red Scarf' from *Red Scarf* (1963), Edwards & Shaw to John Millett. **Glen Phillips:** 'Spring Burning' from *Spring Burning* (2005), Salt Publishing to the author. **Dorothy Porter:** 'PMT' from *Driving Too Fast* (1989), University of Queensland Press; 'Bluebottles' from *Australian Book Review*, April (2002) to the author. **Hal Porter:** 'Obverse' from *The Hexagon* (1956), Angus & Robertson to ETT Imprint. **Peter Porter:** 'Phar Lap in the Melbourne Museum' and 'The Exequy' from *Collected Poems*

(1999), Oxford University Press to the author. **Jennifer Rankin:** 'Burning Off' from *Ritual Shift* (1976), Makar Press to University of Queensland Press. **Elizabeth Riddell:** 'News of the Baby' from *Selected Poems* (1992), Angus & Robertson to ETT Imprint. **Roland Robinson:** 'Casuarina' from Eliot, B. (ed.) *The Jindyworobaks,* (1979) University of Queensland Press to ETT Imprint. **Judith Rodriguez:** 'Nu-plastik Fanfare Red' from *New and Selected Poems* (1988), University of Queensland Press to the author. **Eric Rolls:** 'Sheaf Tosser' from *Sheaf Tosser and Other Poems* (1967), Angus & Robertson to Elaine van Kempen. **Peter Rose:** 'Rattus Rattus' from *Rattus Rattus: New and Selected Poems* (2005), Salt Publishing to the author. **David Rowbotham:** 'First Man Lost in Space' from *David Rowbotham 1945–1993: New and Selected Poems* (1994), Penguin Books Australia to the author. **Gig Ryan:** 'Swoons' from *Heroic Money* (2001), Brandl & Schlesinger; 'Travel' from *The Best Australian Poems 2003* (2003), Black Inc. to the author. **Tracy Ryan:** 'Hair' from *Killing Delilah* (1994), Fremantle Arts Centre Press to the author. **Andrew Sant:** 'Mussolini's Umbrella' from *Tremors – New & Selected Poems* (2004), Black Pepper to the author. **Philip Salom:** 'Barbecue of the Primitives' from *New and Selected Poems* (1998), Fremantle Arts Centre Press to the author. **Jaya Savige:** 'The Master of Small Violences' from *Latecomers* (2005), University of Queensland Press to the author. **John A. Scott:** 'My Favourite Things' from *Smoking* (1983), Scripsi to the author. **Thomas Shapcott:** 'Chekhov's Mongoose' from *Chekhov's Mongoose* (2000), Salt Publishing to the author. **John Shaw Neilson:** 'Love's Coming', 'The Crane is my Neighbour' and 'The Orange Tree' from *Selected Poems* (1991), Angus & Robertson to ETT Imprint. **Craig Sherborne:** 'Strapper' from *Necessary Evil* (2006), Black Inc. to the author. **R. A. Simpson:** 'Diver' from *Selected Poems* (1981), University of Queensland Press to Pam Simpson. **Alex Skovron:** 'The Steeples' from *The Best Australian Poems 2003* (2003), Black Inc. to the author. **Peter Skrzynecki:** 'Migrant Hostel' from *Immigrant Chronicle* (1975) to University of Queensland Press. **Kenneth Slessor:** 'Choker's Lane' from *Darlinghurst Nights* (1933) Frank Johnson; and 'Beach Burial', "Five Bells' and 'Sleep' from Haskell, D. and Dutton, G. (eds) *Collected Poems* (1994), Angus & Robertson to ETT Imprint. **Vivian Smith:** 'Convolvulus' from *Tide Country* (1982), Angus & Robertson; reprinted from *Along the Line* (2006), Salt Publishing to the author. **Douglas Stewart:** 'Silkworms' from *Selected Poems* (1969), Angus & Robertson to HarperCollins Publishers. **Harold Stewart:** 'The Leaf-makers' from Rowe and Smith (eds), *Windchimes: Asia in Australian Poetry* (2006), Pandanus Press. **Randolph Stow:** 'On a Favourite Cat' from *Selected Poems* (1969), Angus & Robertson to Sheil Land Associates. **Jennifer Strauss:** 'Tending the Graves' from *Labour Ward* (1988), Pariah Press to the author.

Bobbi Sykes: 'Cycle' from *Love Poems and Other Revolutionary Actions* (1988), University of Queensland Press to the author. **Norman Talbot:** 'The Uncommercial Traveller' from *Son of a Female Universe* (1971), South Head Press. **Alf Taylor:** 'Moorditj Yorgah' from *Salt* journal (2007), Salt Publishing to the author. **Andrew Taylor:** 'The Gardener and his Garden' and 'Folds in the Map' from *Collected Poems* (2004), Salt Publishing to the author. **Colin Thiele:** 'Radiation Victim' from *Selected Verse* (1970), Rigby Books to Rhonda Thiele. **Richard Tipping:** 'Soft Riots/TV News' from *Soft Riots* (1972), University of Queensland Press to the author. A revised version appears in the anthology. **John Tranter:** 'Voodoo' and 'Lufthansa' from *Urban Myths* (2006) to University of Queensland Press; 'Glow-boys' from *Under Berlin* (1988), University of Queensland Press to the author. **Dimitris Tsaloumas:** 'The Harbour' from *The Harbour* (1998) to University of Queensland Press. **David Unaipon:** 'Narrinyeri Saying', 'Song of the Platypus' and 'the Song of Hungarrda' to Harold Kropinyeri. **Val Vallis:** 'Shipwright' and 'The Mooring Buoy' from *Songs of the East* (1947), Angus & Robertson to the author. **Vicki Viidikas:** 'Future' from *Wrappings* (1974), Wild and Woolley Publications to Ingrid Lisners. **Chris Wallace-Crabbe:** 'Chaos' from *Where the Wind Came* (1971), Angus & Robertson; 'Out to Lunch' from *By and Large* (2001), Brandl & Schlesinger to the author; 'Melbourne' from *Selected Poems* (1995) to Carcanet. **Ania Walwicz:** 'Little Red Riding Hood'and 'buttons' from *Travel/Writing* (1989), Angus & Robertson to the author. **Wangkangurra people:** 'Song of the Knob-tail gecko' from Duwell, M. and Dickson, R. (eds) *Little Eva at Moonlight Creek and other Aboriginal song poems* (1994), University of Queensland Press. **Francis Webb:** 'Cap and Bells', 'Pneumo-encephalograph' from *Cap and Bells* (1991), Angus & Robertson to HarperCollins Publishers. **Williams:** 'Whirlwind: Tatu' from Brandenstein, C. G. and Thomas, A. P. (eds), *Taruru: Aboriginal Song Poetry from the Pilbara* (1974), Rigby. **Frank Wilmot:** 'To a Telegraph Pole' to Melbourne University Press. **Judith Wright:** 'The Company of Lovers', 'At Cooloola', 'Naked Girl and Mirror', 'Request to a Year' and 'Flying Fox on Barbed Wire' from *A Human Pattern: Selected Poems* (1996) to ETT Imprint. **Wullati:** 'Native Poetry' from Threlkeld, L. E. *The Muses – Poetry*. (1974) Australian Institute of Aboriginal Studies. **Fay Zwicky:** 'Bride Drinking from a Pool' from *The Gatekeeper's Wife* (1997), Brandl & Schlesinger to the author.

Every effort has been made to trace copyright holders, but in a few cases this has proved impossible. The publishers would be interested to hear from any copyright holders not here acknowledged.

Index